Humor and the

Healing Arts

A Multimethod Analysis
of Humor Use in Health Care

Humor and the Healing Arts

A Multimethod Analysis of Humor Use in Health Care

Athena du Pré

Southeastern Louisiana University

LEA LAWRENCE ERLBAUM ASSOCIATES, PUBLISHERS
1998   Mahwah, New Jersey   London

Lawrence Erlbaum Associates, Inc., Publishers
10 Industrial Avenue
Mahwah, NJ 07430

Library of Congress Cataloging-in-Publication Data

DuPré, Athena.
Humor and the healing arts : a multimethod analysis of
humor use in health care / Athena du Pré.
        p. cm.
   Includes bibliographical references and index.
   ISBN 0-8058-2647-5 (cloth : alk. paper). — ISBN 0-8058-
2648-3 (paper : alk. paper)
   1. Wit and humor in medicine. I. Title.
R705.D87 1998
610'.2'07—dc21   97-17943
                                                              CIP

Books published by Lawrence Erlbaum Associates are printed
on acid-free paper, and their bindings are chosen for strength
and durability.

Printed in the United States of America
10 9 8 7 6 5 4 3 2 1

To Jordan and Hannah,
my angels

Contents

Preface

Humor and the Healing Arts offers an unprecedented look at health and humor. With dozens of actual examples collected in seven health care settings, this volume shows the ways that humor is used in times of embarrassment, camaraderie, anxiety, pain, and uncertainty. Humor is shown to be a powerful and versatile communication technique. But humor is not an end in itself. In understanding humor better, we also come to better understand the people and situations it involves.

A series of field studies I conducted in the early 1990s provide the primary data of this book. The focus is threefold, centering on the techniques of humor, its effects, and its appropriateness in health care settings. This focus yields insights about the expectations of patients and caregivers, the essential nature of humor, cultural rules for humor use, and the effective management of common health care dilemmas such as helping-by-hurting, complaining-but-cooperating, and chastising-while-befriending.

The book is designed to be thorough and easy to understand. It employs a range of research perspectives (phenomenology, ethnography, ethnomethodology, and conversation analysis) and I do not assume readers are familiar with them all. A chapter at the beginning of each section describes the method used in that section, including its strengths and limitations. Although it is not always necessary to understand the method to appreciate the analysis, I think it is important to acknowledge up front that there are no magic conclusions or mystical insights. At least I don't ask you to trust me on that basis. Better, I think, to follow Moerman's (1988) advice and invite you "into the kitchen so that you can see how the work gets done" (p. 17).

I have been told this is a more conversational book than most. In places, my naivete as an observer is unabashedly evident. I was at times fascinated, frustrated, and utterly baffled and this sometimes shows. Although I was not directly involved in the studied transactions, I was of course, personally involved in understanding them—drawing on my own experiences and expectations, unavoidably filtering the experiences to some extent through the sieve of my own biases. Especially in the ethnographic sections, the reader is seeing through my eyes and hearing through my ears, and I do not pretend otherwise. Yet I propose to present more than a *confessional tale* (Van Maanen's, 1988, term). Although my experiences are subjective, I hope to make a case that they are also *intersubjective*. To do this, I make a great effort to be as specific as possible, to quote actual dialogue, and to cite occurrences that suggest that other people perceived the situations as I did, or acted on a predictable, identifiable set of assumptions. My goal is to substantially explain the basis for all analyses I offer.

Part I describes theory and research on health communication and humor, and explores the relation between health and humor. Part II introduces a Surprise Liberation Theory of Humor and examines the essential differences between "funny" and "not funny."

From an ethnographic perspective (Parts III and IV), joking around seems to serve the same functions in a variety of settings—to mitigate embarrassment, soften or sidestep complaints, display identification, solicit feedback, and good-naturedly insist on compliance with unpleasant routines. However, the tones and topics of humor are sometimes very different. It is bold and public in some settings, quiet and private in others. Practical and cultural reasons for this are explored.

An ethnomethodological look at three medical transactions (Part V) shows how participants collaboratively organize/interpret each experience using humor. Humor is used to (a) rekey a distressful physical therapy episode as a playful one, (b) reduce embarrassment about a patient's nudity, and (c) negotiate a potential confrontation between a patient and caregiver. In each episode, humor appears to minimize the consequences of participating in threatening activities.

Conversation analysis (chapter 21) introduces the idea of laughter-coated complaints, revealing how participants collaboratively manage some complaints as laughable utterances. Part VI offers a conclusive overview and suggestions for practical application and future research.

Acknowledgments

I have been honored with the input of many fine scholars in compiling this book. My deepest gratitude is to Sandy Ragan, who contributed ideas and encouragement at every phase of the process. I would also like to thank others at the University of Oklahoma, including Larry Wieder, Jon Nussbaum, Ling Chen, Eric Kramer, and Susan Marcus-Mendoza.

Thanks also to Sonia Crandall, Ken Brown, Jung-Sook Lee, Gerald Flannery, and Paul Barefield for their assistance in conceptualizing and polishing the project.

Fondest thanks to my family—especially Ginger, Ed, Sarah, Hal, Sidney, Mary, Jordan, and Hannah—and to Cris Berard and Betty Adams, early mentors who inspire me still.

I am grateful to Teresa Thompson and Dolf Zillmann for helpful comments on the manuscript and to the editorial staff of Lawrence Erlbaum Associates, especially Kathleen O'Malley and Sara T. Scudder.

Finally, I am profoundly indebted to the many professionals and patients who graciously allowed me entrance into the fascinating arena of medical care.

—Athena du Pré

I

Background

Chapter 1

▼

Introduction

It is a popular notion that medical settings are as hostile to humor as to germs. The sterile atmosphere makes one get better, but *feel* worse. This is a paradox not to be suffered, said Norman Cousins (1976, 1979), Raymond Moody (1978), Bernie Siegel (1983), and others. With the visibility of their many best-sellers, these advocates of healthy laughter have spawned enthusiasm for humor in the healing arts. There is evidence that their ideas are catching on. Between 1988 and 1992, the nonprofit HUMOR Project in New York awarded grants to launch 125 humor programs in hospitals, nursing homes, and other agencies (Suchetka, 1992).

This study represents an effort to identify the emerging roles of humor in health care. Although it is shown here that confidence in medical humor is growing, it is also true that much uncertainty still surrounds the issue. Questions about the appropriateness of humor, its effects, and its functions remain unanswered. Most humor programs encourage caregivers to use humor with patients when it seems helpful and appropriate. These are vague terms, however, and research to date is inadequate to explain what factors determine the helpfulness and appropriateness of humor.

Overall, my interest in humor is both applied and theoretical. The subject was initially posed to me by medical practitioners who wished to understand humor more fully. Considering the importance of medical communication, I feel it is important to pursue answers to their questions. I think research is at its best when addressed to real-life concerns. Furthermore, I am convinced that our ignorance about

3

humor represents a serious gap in our understanding of communication and human nature. Many hours of observation have convinced me that humor is an extremely versatile and effective communication technique worth serious attention.

BACKGROUND ON THE HEALTH CARE HUMOR MOVEMENT

Research suggests that humor and verbal play are already prevalent between some patients and caregivers. Indications are that joking around serves several objectives of medical care; it reduces the face threat of medical exams (Ragan, 1990); allows patient and caregiver to show that they identify with each other (Beck & Ragan, 1992); reduces embarrassment, bolsters rapport, and encourages attentiveness (Smith-Dupré, 1992).

Sometimes a funny situation occurs accidentally. Robinson (1975) described the mirth unintentionally created by a young nurse unfamiliar with the colloquial term *vase* for a bedpan: "When asked by a patient for a 'vase,' she looked around and finally asked, 'Well, how big is your bouquet?'" (p. 57)

In an increasing number of cases, however, humor is not an accidental occurrence. Health care centers across the country have begun implementing in-house humor programs. A Laugh Mobile at Duke University Medical Center offers cancer patients a selection of humorous tapes, books, and puzzles (Bost & Foltz, 1990). Humor programs are also underway at Baptist Medical Center in South Carolina (Scott, 1992), Babies Hospital in New York (Williams, 1990), the Ethel Percy Andrus Gerontology Center in South Carolina (Adams & McGuire, 1986), and the Rehabilitation Institute in Detroit (Banner, 1988), to name a few.

Cousins is frequently lauded as a pioneering advocate of health-related humor. In *Anatomy of an Illness as Perceived by the Patient* (1979), Cousins described how he used humor and vitamin C to overcome intense pain, and to recover from a paralyzing disease that kills about 499 out of every 500 people who contract it. After *The New England Journal of Medicine* published Cousins' story (1976), he received 3,000 letters from physicians, most of them expressing confidence in the unconventional treatment he described (Cousins, 1979). And although Cousins was not a physician, he sufficiently impressed the staff of the

UCLA School of Medicine, who offered him a position as adjunct professor of medicine, law, and human values. Cousins held that position for many years before his death in 1990 (Buckeley, 1990).

Cousins' story is representative of much humor literature. Anecdotal and philosophical accounts abound. The health care professionals I interviewed are unanimous in the conviction that patients who maintain positive attitudes feel better and heal more quickly. Likewise, the patients I meet almost always describe their favorite caregivers as the ones who smile and joke around with them. But believing in humor is not the same as understanding it. After surveying a random sample of 204 nurses, Sumners (1990) reported that a majority were willing to incorporate humor in patient care, but felt uncertain how to go about it. Vera Robinson, a nurse with more than 30 years experience, asserted in the preface to her 1975 dissertation:

> It [humor] is part of our lives even in times of stress, danger and death. Yet, despite our recognition of its value, we don't take humor seriously. Somehow, we are afraid to look at it, to analyze it and to make conscious, deliberate use of humor as a tool in communication, as a way of intervening in the stresses of living. We allow it to happen by chance. And, particularly in health professions, there's generally no attempt at a planned use of humor. (p. ix)

Other research seconds Robinson's assertion that humor is part of everyday life. In an early study (Kambouropoulou, 1926), an all-female sample of college students kept humor diaries. They recorded an average of 15 to 21 humorous experiences per day. Young (1937) reported even more extravagant use of humor. On a self-report questionnaire, 184 undergraduates noted that they laughed "hundreds of times," sometimes "500 times," in a typical 24-hour period (p. 319). There is obviously some disparity between the studies, and the larger figures may be somewhat exaggerated. Yet even the most conservative results point to a strong presence of mirth in daily life.

Goodman (1983)—director of the HUMOR Project—proposed that "the human condition is inherently funny" (p. 15). Zijderveld (1983), a humor researcher, asserted "one should never underestimate the serious nature of play" (p. 6). And Robinson (1975) made a case that "humor is not just a laughing matter, it is serious business" (p. 3). All point to people's instinctive reliance on mirth as a coping mechanism. If these claims are valid, it seems artificial and perhaps destructive to exclude humor from the emotionally charged atmosphere of a health care setting.

GOALS AND RATIONALE

My goal here is not to design a prescriptive program for humor use, nor to advocate or discourage the use of humor in medical settings. I wish only to understand humor better and to help others understand it. I think this goal is particularly important now, when so many people wish to understand and use humor.

I also wish to extend the study of health communication beyond patient–physician transactions to include transactions between patients and a wide range of caregivers. Included primarily in this study are radiology technicians, nurses, a physician, physical therapists, and student aides. Occasional references are also made to nurse aides, physicians, therapists (physical, occupational, recreational, respiratory), phlebotomists, and orderlies. (The communication of the later caregivers is examined more fully in Smith-Dupré, 1992).

My studies to this point convince me that the choice to use humor is, and should remain, personal and situational. But I am also convinced that one need *not* be "born funny" to use and understand humor. When I mention to people (scholars and laypersons) that I study humor, their reaction is often part surprise and part suspicion. They are surprised that the topic is, as they say, so "fun" and so "real life." But they are suspicious: "Can you teach people to be funny?" Their reactions reflect the common viewpoint that humor is one of life's mysteries: Some people are funny and some are not. I submit that it is only our ignorance of humor that has made it seem ethereal—an enigmatic gift bestowed on some but not on all. Although there is a creative element to humor that is developed with practice and sensitivity, being "funny" is largely a matter of observing explicable rules. I describe some of those rules in this book.

Some people seem to understand the rules of humor use without really trying, just as some people find it easy to be good listeners or effective lecturers. One difference between listening, public speaking, and humor is that scholars have given careful attention to the first two but not to the later. Thus, we are able to speak fairly knowledgeably about the skills and guidelines helpful in becoming better listeners or speakers. I believe we can eventually do the same with humor. Furthermore, I do not believe we compromise the magic of humor by understanding it. After all, people who use humor do understand it. My goal is to make their implicit, often unconscious understanding of humor accessible. I am especially interested in the techniques with which people create and interpret humor, the effects of humor on medical transactions, and the cultural codes that determine humor's appropriateness. Overall, I hope to say something about the assumptions and subtle techniques that make humor possible, useful, and appropriate in health care settings.

TERMINOLOGY

I have largely resisted assigning empirical definitions to the phenomena described here. To do so, I felt, would obscure the answer to a more interesting question: How do the people studied regard humor? This question seemed much more to the point, but it was not easy to answer. For one thing, most people seemed to equate the word *humor* with comedy. Most health care professionals shook their heads decisively and said some version of: "No, I don't use humor. You mean like jokes and stuff?" (Their tone seemed to suggest I had mistaken them for Jerry Seinfeld or Whoopi Goldberg!) But people could nearly always suggest another caregiver who they said did use humor (invariably, a person said to be much loved by co-workers and patients for his or her good humor). But I would receive the same "not me" response from that person.

Meanwhile, I was watching these people interact with patients and I could not write quickly enough to note every time they laughed together. They did not tell jokes, but they frequently engaged in playful banter relevant to the situation. For instance, one nurse brandishing a patient's chalky barium swallow joked, "Ready for your cocktail?" Humorous puns, comical expressions and actions, exaggerations, absurdities, and effusive compliments were plentiful. To my mind, caregivers and patients were using conversational humor almost constantly. Yet they claimed not to. How to explain this? I began to consider that (a) admitting to humor use represented a type of boasting and people were being modest with me, (b) they did not realize they were using humor, or (c) what I was interpreting as humor was not humor in their minds. Only after 2 years of study did I hit on a solution to the dilemma. I began asking the question differently: "Do you joke around with patients?" "Oh yes," they would often exclaim, "all the time." Thus, I present that—in vernacular terms—this is a study of joking around. Roughly translated to scholar-ese, joking around includes what I call *conversational humor* (statements and actions that draw a laugh) and verbal play (instances of feigned emotion and exaggerated playacting not necessarily punctuated with laughter). In the terminology used by Long and Graesser (1988), almost all the medical humor I observed can be categorized as *wit*. That is, it is situational and seemingly spontaneous. I have never heard a patient or caregiver tell the other a joke. I am sure it happens, but it is certainly less prevalent than situational witticisms. In other words, the patients and caregivers I studied never told each other jokes, but they did joke around. (In chapter 7, I address fundamental differences between contrived and spontaneous humor.)

In summary, I use the terms *joking around* and *humor* to describe the playful transactions of patients and caregivers. It is difficult (and perhaps misleading) to be more empirically specific than that. Sometimes people laugh while they joke around; sometimes they pretend to be angry. But to one familiar with the setting and the people involved, it was easy to know when people were joking around. Their smiles, laughter, and posture were clues, as were the outlandishness of many humorous comments and the relational patterns of the people conversing. So the reader may better judge the humorousness of a situation for him or herself, I make an effort to include relevant contextual details and verbatim dialogue throughout the book.

Chapter 2

▼

Related Literature
in Health Communication

Few situations are so paradoxically personal and alien as a medical transaction. Caregiver and patient go behind closed doors for a brief time and attempt to overcome the constraints of status difference, unfamiliarity, anxiety, and language. Research suggests that ineffective communication can leave patient and healer frustrated and dissatisfied (Ben-Sira, 1976, 1980; Buller & Buller, 1987; Frankel, 1984; Street & Wiemann, 1987) and reduce the likelihood that patients will cooperate with treatment plans (Frankel & Beckman, 1989; Fuller & Quesada, 1973; Korsch & Negrete, 1972; Lane, 1983). The importance and difficulty of communication in medical transactions presents health as an important theme for communication research. A review of health communication literature is presented here, prefaced by a brief discussion of its significance.

IMPORTANCE OF HEALTH
COMMUNICATION RESEARCH

Communication is particularly important considering the diverse interpersonal challenges of the patient–caregiver relationship. A caregiver's schedule is physically and emotionally exhausting. A physician may have to tell a patient he or she has a brain tumor, then minutes later devote attention to a case of tonsillitis. In this context, tonsillitis may seem trivial to the doctor, but not to the patient. Moreover, the patient may have more serious concerns that he or she will not divulge if he or she perceives the physician to be indifferent. Korsch and Negrete (1972) found that more than one quarter of pediatric patients' parents did not share their greatest concern with the doctor because they felt the doctor was unreceptive. For similar reasons, less than half the patients Korsch and Negrete studied complied with the doctors' recommendations.

Both patient and physician feel the repercussions of dissatisfying communication. Patients may feel dehumanized and think their money and time have been wasted. Diagnostic information may be lost and treatment success jeopardized. Patients who are not satisfied with the medical exam may make return visits and phone calls, or begin to doctor shop. Baker (1987) described the negative implications when a patient and physician do not communicate satisfactorily:

> Families who disagree with the clinician's plan may doctor-shop, leave the hospital against medical advice, bring a lawsuit, or openly disagree and try to negotiate. Covert ways of expressing differences would be noncompliance, attempts at manipulation, or criticizing the professional to other people without his/her knowledge. (p. 99)

By contrast, wrote Baker, "when families and the healthcare [*sic*] team agree on the patient's care, families may compliment clinicians and recommend them to other people" (p. 99).

The doctor's goal is presumably to get the information he or she needs for a diagnosis as efficiently as possible. But we should not be hasty in equating efficiency with the length of a patient visit. Numerous studies show that limiting patients' input costs physicians dearly. Without thorough and accurate information, they are less able to help patients heal. Disgruntled patients are often less cooperative and more critical. These factors may endanger the physician's effectiveness and his or her professional reputation. There is also evidence that ineffective communication costs time and money. National figures (U.S. Department of Health and Human Services, 1983) show that the time spent in a medical exam is commonly magnified fivefold by follow-up calls and visits from patients requesting more information. Consequently, physicians' schedules become clogged with unnecessary follow-up exams and inconvenient "nuisance" calls. Thus, strict time constraints on medical exams may be counterproductive. It is presumably the large number of additional contacts, not the original exams, that crowd physicians' schedules and interrupt their personal time. If more effective communication techniques in the exam room can minimize dissatisfaction and unnecessary follow-ups, those techniques would certainly save millions of dollars and improve health care.

In summary, evidence suggests that dissatisfying communication is not only bad medicine, it is bad science, and it is bad business. Some amount of conflict and disagreement is inevitable in medical exchanges. Patient and caregiver face extraordinary challenges. But if communication can be used to minimize standoffs, patients—as well as caregivers—stand to gain.

Communication between patients and medical professionals may be especially problematic. Barnlund (1976) cited 10 universal obstacles to communication: ego involvement, differences in knowledge, social status differences, disparate communicative purposes, emotional distance, one-way communication without effective feedback and clarification, verbal manipulation, ambiguity and inadequacy of language, jargon, and time constraints. It is difficult to imagine a medical encounter unaffected by nearly all these.

The following literature review examines two factors: the different expectations harbored by patients and physicians, and the less symmetrical power balance in patient–caregiver conversation. Following discussion of these factors is better news—what works well and what can be done to improve patient–caregiver communication.

PATIENTS' EXPECTATIONS

The literature suggests that patients value interpersonal over technical skills when it comes to physicians. In a survey of 16 hospital patients (Fuller & Quesada, 1973), only 2 mentioned medical skills in their descriptions of an "ideal doctor." Ben-Sira (1976, 1980) demonstrated that pleasing affective behavior was a better indicant of satisfaction than perceptions of a physician's technical competence. Other studies show patients' preference for physicians who are affiliative rather than domineering (Buller & Buller, 1987; Street & Wiemann, 1987), courteous and good listeners (Burgoon et al., 1987; Comstock, Hooper, Goodwin, & Goodwin, 1982), and involved and expressive (Street & Wiemann, 1987).

Frankel (1984) suggested that—from the patient's perspective—the success of a medical visit often hinges more on interpersonal factors than medical ones. He cited national estimates that four of five office visits result in "no problem" or "minor problem" diagnoses. "This type of visit is of interest behaviorally, since it represents a type of healthcare transaction in which problems and complaints are most readily dealt with in social rather than biological terms" (p. 137). This is not to suggest that technical skills are not important. They are perhaps just hard to measure. Patients in most cases seem to take medical competence as a given. Ben-Sira (1976, 1980) suggested that patients judge a physician by his or her affective displays because they are unable (at least immediately) to judge the physician's technical competence.

Whether this is a valid way to judge a physician, patient satisfaction seems to be linked to patient cooperation. Patients' cooperation with treatment advice is strongly correlated (0.72) to the physicians' communication tactics, according to Lane's (1983) study of 16 junior podiatrists and their patients. In Korsch and Negrete's (1972) study of 800 patients and their parents, only 42% complied completely with pediatricians' instructions. The most frequently given reason was dissatisfaction because the doctor failed to address the parent's feelings of concern and anxiety.

Based on three case studies, Frankel and Beckman (1989) proposed that patients may distrust diagnoses, therefore not adhere to prescribed treatment plans, if they are not allowed to voice all their concerns or if concerns they voice go unaddressed. Patients they studied also reported that doctors prescribed treatment without considering if they were able to, or could afford to, carry it out.

Overall, it seems that patients expect physicians to be more than technically competent. They look for attentiveness and empathy, and when their expectations are not met, patients may withhold information and distrust diagnoses. A corresponding lack of cooperation can interfere with medical success and no doubt frustrate both patient and physician.

PHYSICIANS' EXPECTATIONS

Research has almost completely overlooked the expectations and satisfaction levels of physicians. Yet physicians may naturally feel exploited when interactional partners (patients) fail to provide feedback, and render the relationship ineffective by refusing to negotiate or carry out treatment advice (Fuller & Quesada, 1973). Physicians in Lane's (1983) study attributed twice as many compliance factors to patients as to physicians. If patients expect comfort and understanding, it seems physicians expect respect and cooperation.

That patients and physicians misunderstand each other is illustrated by McKinlay (1975). In that study, physicians significantly underrated patients' ability to understand 12 of 13 health-related words. But they used the words with patients nonetheless. For example, the doctors judged that patients would not understand the word *membranes* but reported using it 44.4% of the time, nonetheless.

In a random study of 336 patients and their physicians, Waitzkin (1984) found that patients wanted the same amount of information regardless of education or socioeconomic status. Physicians, however, offered less information to less educated, poorer patients because they asked fewer questions than others.

Finally, studies suggest that the expectations of patients and caregivers are affected by cultural differences. Medical jargon is an obvious symbol of the language barrier between medicine and lifeworld. Although such jargon provides the benefits of efficiency, precision, and emotional detachment, it can render a patient ignorant and passive (Coleman, 1983). Unable to comprehend what is being said, a person is powerless to dispute or contribute to statements made. According to Coleman, "There is an inherent weakness—in some cases an eliticism—in any semantic environment. In healthcare, [*sic*] this weakness could lead to death" (p. 407).

Other literature suggests that institutional agendas have a strong and sometimes perplexing influence on medical transactions. An anthropologist, Firth (1977), shared an analytic diary she kept while undergoing diagnosis in a tropical disease hospital. It describes her adaptation to the hospital culture with its unfamiliar orientation to obedience and bodily functions:

> The constant concern with defecation, along with other prohibitions, is strangely regressive-making. Yet one comes to see that one obeys and accepts if not directly to avoid harassment, then indirectly for the sake of someone else, who will suffer for your non-conformity, [*sic*] in this case a nurse on whose good offices I am dependent. (p. 147)

Hospital patients are not the only ones socialized to medical routines. After observing more than 250 episodes of obstetric care, sociologist Danziger (1980) concluded that the doctor's office caregivers socialized patients on how "pregnancy ought to occur" (p. 274), including what complaints were legitimate at each stage. Danziger said the patients were expected to play along with the "normalcy" theme in early pregnancy, then conform to a "medical crisis definition" (p. 293) of childbirth. She argued that the power of medical expertise was used to control the pregnancy and birth experience in keeping with a medical agenda, minimizing the patient's personal agenda and input.

Long (1985) also attested to the rigidity of medical routines. His video observation of 200 general practitioners showed that—even when patients were widely diverse—some physicians used nearly identical greetings, questions, and statements. Long suggested that rigidity is an artifact of medical education largely devoid of interaction skills training, compounded by negligible opportunities for physicians to receive feedback once in private practice.

The disparity between medical and lifeworld cultures may be heightened by patients' isolation from familiar contexts. In "The Moral Career of the Day Patient," Weir (1977) offered a thick description of a day-long outpatient experience in a men's surgical ward. He described the patient first as a neophyte, excluded from regular inpatient routines and isolated from other day patients. The power of the institution is underlined in Weir's humorous account of a mealtime ritual, "When he [postoperative patient] requests lunch he may be referred to the ward sister who has then to adjucate his 'medical' condition and determine whether the administration of boiled beef, mashed potatoes and cabbage is likely to prove fatal" (p. 138). The outpatient's "instant career" involves a rapid socialization and then a sudden expulsion at the end of the day back into "normal" society (p. 140). The middle time is choreographed to suit medical routines. Weir described the staff's obvious disappointment when a patient did not progress through a series of "normal" stages.

Culture may also influence how and when a person visits the doctor, and the way he or she describes symptoms. Zola (1983) and his assistants conducted open-ended interviews with patients in the waiting rooms of Massachusetts clinics. He found that Italians complained of more symptoms, more affected body areas, and more serious effects than did Irish patients. The Irish were more specific, the Italians more diffuse. Zola suggested that the Italian culture encourages dramatization as a coping mechanism, thereby affecting the presentation of health concerns. He also found that Italians were more likely to seek medical aid during an interpersonal crisis (often unrelated to their symptoms) or when their symptoms interfered with social activities. Irish were more apt to see a doctor when someone urged them to and Anglos when they perceived that their conditions were interfering with work and physical activity. Zola speculated that one's physician may represent a cure-all for everything that ails—even, perhaps often—when the ailment is more social than biological. He concluded that "health and illness *are* social phenomena" (p. 120).

In summary, there seem to be many reasons why patients and physicians harbor disparate expectations. From the physician's standpoint, it may seem unrealistic that patients seek solace, support, and medical cures in the limited frame of a doctor's visit or hospital stay. Limitations are necessary to manage the emotional and time demands of medical practice. Furthermore, physicians are not entirely to blame if patients yield the floor and remain mute about their concerns and questions. Patients, on the other hand, may be quick to assume that a physician is insensitive and domineering. It can be embarrassing and insulting to have personal concerns shrugged off as unimportant. Moreover, a comforting word may be better tonic than a painkiller. All in all, patients may often leave medical exams wondering whether the doctor really understood the problem.

In Barnlund's (1976) terms, patients and physicians approach the transaction with somewhat different purposes. They may perceive different time constraints and be separated by the differences and inadequacy of language. Overcoming these obstacles would seem to require a great deal of interpersonal negotiation. But as the following section demonstrates, patients and physicians typically forsake the conventional give and take of everyday conversation.

CONVERSATIONAL POWER DIFFERENCES

Research supports that the high control style of interviewing many doctors learned in medical school discourages disclosure and questions by patients. One result is less diagnostic information (Friedman & DiMatteo, 1979; Weston & Brown, 1989). With a series of observations and interviews, sociologist Todd (1993) revealed what five gynecology patients did not tell their gynecologist. The women admitted lying about their contraceptive use to avoid the doctor's disapproval or to mask their own embarrassment. Explained one patient: "I think he'd rather see me take the pill . . . and so instead of getting into confrontations with him, because he's pretty strong willed . . ." (p. 278).

Discourse analysis shows that physicians consistently breach turn-taking sequences, dominate questioning, and abruptly shift topics. Roter's (1989) meta-analysis of 80 studies shows that physicians talk about 10 times as much as patients, mostly giving information and asking close-ended questions. Roter concluded that current medical communication is neither open nor patient-centered. A collaborative pattern often emerges in which the patient offers only brief replies to close-ended questions, forsaking the interactive feedback of casual conversation. The following studies describe the lopsided nature of many medical transactions and the methods of interaction that make that imbalance possible.

West (1993) reported that the family physicians she studied asked 91% of the questions in medical exams. Furthermore, physicians *answered* only 87% of the patients' questions, sometimes countering with questions of their own, other times referring silently to medical notes without explanation. Likewise, Arnston and Philipsborn (1982) reported that pediatricians they studied asked twice as many questions as patients' parents, issued twice as many commands, and made 61% of the utterances.

The work of Frankel and associates illustrates how physicians use interruptions to reject information they do not desire, cutting short what patients would like to have known about their conditions. Of 74 patients observed by Beckman and Frankel (1984), only 17 were allowed to complete their opening statements of concerns. Physicians interrupted most patients after about 18 seconds, although completed statements never exceeded 2½ minutes. Usually, physicians claimed the floor with specific, close-ended questions.

Moreover, Frankel (1984) reported that patients yielded the floor 15 out of 16 times analyzed when a physician's speech overlapped their own, and patients did not recycle utterances they abandoned. This acquiescence contributes to the one-sidedness of many medical interviews.

It has also been noted that physicians shift topics and ignore questions. Paget (1993) analyzed three conversations between an internist and a former cancer patient. The report describes the physician's inattentiveness once he dismissed the patient's complaints as "just nerves." The physician displayed almost no forms of conversational politeness. He ignored questions, abruptly shifted topics and in many ways short-circuited open communication. Likewise, Shuy (1993) reported that physicians in his study initiated 27 of 30 topic shifts.

In summary, there is much to say about how communication is structured in medical settings. Transaction analysis suggests that the patient and physician may collaborate in conversational patterns involving interruptions, topic shifts, and acquiescence. These patterns suggest substantial power differences, often in the physician's favor.

THE GOOD NEWS

On the bright side, a few studies point out communication strategies that work well in medical contexts. Drass (1988) described the adeptness with which nurse practitioners in his study educate patients while attending to their health, emotional, and social concerns. And several studies show that medical students who learn to conduct gynecological exams with feedback from trained mock patients are more considerate and less anxious than those who learn on plastic models (Fang et al., 1984; Lesserman & Luke, 1982). Following is a description of other strategies with positive results.

There is some indication that caregivers can improve patient recall by using highly expressive language. This effect was strong for same-gender dyads, but less evident between men and women (Bush, 1985). Bush's advice to caregivers is "develop a relatively expressive communication style if you want to improve recall of your instructions, but tone it down a bit for the opposite sex" (p. 114). He suggested that members of the opposite gender may be distracted by the interpersonal attractiveness of expressive speakers.

There is also evidence that priming patients to ask questions may help balance the conversational scales. Finney et al. (1990) found that, following preappointment interviews, the parents of pediatric patients asked the doctor more questions than did other parents. The authors reported that these additional bids for information did not interfere with clinical routines. This suggests that it may be more efficient for patients/parents to ask questions than for a doctor to provide information blind to their concerns. In the preappointment interviews, researchers asked the parents about their concerns and questions and encouraged them to address those issues with the caregiver. They suggested that nurses and receptionists may help with this task.

One particularly promising technique is the use of humor and verbal play in medical settings. Although verbal play has received little attention so far, early studies by Ragan (1990; Beck & Ragan, 1992) and associates suggest that levity accomplishes many goals without prolonging or disrupting medical routines. For instance, Beck and Ragan studied the way gynecology patients and a female nurse practitioner used playful asides during exams. They concluded that the women used verbal play to demonstrate politeness in an awkward situation and to show their identification with each other. The interactants switched easily from verbal play to medical talk without prolonging exams. In a similar study, Ragan noted frequent instances of shared laughter in audio recordings of 41 gynecological exams. Verbal play seemed to reduce the face threat of the exams. Ragan concluded that play may ease the problematic nature of health care experiences for both patients and caregivers.

In summary, it appears there are communication techniques that minimize the effects of status difference, unfamiliarity, and embarrassment common in medical transactions. As suggested before, these may be used to facilitate more open, less asymmetrical communication between patients and caregivers. The benefits may serve them both.

Chapter 3

▼

Related Humor Literature

While tracing humor through available literature one clutches at many strings and finds most of them dishearteningly short. There is some research, but not a lot. However, for the researcher willing to disregard disciplinary lines and hurdle great periods of apparently "humorless" scholarship, there is much of interest. For one, the functions of humor seem remarkably similar across the world and in many situations. In a wide variety of cultures, people use humor to foster relationships, vent emotions, and exert social control. Although this review is informed by the study of humor in many settings, it is focused most directly on medical setting humor. Overall, I summarize literature about the ways humor affects/reflects physical health, psychological well-being, embarrassment, interpersonal rapport, attention-getting efforts, and cultural norms.

PHYSICAL EFFECTS

A range of indicators suggests that laughter and humor may improve physical well-being. This section describes early evidence that humor may enhance the body's immune system, heart, and lungs, as well as reduce pain and improve mental and physical health.

The physical arousal of laughter may be viewed as a type of stress. However, it is stress of a positive sort, according to Berk et al. (1989). By taking blood samples from participants every 10 minutes, Berk et al.

19

found that cortisol levels dropped significantly among those watching a funny video, but not among members of a no-video control group. Cortisol is typically secreted by the body during stress, and excessive amounts are believed to suppress immunal functioning (for a review of the literature, see Halley, 1991). Thus, laughter may represent a type of healthy stress or "eustress" capable of counteracting the negative effects of classical stress.

Another way to assess the body's resilience to disease is to analyze saliva for the presence of a natural virus-fighting substance called immonoglobulin A (IgA). IgA levels have been shown to increase while participants watch humorous videos (Dillon, Minchoff, & Baker, 1985; Lambert & Lambert, 1995; Lefcourt, Davidson-Katz, & Kueneman, 1990), and maintain higher and more stable than normal levels among regular humor users (Dillon et al., 1985). Additionally, high humor users seem to suffer less from chronic stress. Martin and Dobbin (1988) found that, among low humor users, IgA levels dropped during stressful life episodes, but the levels of high humor users remained relatively stable despite life's hassles. These studies contribute to the idea that humor helps to sustain and even to bolster the body's immune system.

Pointing out that "laughter is essentially a respiratory act," Burton (1986, p. 164) reviewed evidence that laughter is accompanied by increased lung volume. Her literature review also suggests that laughter produces temporary rises in heart rate and blood pressure, followed by drops below prelaughter levels. The same effect is noted in muscle activation (Robinson, 1983) and stimulation of the sympathetic nervous system (McGhee, 1983). The temporary tension of laughter is followed by greater than normal relaxation.

This relaxation may contribute to humor's effectiveness as a pain reliever. As mentioned in chapter 1, Cousins (1979) used humor to overcome the pain of a potentially crippling disease. He attested that 10 minutes of belly laughter afforded him 2 hours of pain-free sleep. Likewise, elderly chronic pain sufferers in Adams and McGuire's (1986) study requested less pain medication and reported more positive affects after watching a series of funny videos over a 6-week period.

This pain-buffering effect may not be exclusive to comedy, however. Participants in a pain threshold study were able to tolerate more compression of a blood pressure cuff after watching a humorous video than before, particularly when they found the video to be highly absorbing (Zillmann, Rockwell, Schweitzer, & Sundar, 1993). No effect was noted among participants who watched dramatic or instructional videos.

However, a tragic video was as effective as the comic videos at raising participants' thresholds for pain. The researchers speculate that the affective intensity of both comedy and tragedy may make physical stimuli seem less intense, or may evoke changes in the sympathetic nervous system that reduce tactile sensitivity.

There is also some evidence that everyday humor use correlates with good health. Carroll and Shmidt (1992) compared 51 college students' responses on a Situational Humor Response Questionnaire and a 13-item health inventory. Students who reported using humor as a daily coping strategy listed fewer health problems (-0.34 correlation). Simon (1990) reported that elderly individuals who use humor as a coping strategy usually score higher than others on perceived health inventories. Similarly, efforts to promote a positive state of mind are often linked to health improvements (Halley, 1991). Strategies shown to have especially positive indications for health include relaxation, massage, meditation, and humor use.

It remains to be seen what health care professionals will make of the possible link between health and humor. Robinson (1983) predicted that humor will become more professionally acceptable as the focus of health turns from negative indicators (that health is not present) to positive, holistic indicators (that health is being maintained). If this is true, the emerging emphasis on prevention may lead medical professionals to regard laughter as a more legitimate feature of assessment and treatment than in the past.

PSYCHOLOGICAL EFFECTS

Particularly with humor, it is difficult to distinguish between physical and psychological effects. The following research from psychology and psychotherapy examines humor's place in the connection between state of mind and state of body.

Psychotherapist Richman (1995) credited humor with prolonging the lives of many suicidal patients. He reported numerous incidents in which laughter at a stressful subject seemed to quickly and effectively reduce a patient's anxiety. Particularly salient, he wrote, is the elderly's use of storytelling, which builds enjoyable bonds between them and others. "Humor must be communicated to others, and its simple presence reduces isolation" (p. 273).

O'Connell (1987) put a similar idea into practice with his Natural High Therapy program, designed to help troubled individuals reconcile the frustrations of life by laughing about their problems. After many years practicing the method, O'Connell is convinced that that high humor users are more tolerant of imperfection, less guilt-ridden, and more interested in social interaction than others.

Based on a series of self-report inventories, Kuiper and Martin (1993) reported that people who use humor as a coping mechanism and are quick to laugh in commonplace situations enjoy a number of psychological benefits. High humor users tend to judge themselves by less harsh and rigid standards. They tend to enjoy a more stable and positive sense of self and regard themselves as more social and less given to depression. Humor's effectiveness in easing depression has been documented by others as well (Danzer, Dale, & Klions, 1990; Nezu, Nezu, & Blissett, 1988).

Likewise, there is mixed evidence that people who use humor frequently have higher morale (Simon, 1990) and fewer mood swings (Martin & Lefcourt, 1983). In a series of three studies, Martin and Lefcourt found that high humor users were less disturbed than others by negative life events. Some argue that humor's effects are less sweeping, however. Nezu et al. (1988) performed a study similar to Martin and Lefcourt's. They found that humor seemed to reduce depression but not anxiety, although both are commonly regarded as components of stress. Porterfield's (1987) findings are also slightly at odds with Martin and Lefcourt's. His replication of their 1983 study suggests that humor users are less prone than most to depression, but Porterfield did not find a direct link between humor use and resilience to unfavorable life events. The implication is that humor helps in a general, but not a specific way. All in all, these studies buttress the common belief in humor's beneficial effects, although scholars have yet to reach consensus on the precise nature of those effects.

As a health-related coping strategy, humor is being incorporated into programs concerning AIDS. Programs across the country have begun using humor to reduce the threatening atmosphere of AIDS treatment and education (see, e.g., Fennell, 1993). In less formal circumstances, patients and friends sometimes use humor to deal with devastating diagnoses. Peterson (1992), an AIDS researcher, recalled the last years of a dying friend's life as the most laughter-filled in her memory. Callen's (1990) book, *Surviving Aids*, is filled with the playful, apparently therapeutic, comments of 14 long-term HIV/AIDS survivors.

Humor may be a particularly effective technique for dealing with unavoidable hardships. Coles (1989), a physician-researcher, attested:

> I am still constantly surprised at the ability of my seniors [elderly patients] to laugh at their problems, to separate themselves, as it were . . . that's the beauty of humor. It allows us to express our deepest concerns, our passions and our doubts while asserting control over those feelings—no matter what our age. (p. 85)

Consistent with this perspective is Lefcourt and Martin's (1986) study of humor use and physical disability. After surveying and observing 30 severely disabled persons, Lefcourt and Martin reported that those who demonstrate a willingness for humor are more vital and confident than others. The researchers were initially surprised when the high humor users rated themselves only minimally in control of life events. On reflection, they suggested that an external locus of control may allow disabled persons to "come to terms" with their conditions without blaming themselves. Lefcourt and Martin would not be the first to associate a forgiving quality with humor appreciation (viz., Kuiper & Martin, 1993; O'Connell, 1987).

Stress can also lead to burnout, employee turnover, emotional detachment, and dissatisfaction among caregivers (DesCamp & Thomas, 1993). Using a series of self-report questionnaires, DesCamp and Thomas found that nurses who engage in physical play at work experience less job dissatisfaction and less work load stress. They suggested that we rethink concepts of professionalism that restrict people from engaging in lighthearted, stress-relieving activities. Some amount of "goofing off" may serve a useful function. Burton (1986) described the role of humor in the high-stress environment of a critical care unit:

> Where minute-to-minute stress is most pronounced, where patient lives are temporarily or permanently suspended in a technological holding pattern, and where the demands on the accompanying nurse can be unrelenting, humor is often present, and is often found to make a positive difference. Not because illness, hospitalization, suffering, and death are funny, but because somehow, through humor and laughter, we adapt to them. (p. 162)

These conclusion are not new. Nearly 40 years ago, Fox (1959) described the stress of 11 young physicians working on a research metabolic ward, asserting that the doctors developed a "highly patterned and intricate form of humor" (p. 76) to offset their anxiety. At about the same time, Coser (1959) identified similar coping strategies among hospital patients. Patients shared what she called "griping humor" to relieve anxiety about themselves, the rigidity of the hospital, and the inflexibility of hospital routines. Similarly, Coombs and Goldman (1973) found that humor was a key method of lightening tension in an intensive care unit, and that veteran personnel were most adept at comic relief.

To conclude, there is evidence that humor has positive indications for physical and emotional health. We do well, however, to remember that humor has limitations and research about it is in early stages. Although long an advocate of humor and psychotherapy, Goldstein (1987) wryly observed that comedians do not seem to live any longer than do other people. He suggested that, in the end, mirth may more reliably increase the quality—rather than the length—of life.

EMBARRASSMENT

Humor performs a face-saving function. Metts and Cupach (1989) noted that humor is one of the most common responses to embarrassing accidents. Even more grandly, Duncan (1962) called comedy one of the great societal arts, alongside religion and drama. In his book *Communication and Social Order*, Duncan described humorous expression as a way of airing fears and rallying support.

Medical care often requires a patient to air or confront fears. It also violates many taboos of daily life. Relative strangers have license to see and touch nearly any part of a patient's body. It is necessary at times to speak openly about such topics as bowel movements and sexual history. It is not surprising then that patients (and caregivers) may experience awkwardness or an embarrassing loss of poise.

In anecdotal terms, Armour (1972) applauded those who trade mirth for health-related chagrin:

> Happily, I travel (rather slowly) in a group of friends who are very frank about their prostate glands. One, who had a prostatectomy when he was in his early 70s, is not only happy to talk about it but proud. . . . "It was as big as a grapefruit," he will tell anyone. . . . I have been told I have a size 2 [prostate] which is large enough to call for occasional treatment but not big enough to be proud of or to dominate the conversation with. (p. 126)

Few people are so bold as that. But studies suggest that less extreme measures are helpful in reducing embarrassment in medical situations

(Beck & Ragan, 1992; Ragan, 1990; Robinson, 1975; Smith-Dupré, 1993). Overall, this research suggests that people commonly use humor to manage face-threatening situations. In doing so, they downplay the solemnity that might accompany a loss of dignity, reframing the episodes as affiliative and unserious instead.

LAUGHTER AND AFFINITY

The socially pleasing aspects of humor are widely touted. A sense of humor is among the most coveted traits in a perspective mate. It ranks in the top four, along with kindness, consideration, and honesty (Goodwin, 1990). Humor also seems to affect work relationships. After studying employees in a London department store, Bradney (1957) remarked:

> Those who joke readily are obviously very much more popular than those who do not. They are approached more often by others. They elicit a more favorable reaction than others when they make an approach themselves and they are never seen to sit alone at meal breaks. (p. 180)

Humor's role in establishing friendly medical relationships is supported by Beck and Ragan (1992), Coser (1960) and Smith-Dupré (1992). Coser noted that shared humor seemed to diminish social distance between senior and junior staff members at a mental hospital. In a similar way, hospital patients and caregivers use humor to build rapport and to reframe threatening encounters as friendly exchanges (Smith-Dupré, 1992).

In a dissertation urging the cultivation of humor in health professions, Robinson (1975) reflected on her experience as a nurse, and on research observation in a hospital. She posited that humor in the hospital improves communication, fosters friendliness, and soothes emotions. Robinson urged health care professionals to be generous with their smiles: "It says to the patient, or colleague or student, 'Relax, I'm a friend, you can trust me. This isn't such a terrible place'" (pp. 52-53). Her words echo a theory proposed by Hayworth, an anthropologist. Hayworth (1928) suggested that laughter is an instinctual sign of safety predating verbal language. "Laughter was originally a vocal sign to other members of the group that they might relax with safety" (p. 370). His theory helps to explain why laughter is contagious. By joining in, we relay the signal.

There is also evidence that good-humored patients get better treatment. Coombs and Goldman (1973) found that intensive care personnel listed pleasant and cooperative patients as their favorites. Said one informant:

> I tend to give a greater amount of care to patients whom I feel more comfortable with. I tend to make an extra effort to cater to the needs of patients who "hit me" the right way. It is not that I don't make an effort to care for each of my patients, but I seem to put a little extra into catering to the needs of patients with whom I can relate well. (pp. 352–353)

In a keynote address before members of the Nursing Society, Metcalf (1987) challenged caregivers to acknowledge their own humanity. "You are not a job with a person inserted in it, any more than a cancer patient is a disease with a person stuck in it" (p. 20). He maintained that caregivers who lose humor and the zest for living "cease to be part of the healing, and become part of the illness" (p. 20).

The affinity function of humor extends beyond medical settings. In his work on humor in the workplace, Kahn (1989) identified a "sliding scale" of humor, with which people may either create a social distance or bridge interpersonal gaps. This idea is echoed in different ways within many studies. Seckman and Couch (1989), for instance, noted that factory workers accomplish much of their "relationship work" with humor. They observed employees using jocularity to solidify existing relationships and to include new employees in social circles. Similarly, Vinton (1989) suggested that workers use humor to socialize new members, hint about work performance, and relax status differences.

In summary, humor use seems to be a particularly attractive quality. Typically, people who laugh together feel comfortable together. This may be a result of custom, or as Hayworth suggested, an instinctual reaction to laughter as a sign of safety.

HUMOR AS ATTENTION-GETTER

Most studies of health communication treat the transaction as primarily therapeutic, not educational. But my observations suggest that caregivers spend a good percentage of their time teaching patients. In Smith-Dupré (1992), I noted that they use humor to make statements memorable and attention-getting. One physician, for instance, admonished a patient, "Don't lift anything heavier than a peanut butter and jelly sandwich. And then it depends on how much peanut butter is on it!"

Although this attention-getting function of humor is not mentioned in many health studies, it does come up in education literature. Robinson (1975) recalled a memorable-because-comical example from her medical studies, "The classic definition of menstruation as 'the weeping of a disappointed uterus' not only produces a laugh, but conveys in one short sentence the physiology of the menstrual cycle to which the student can always relate" (p. 120). Unfortunately, the case for classroom humor is similar to that of medical humor. Many people go to bat for the idea, but little research is available to explain it.

HUMOR AND CULTURE

Raddcliff-Brown (1940/1959) was perhaps the first scholar to recognize the cultural importance of joking relationships. Such relationships consist of "two persons in which one is by custom permitted, and in some instances required, to tease or make fun of the other, who in turn is required to take no offence" (p. 90). Raddcliff-Brown noted that who-jokes-with-whom says much about social hierarchy and expressions of respect. Scholars have applied the same analysis to other cultures. In U.S. hospitals in the 1950s, for instance, bosses initiated humor with subordinates, but seldom the other way around (Coser, 1960).

In light of studies (e.g., Zola, 1983) that depict medical transactions as cross-cultural, it is interesting to examine how humor is used to negotiate social expectations. In his well-known "Jokers Wild" study, Linstead (1985) proposed that humor characterizes the culture of an organization and provides a means to continually refine that culture. He observed that humor is a socially acceptable way of marking violations and challenging social hierarchy and rules. This premise is illustrated well in Peterson's (1975) account of one-sided and two-sided joking in a newly integrated school. Peterson described ways that African-American and Euro-American teachers used joking behaviors to comment on and change the expectations of others:

> A meeting of faculty from all schools had been called and a white teacher passed by a group of black male teachers as she left the building. One of them, with whom she had established a one-sided joking relationship,

called "Good-bye, see you tomorrow." She asked, "Aren't you going to the
meeting?" He replied, "Yes, but you won't see us there. You will be sitting
with your white friends, so I'm saying good-bye now." (p. 35)

The teacher reported later that the jest made her so indignant she rode
to the meeting with the African-American men and sat with them during
the assembly. The man's joke had the effect of calling attention to (and
breaking) a pattern.

Furthermore, ethnographies of humor show striking resemblances
between humor used around the world. Miller (1967) reported that
Chippewa use humor to promote social unity in the tribe, validate
friendships, allow good-natured hinting, and relieve tension. Similarly,
in the South India village of Koya, teasing behaviors are used to unite
"constellations of individuals" (Brukman, 1975).

Overall, it seems that humor is an indicator of cultural patterns and
a useful way to shape those patterns. Within organizations and broader
contexts, humor seems to be a valuable tool of social negotiation. U.S.
medical personnel use humor to establish friendly relationships in the
same way that Chippewa trade amiable quips. The Koya in South India
use jokes to communicate social norms as do the Hopi in Arizona, U.S.
school teachers, and patients in hospitals. The idea that humor creates
and affects organizational climate is salient to medical settings, where
caregivers must socialize patients to the rituals of a medical institution
(and patients must often negotiate subtle changes in the rituals). This
may explain, in part, why the hospital humor I observed is particularly
prevalent and bold.

VERBAL PLAY

Much of what caregivers call "joking around" falls within the category
of verbal play. Goffman (1974) and Bateson (1956) suggested that play
arises when people tacitly agree to treat some activity as "other than
usual." An exaggerated wink, for instance, may signal that one is not
serious, but "only kidding." Playful episodes may also be marked by
frequent role-switching and deviations from routine. As Glenn and
Knapp (1987) reported, a routine sequence can be made to seem playful
by altering, repeating, or skipping steps in the sequence. I have observed
that patients often introduce humor into medical exchanges by responding to routine questions in unexpected ways. For instance, when asked

if anyone had drawn blood from him that day, one patient responded with a grin, "Oh yes. If they take any more I'll be fresh out!"

Ellis (1973) summarized different theories about play. Some say that play serves to expend surplus energy and provide relaxation, and that playacting is a way to prepare for and reenact important life events. Otherwise viewed, play seems to be a relational barometer reflecting/affecting interpersonal intimacy. Baxter (1992) reported a high correlation between closeness and playfulness in both friendships and romantic partnerships. Verbal play may also function in conflict situations. Alberts (1990) found that the 40 couples she observed frequently used humor when managing disagreements, but the couples had mixed ideas about how effective the humor was at controlling conflict.

Thus, it seems that play surfaces in many situations for a variety of reasons we are only beginning to understand. Researchers are still divided about the distinction (and, if distinct, the relationship) between verbal play and humor. Some (e.g., Cheatwood, 1983; McGhee, 1979) treat humor as a subset of play, and some (e.g., Long & Graesser, 1988) view play as a particular type of humor. Moreover, although many embrace the view of play as other than usual how removed is it from the activities of "life as usual"? Huizinga (1970) characterized play as something "standing quite consciously outside ordinary life" (p. 32), an activity that engages one only during "free time" (p. 26).

I do not attempt to distinguish between humor and verbal play in the episodes described here. There is a case to be made that "joking around" sequences are sometimes funny (humorous) and sometimes only fun (playful). But in my experience, this is a difference of style, not of function. I also believe it is self-evident in my data and other data (e.g., Baxter, 1992; Beck & Ragan, 1992; Betcher, 1981; Glenn & Knapp, 1987; Ragan, 1990; Ragan & Glenn, 1990) that play is not merely a leisure-time activity. That is, although playful episodes are bracketed as not serious, they are often embedded within serious, routine sequences of daily life. The data I present suggest strongly that humor and verbal play are often present in tense, even life-threatening, situations.

SUMMARY

The (albeit limited) research on humor in health care settings points to several recurring functions of mirth. Humor serves as an invitation to greater social intimacy, and a means of buffering such emotions as anxiety, anger, fear, and embarrassment. As a means of reducing social distance, humor can help caregivers dispel the stiff formality of medical institutions. Verbal play provides a means of exerting energy, experimenting, and displaying/encouraging greater intimacy. Overall, there are indications that joking around may encourage open communication between patient and caregiver, and help the patient feel less alienated.

Chapter 4

▼

Conceptual Foundations

Although this book is not addressed to any one theory of communication, it is informed by many theories and many approaches. For instance, in addition to theories of humor and social transaction, each perspective I use is grounded in its own assumptions about the nature of knowledge and humanity. I describe these theories and approaches as the analysis unfolds. But there is an even deeper theoretical grounding worth explicating here.

At a fundamental level, this book is influenced by my beliefs about the nature of communication and the best ways to understand it. My beliefs contribute to a conceptual framework which influences the methods I use and the questions I explore. The approach I take has roots in Bateson's (1972) idea of interactionism or relational communication and Rawlin's (1989) work on dialectics. As described here, I hold that communication is a process of collaborative transaction characterized by interpersonal negotiation and contextual considerations.

RELATIONAL COMMUNICATION

Bateson (1972) proposed that communication involves more than simple message transmission. Indeed, from the viewpoint of relational communication, message transmission is anything but simple! As Barnlund (1981) attested, "We are born into an environment so varied, so complex, so devoid of inherent meaning as to overwhelm the senses. Yet

31

no matter how chaotic it seems, we make it intelligible" (p. 92). Vested with the need to share a sensible understanding with others, yet constrained by the limitations and ambiguities of language, we do what we must to achieve some measure of mutual understanding.

What we must do, according to Bateson, is offer (and attend to) clues which reduce ambiguity to a manageable level. To do this we not only communicate with others, but communicate *about* our communication. That is, we plant clues so that we may present a less puzzling mystery to those who attempt to understand us. These clues (or cues) suggest how the message should be (and is being) interpreted. And because we are concerned about more than message transmission, we also swap metacommunicative cues suggesting how the message is relevant to the relationship and to the situation of the interactants. Such metacommunicative cues act as subtle guides to interpretation. To use Bateson's terminology, they contribute to the context or the "frame" of the transaction and make understanding possible. (See chapter 19 for a more thorough explanation and application of Bateson's concept of *framing*.) Moreover, this process of metacommunicative cuing is simultaneous and continuous. Watzlawick and Beavin (1977) wrote that "Persons act and react, 'receive' and 'send,' in such detail and complexity that these terms lose their meaning as verbs of individual action" (p. 57).

I found the premises of relational communication to be justified and useful in my research. The people I observe do seem to offer cues about how their utterances and actions are to be interpreted. For instance, it is informative to examine the ways that social actors display to each other that an action or utterance is "humorous" or "playful" rather than "serious."[1] In the data I present, I show evidence of a sophisticated system of metacommunicative "humor cues," including slightly raised eyebrows, exaggerated facial expressions, and idiosyncratic word choice, to name a few. (The presence and significance of these cues is even more interesting considering that participants themselves are often only tacitly aware of them, and seem to attend and present cues in a manner that seems almost effortless.)

I find it useful as well to consider communication as a collaborative process. For instance, it is worth noting that apparently serious messages are sometimes treated as funny after humor cues are included in

---

[1]This reliance on metacommunicative cuing extends even beyond the realm of human transaction. Bateson (1972) noted that monkeys (and apparently a whole array of other animals) display metacommunicative cues that make it possible for others of their species, and even humans, to distinguish between their play fights and earnest fighting.

feedback. Furthermore, messages delivered with laughter may be taken up as serious. It often seems that the receiver has as much (or more) influence than the sender on the *meaning*[2] ultimately attributed to a message. These observations support the idea that communication is a collaborative process and that meanings are mutually managed, not simply imparted.

DIALECTICS

The dialectic viewpoint considers that people both influence, and are influenced by, their environments (Rawlins, 1989). Historically, the idea of a society–individual dialectic grew from discontent with Marxism, at one extreme, and Freudian psychoanalysis at the other. Alone, neither view could completely explain human behavior. "Marxism was heavy on the side of society and short on the individual, while psychoanalysis had the opposite emphasis" (Buss, 1979, p. 317).

Dialectics presumes that "reality" is shaped—not by one force—but by many forces. Everything exists in relation to something else. It is misleading or impossible to consider people or things in isolation. Rawlins (1989) wrote: "Discrete 'things' are inconceivable...what comprises reality are relations" (p. 158).

From a dialectic perspective, social actors continually negotiate to achieve a satisfactory balance between such relational opposites as dependence and independence, judgment and acceptance, and expressiveness and protectiveness. (I argue as well that medical transactions are shaped by a dialectic between helping and hurting.) Because relationships are continually managed by the people involved in them, they are products of mutual influence. This includes the relationship between an individual and the social world—a dialectic Rawlins (1989) called *praxis*. Praxis is the process by which people shape their environments and are simultaneously shaped by them. Rawlins offered the following example: "How one elects to treat one's friend will result in changes in the composition of the friendship, which will change or limit one's options for communicating with the friend at another social juncture" (p. 163).

---

[2]I italicize the word *meaning* to make the point that I am speaking in relational terms. That is, I consider meaning to be a collaborative accomplishment of the transaction—a product of both parties' treatment of an action or utterance—not in terms of what either party might intend to communicate.

In this way of thinking, "caregiver" and "patient" are not ready-made roles into which people simply step. The caregiver and patient help to fashion the roles themselves, and in so doing create a relational reality that sanctions certain behaviors. Thus, doctors and patients are partly correct when they say that the situation limits them. But they may fail to realize that they play a part in creating the situation.

Rawlins (1989) also said that friendships are often "fraught with ambiguity" (p. 169). Without institutional guidelines to define friendship, the relationship is one of interpersonal interpretation. Research suggests that medical communication suffers from the opposite extreme. It is often fraught with inflexibility. This inflexibility is achieved conversationally by patients' acquiescence and physicians' dominance (Arnston & Philipsborn, 1982; Beckman & Frankel, 1984; Frankel, 1984; Paget, 1993; Roter, 1989; Shuy, 1993; Todd, 1993; West, 1993). It is underscored by the mutual acceptance of institutional agendas and routines (Danziger, 1980; Firth, 1977; Weir, 1977).

Several studies include the bewildered comments of patients who perceive that actions are prescribed for them by members of the medical institution. For instance, Firth (1977) recalled of her hospital stay:

> I put on a dressing-gown and strolled onto the balcony. A nurse reproved me: "You should not go onto the balcony in your dressing-gown. You might catch cold." "I think it's warm enough!" I replied. "Well, that's up to you," was her sharp retort. Am I an adult seeking specialist advice in this hospital, or a child who knows nothing of what is good for it? (p. 153)

To the degree that patients and caregivers accept institutional routines, those routines are confining. Put another way, medical transactions can change only if patients and caregivers realize that they are agents of change. Some constraints are beyond their control. But to an extent, they negotiate the tensions that define their relationships.

Important in this outlook is the theoretical position that people can and do change. One must go beyond a purely behaviorist mind set to accept that people are actively involved in creating their social environments. In the words of Rawlins (1989):

> Individuals are depicted as conscious, active selectors of possible choices from a field that is partially conceived by them, partially negotiated with others, and partially determined by social and natural factors outside of their purview. In any case, the choices a person makes simultaneously engender and restrict options. (p. 185)

Unless we accept that patients and caregivers are to some extent capable of changing their communication patterns, the study of medical transactions is purely speculative. We can have no hope of improving the process. At the same time, a dialectic perspective reminds us that change requires more than an individual effort. Physicians cannot change if patients do not collaborate with them to do so. And wide-sweeping change requires more still. Institutional, systemic factors will not change without the concerted effort of many people.

IMPLICATIONS

There are several implications of the conceptual framework I have adopted. First of all, the focus is directed to outward manifestations of communication and less (or only very tentatively) to participants' intentions. Second, assuming as I do that people are more than reactive agents, I must also accept that human action is not strictly predictable. Each transaction is managed in a unique context in a unique way. Although I may comment on the contextual features which often characterize transactions, I cannot say how those features will combine to affect any particular person or conversation. Thus, my work is aimed more at description and awareness than at prediction.

On the other hand, there are several advantages of this approach. If people are indeed teleologic beings, research may be able to do something more than predict. It may provide a basis for awareness and development. This is particularly important in health communication, where so many bemoan the ineffectiveness of patient–caregiver transactions. Second, by considering communication as a phenomenon that exists between (not within) people, I am able to ground my claims empirically. I can quote conversations and even play recordings as evidence of the claims I make.

Perhaps most importantly, an orientation to communication as relational and dialectic admits the complexity of life, health, and medical transactions. It allows inclusion of many factors and makes few presumptions about people based solely on age, gender, illness, and so on. I suggest that a developmental approach may provide a badly needed antidote to the rigid biomedical model, which places emphasis on objective signs and laboratory tests. If we acknowledge that people are affected by complex dialectics including emotional, social, and biological influences, it is inadequate to base decisions solely on biological indicators. As Nussbaum (1989) asserted, "one cannot hope to understand human beings interacting or the communicative significance of that transaction without first coming to grip with the life-span context framing each interaction" (p. 3). Within the conceptual framework I present, people are viewed as constantly developing, both affecting and reacting to the contexts of their lives. This, it seems to me, is the starting point for understanding and ultimately improving health communication.

Chapter 5

▼

Overview of Humor
in Health Care Settings

Health care settings provide a rich and demanding setting for the study of communication. The medical exam is a particularly accessible phenomenon because it repeatedly replays itself. With patience (and permission) one can watch and/or record an almost infinite number of patient encounters. But the researcher is also confronted with certain restrictions. Issues of confidentiality, ethics, and access govern the methods available to study health communication. Causality is difficult to assert given the complex nature of medicine, illness, and human transaction. It is not often easy or ethical to manipulate the conditions of someone's health. Confounding variables such as health history, treatment, and state of mind make healing itself more a humanistic art than a predictable science (McWhinney, 1989). The task is to select research methods that maintain the integrity of the phenomena without jeopardizing the processes at work.

With this book, I present a multimethod analysis of humor in medical settings that is immediate to health communication but does not interfere with it. Because I observed (and often audio recorded) medical transactions *in situ*, my data reflect the natural situations and sequences of the phenomena. I took many steps (see chapter 9) to minimize the effects of my presence on the transactions, to further ensure that neither the integrity of the data nor the quality of medical care was jeopardized.

Another advantage of this analysis is that it examines the data from several perspectives: phenomenology, ethnography, ethnomethodology, and conversation analysis. I believe the relative merits of these perspectives contribute to a thorough analysis and outweigh the disadvantages of using any one approach alone. A description of the assumptions, advantages, and limitations of each perspective is provided in later chapters.

Following is a brief rationale for the perspectives I have chosen, followed by an explanation of the sampling technique and methods of data collection used in this study.

PERSPECTIVES

Husserlian phenomenology is advantageous because it transcends empirical indicators. The phenomenologist suspends consideration of a phenomenon as it supposedly exists in time and space, and considers instead how the phenomenon is experienced (Harvey, 1989). Moreover, the phenomenologist is concerned with intersubjective experience—shared perceptions that allow members of a community to consistently distinguish between one type of phenomenon and another. In this study, how is something funny distinguishable from something not funny? And how is it that—even among strangers—we are usually able to agree on the difference between serious and funny? In short, the focus is on what, essentially, characterizes the experience of "funny." By employing phenomenology, I am able to acknowledge and examine humor as a pervasive but intangible presence in social intercourse. This approach transcends the inexact assumption that something is "funny" when, and only when, someone laughs at it.

However, as so often happens, the strength of phenomenology is also a limitation. By bracketing out empirical suppositions, we may examine the phenomenon of funny as it is essentially experienced, but in doing so we lose contextual details that—in any one case—contribute to the experience of a thing as funny. Ethnography supplies the contextual details excluded from phenomenology. It provides a look at humor—not as it exists at an essential level of consciousness—but as it is manifested in a particular culture or situation. Put another way, although the experience of "funny" is essentially the same in any context, it may take different forms and surface at different times depending on the expectations of people involved. Using ethnography, we become aware that humorous utterances in the breast care center studied are strikingly different than humorous utterances in the physical therapy department. Through naturalistic observation we can identify cultural consistencies which show that actors in each situation demonstrate a shared sense of what is useful and correct in that culture. In Part III, I identify consistent innercultural agreement about the topics of humor, the tone of humorous interactions (subtle or bold), and the appropriateness of humor in different situations. In summary, ethnography provides a richly contextual look at the health care settings studied, and makes it possible to examine humor as a cultural medium.

Once we move beyond phenomenology, we are forced to examine funny as it is displayed, not as it is experienced. This is a limitation of ethnography. Moreover, it is a limitation we live with every day as social actors. Ethnomethodology and conversation analysis are based on the assumption that people must display to each other what they expect and what they mean. Elements of another person's consciousness are no more explicitly available to neighbors than they are to scientists. Faced with the complex and ambiguous task of constantly displaying and receiving, social actors manage social transactions as they must—by collaboratively constructing/interpreting them as sensible. This achieved orderliness serves adaptively as a guide to interpretation and a guide to action. To illustrate, if we expect a physician to enter the room wearing a lab coat we might be surprised to see her pop in wearing Hawaiian print shorts. If we are sufficiently and pleasurably surprised, we find her appearance funny. (This proposition, that funny is the result of a pleasurable surprise, is explored more fully in chapter 7.)

One might say that, without a sense of orderliness, there could be no humor. Indeed, there could be no communication! Of course, cultures differ in their expectations and the codes that they uphold. This is the interest of ethnography. But they are alike in the sense that social actors anywhere can only communicate by rendering sensible the actions of themselves and others. This ever-present sense-making is the focus of ethnomethodology and conversation analysis. In this book, ethnomethodology helps to explain the Gestalt effect of humor—the way a laughable utterance sometimes transforms the way a medical transaction is managed and interpreted. I propose that humor is a persuasive guide to interpretation, suggesting that actors interpret the situation as funny or absurd rather than serious. Conversation analysis provides a close-up look at laughable complaints—one conversational technique for sharing humor.

ADVANTAGES AND LIMITATIONS
OF MULTIMETHOD RESEARCH

I believe the multimethod[1] approach of this book is its main strength. Each chapter is strengthened by others, which offer complementary examinations of the data. Indeed, in collections such as this one, it is intriguing to wonder if different methodological paths will lead to the same theoretical conclusions. Such comparisons are heralded as the main advantage of triangulation, and it is often suggested that it is a hallmark of validity for two perspectives to yield the same result. I do think multiple perspectives can and should complement one another, but I would like to caution the reader not to expect exact synchronicity. The comparative process is not so simple as that, and this is not a collection of replications. Although the gross data are the same, each perspective examines slightly different phenomena within that data. In other words, the perspectives are not designed to be different paths to the same goal. The goals, and the paths, of each are different. From different standpoints, different elements of the same data are more or less interesting and salient.

Debates are ongoing between those who wish to synthesize methods, or straddle multiple paths, and purists who defend the advantages of maintaining a singular focus. Of particular relevance here is the issue of whether context is informative when examining conversational structure. (See Appendix A for a synopsis of this debate.) I have chosen to present different analytic perspectives side by side. In this way I hope to maintain the advantages of each perspective and minimize distractions. As a result, I do not promise that every chapter ends up in the same place, but I do propose that every chapter contributes in a different and complementary way to an overall understanding of humor as an element of communication in medical transactions.

THEORETICAL SAMPLING

In all, I have collected data through naturalistic observation and occasioned interviewing in the following settings:

---

[1]It is more accurate to say that I have employed four perspectives rather than four methods. Each represents a unique way of viewing phenomena, not merely a way of collecting or analyzing data. But because the methodological consequences of these approaches are so compelling, I treat them here as methods.

- a breast care center,
- the office of a family physician,
- an outpatient physical rehabilitation unit,
- an inpatient physical rehabilitation unit,
- a hospital pediatrics department,
- a hospital orthopedic/general medicine unit, and
- a hospital surgical unit.

In chapters to come I concentrate mainly on the first three settings, using the hospital observations as a basis for comparison and contrast. (For more on the last four settings, see Smith-Dupré, 1992.)

To obtain data rich in comparison, I chose the sites using theoretical sampling, as described by Glaser and Strauss (1967). That is, I chose settings—not randomly—but purposefully, considering their theoretical significance. For instance, I believed there might be important differences between the humor caregivers share with day-patients and inpatients, patients of different ages, patients with differing degrees of infirmity, and in mixed-gender and same-gender dyads. I reasoned that humor use might be significantly affected by these factors and chose a diverse sample to see if those differences were indicated. Because there is so little research about humor in health care settings, I also believed a diverse sample would provide a valuable basis on which to build.

Within the chosen settings, my sample of patients and caregivers consisted of all who agreed to be observed. This method of volunteer sampling is admittedly susceptible to systematic internal bias. People who agree to take part may be systematically different from others. But out of hundreds of people I approached, fewer than six declined to be observed. For this reason, I believe that selection bias is not a serious threat to the trustworthiness of the data.

DATA COLLECTION

In every setting, I made a disciplined effort to be as unobtrusive as possible. In situations (such as the physical therapy units) where I could observe a number of patient transactions at one time, I found an inconspicuous, central location where I could listen and observe without making it obvious whom I was observing. When it was necessary for me to accompany caregivers into patient rooms (as in the hospital and doctor's office) I positioned myself so I could see the participants but was not within their gaze at each other. I carried a clipboard and, in some settings, a small audio recorder.

This method of on-site observation allowed me to observe medical transactions fairly unobtrusively. Sanjek (1990) labeled this observational strategy "informant's turf, informant in control" or "situated listening" (p. 245). It was especially useful in my study because it was important not to compromise the success of medical procedures, and because the phenomena I studied were unavailable through other means. The participants were not able to enunciate the cultural rules of humor use. Although their actions showed the embodiment of such rules, they could not make those rules directly available to me through interviews or surveys.

My study was initially described to staff members and patients simply as a study of health-related communication. Staff members were briefed on the study in advance and assured of anonymity should they choose to participate. All staff members agreed to be observed, and were assured they could cease to participate at any time.

Patients' verbal consent was obtained by staff members with a statement such as: "We have a student observer in today. Do you mind if she comes in?" Caregivers were instructed to accept any declinations without question. I was always present to answer questions about the study (omitting only the humor focus). The staff (and some patients) were apprised of the humor focus near the study's completion. After that, I solicited their views about humor using conversations and open-ended interviews.

Overall, I have collected several hundred pages of typed fieldnotes and transcripts, about 15 hours of taped dialogue, and a huge stock of memories and mental impressions (for more on the value of "headnotes" see Ottenberg, 1990). Shortly after leaving the field every day, I typed my notes, using the audiotapes when available to fine-tune handwritten sections of dialogue. As a result, my typed notes include observations and contextual information as well as verbatim bits of dialogue. I later reviewed select sections of dialogue more intensively to create detailed transcripts.

TRANSCRIPTION

Some of the same excerpts and examples appear in different places throughout the text. I have labeled each dialogue excerpt with an alphabetical letter (or combination of letters) in parentheses so that it is possible to identify repeated use of it. Although I make an effort to present every transcript excerpt verbatim, I use varying degrees of transcription, depending on the requirements of the analysis and the availability of taped records. For purposes of conversation analysis, for example, it is informative to note speech overlaps, the length of pauses, and even elements of speech which are almost imperceptible. In noting these, I use the method of transcription developed by Jefferson (see Appendix B, Transcription Guide). In an ethnographic analysis, however, such details may detract from the overall effect of the utterance. The humorousness of the utterance may become lost in a complex diagram.

SIGNIFICANCE AND ORGANIZATION

Although many (cf. Brewer & Hunter, 1989; Polkinghorne, 1983) laud the merits of triangulation, there are yet few examples of extensive multimethod research available. Thus the organization of this book is somewhat novel. In each section, I introduce the perspective used, then present the analysis. For example, in Part II, I outline the phenomenological perspective, then present a phenomenological analysis of funny, so on with Parts III and IV (ethnography), Part V (ethnomethodology and conversation analysis). Part VI provides overall implications, comparing the results of different analyses, and suggesting avenues for further research and practical application.

II

The Nature of Funny

Chapter 6

▼

About Phenomenology

A basic question confronts people who wish to create or understand humor: What makes a thing funny? Although most of us know "funny" when we see or hear it, it is hard to say generally what distinguishes something funny from something not funny. And to make matters more perplexing, what is funny once is often not funny twice. And an experience once harrowing may seem hilarious in retrospect. In my work, I continually confront the dilemma that, although I see and hear humor manifested in words I can repeat, the words are insufficient in themselves to explain humor. Funny is an interpretation, not an utterance.

In light of this, I begin by examining "funny" at its most essential level—the level of consciousness. The question is: How is something "funny" essentially different from "not funny?" I pursue the answer using Husserl's method of phenomenological reduction (summarized by Spiegelberg, 1982).

Husserl's method prescribes that we imaginatively bracket or suspend the assumptions of life as usual so that we may identify the essential properties of a phenomenon. The aim is to find what, at the most basic and essential level, distinguishes one type of awareness from another. Finding this basic level requires an excavation of sorts, because through experience, we begin to build layers of assumptions about a phenomenon. That is, we begin to attribute traits to the phenomenon that, although related to it, are not essential to it. These assumptions form what Husserl called the "sedimentation" of the natural attitude (Harvey, 1989, p. 61). Sediment builds up in the form of taken-for-granted notions about things. This sedimentation, although useful and unavoidable in daily life, obscures the essential nature of the phenomenon. For instance,

47

we may come to believe that comedians are funny, and jokes are funny, and funerals are not funny. Or we may say, "A thing is funny if it makes me laugh." These assumptions are practical, but they obscure the otherwise obvious conclusions that "comedian" does not equate with "funny." We do not laugh at all things funny—and for politeness or other reasons—we laugh at some things that are not funny. Thus, although we may get a sense of funniness listening to Jerry Seinfeld (or to a eulogy, for that matter), funniness is a phenomenon not sufficiently explained by the presence of outside influences or by our own physical demonstrations.

In the following analysis I propose that there are essential differences between spontaneous humor and contrived humor, and that "funny" is the result of a pleasurable, surprising deviation from what is "expected."[1] I propose, as well, that there are upper and lower thresholds of funniness. A surprise that is too trivial or too threatening is not funny.

In examining the way that a "funny" episode is experienced, I examine and describe some of my own funny experiences. I cannot think how to proceed otherwise. The content of these experiences is provided for the purpose of illustration, but the content is nevertheless rather inconsequential. If this is a valid phenomenology, the essence of the experiences I describe should be the same for any funny experience, regardless of the circumstances. Thus, for the reader who wonders mid-chapter what this examination of funny episodes has to do with medical setting humor, I beg patience. At an essential level, I argue that there is no difference between medical humor, gallows humor, airplane humor, and so on. If my examples appear to be "school days humor" or some other categorization, it is only because those are experiences most available to me at this time. The essence—if not the outward manifestation—of all funny experiences is the same. To further make this point, I conclude the chapter with suggestions for an all-inclusive theory of humor, and discuss the relevance of this analysis to an examination of humor in health care settings.

---

[1]I am faced with the semantic dilemma of having no word to accurately describe the sensation of "expecting" an occurrence without being conscious of the expectation. Typically we think of an "expectation" as being the conscious anticipation of something likely to happen. However, I find that many times we are amused when something "unexpected" happens, although we are not quite sure what we did "expect." If asked, we might say, "I don't know what I expected, but not that!" It also happens that we become aware of some "expectations" belatedly, only if events take a surprising turn. Goffman (1974) described it this way: "Observers actively project their frames of reference into the world immediately around them and one fails to see their doing so only because events ordinarily confirm these projections, causing the assumptions to disappear into the smooth flow of activity" (p. 39). For lack of a better word to describe this phenomenon, I use the words *expect* and *expectations* in quotations to signify that what I write of is not necessarily the conscious anticipation of a specific occurrence.

Chapter 7

▼

The Essence of Funny

Many things are said about humor. Proverbially we are encouraged to laugh our cares away, have the last laugh, grin and bear it, and sometimes, to laugh to keep from crying. Humor is a central part of the folk wisdom and practice of everyday communication. Yet humor remains largely enigmatic. How is something funny essentially different from something not funny? With the following phenomenological analysis, I attempt to answer that question. In the process, answers to several other questions are suggested. For instance, how is a joke essentially different than a funny life episode? Why is a punch line usually funny only once? And why is a thing funny to some people but not to others?

To understand the nature of funny we may first examine it from a stimulus–response perspective. From that perspective the theoretical question is: What stimuli trigger a perception of funny? This analysis distinguishes between contrived jokes and situational humor. Next, eidetic reduction reveals how a phenomenon is constituted in consciousness to be funny. I propose a Surprise Liberation Theory of Humor that suggests that funny is the result of a perceived liberation. It requires, first, an "expectation"; then a surprising deviation; and concurrently, a pleasurable feeling of liberation relative to the surprise. These ideas are discussed more fully on the following pages.

STIMULUS–RESPONSE PERSPECTIVE

We may distinguish between two types of funny stimuli: the contrived and the uncontrived. Contrived humor often takes shapes as jokes. Jokes are contrived in two ways. First, they are planned, mentally rehearsed. Second, they rely on a contrived, hypothetical situation.[1] The hypothetical set-up often begins "There was a one-legged man . . ." or "There was this traveling salesman. . . ." At other times a joke pretends to be "real" until the punch line reveals it as a spoof. The "punch" is—or is meant to be—a surprise wallop that disputes one's "expectation." In either case, the surprise refers to the set-up, not specifically to the lifeworld context in which the participants find themselves. This is an essential difference between contrived jokes and uncontrived, situational humor. Consider the following joke:

> Two ropes walk into a bar. The bartender says to the first one, "You'll have to go elsewhere. We don't serve ropes here." The first rope wanders dejectedly away. The second rope makes some quick adjustments and demands assertively, "I'll have a whiskey." The bartender thunders, "Didn't you hear what I told your friend? Aren't you a rope?" Comes the reply: "Nope, I'm a frayed-not."

The punch line relies on the set-up. It is funny only within the reality of the joke (if then!). To "get" the joke one must entertain the reality of the scenario. In this case, one must consider a fantasy situation in which two ropes walk, talk, and order drinks in a bar. Punch lines are characteristically nonsensical, or at least unfunny, out of the context of the joke.

By contrast, situational humor refers to statements and actions relative to the experience of a lifeworld situation. They are set up only incidentally. I remember, for instance, a funny incident that occurred during a high school field trip years ago. While leading the class across a sidewalk on the nearby college campus, our teacher, Mrs. Adams, slipped on a wet leaf. Her arms and legs flailed for a brief moment before she landed, sitting flat on her bottom, in the middle of the street. I believe we managed temporarily to choke back our guffaws, but my classmates and I found the incident immensely comical. Even now, nineteen years later, I still find it funny when I mentally replay the scene as I saw it then. In contrast to the self-made reality of a joke, such spontaneous humor relies for effect on the context of the transaction as lived. It directly relates to (and, I argue, challenges the assumptions of) everyday expectations.

---

[1] I should emphasize here that, as I experience them, a "joke" and "joking around" are different phenomena—the first being, to some extent, a staged event and the second usually spontaneous.

In summary, we can categorize funny things within two categories—contrived, self-contextual jokes and spontaneous occurrences. Of course, hybrids of the two are common. Practical jokes, for instance, are contrived set-ups designed to alter the context of a natural situation. Episodes of *Candid Camera* are replete with this type of contrived humor (e.g., the talking mail box, the woman's enormous hat feather that swishes through a man's soup). The humor often arises from the victim's efforts to deal with inexplicable anomaly in a supposedly natural situation.

There is more to say about the types of stimuli generally believed to trigger a "funny" feeling. However, this analysis is aimed at a phenomenon still more essential to funniness. The remaining analysis brackets out the metaphysical presuppositions of stimulus–response theory—chiefly that there are free-standing things to which funniness is an incarnate reaction. Eidetic reduction dispels the idea that funny entities exist separate from our conscious awareness of them. Thus, the analysis moves from the consideration of what triggers a funny feeling, to the funny feeling itself.

THE FUNNY FEELING

It must be noted initially that "funny" is constituted within consciousness and is not necessarily identifiable by a laugh or smile. We may offer a nervous or obligatory laugh, and refrain from a smile when something strikes us as funny. Neither is funny sufficiently defined by the thing that triggers it. As illustration, I return to the example of my fallen teacher.

Expectations and Perspective

As mentioned, I still find it funny when I mentally replay the "great fall" as I viewed it then. But since that time, this teacher (whom I always liked despite my mirthful reaction) has proven herself to be a sincere and caring friend to me. The last time I saw her she hugged me tenderly and shed a few tears as she congratulated me about recent accomplishments (accomplishments touchingly larger in her estimation than in my own). When I consider her now—through eyes 19 years older and perhaps wiser—she is a person-friend, and it is not nearly so funny that she fell down. Indeed, I feel a certain sense of empathy and protectiveness. She is no longer just the leader and I the follower. My orientation to teachers and my orientation to this teacher, has changed. Thus, depending on my orientation to it, the memory is either funny or faintly sad.

I submit then that funny relies, in essence, on one's orientation to the phenomenon. We have different sympathies and expectations based on our perspectives. As I have implied, we may consciously switch from one perspective to another. As we do, our awareness of an event is reconstituted. Although we recognize it as the same event, our sense of it may be notably different. A memory may thus be funny from one angle and tragic from another. Sometimes a shift in perspective may itself provoke a "funny" feeling—as when we belatedly see the humor in an otherwise embarrassing situation.

From my perspective as a 15-year-old, there was something immensely unexpected and funny about seeing my teacher slip and fall. It was hardly to be believed. My "expectation," my prejudice, was that teachers did not perform such ignominious acts. Adultness and especially "teacherness" were defined by dignity and control. It was what separated us from them. It was part of the omnipotence, the power, that qualified them to be leaders and us only to be led. The assumption, quite frankly, chafed a bit.

As I found out, it is sometimes quite pleasurable to have a prejudice exposed. It was a heady and liberating sensation to see a teacher behave in such an "uncharacteristic" way. Put another way, it was funny. My prejudice of teacher dignity—and by association other prejudices—were suddenly exposed as just that, prejudices. What of omnipotence if this teacher, leading us grandly into the unknown, is suddenly flat on her butt?

Looking back, the fallen teacher episode represents an epoche of sorts. It was as if a bubble burst and many of my assumptions with it. If the teacher image of infallible leader was dispelled, I in turn, was liberated from the antithetic role of fallible follower. The event did not reduce my estimation of Mrs. Adams exactly. In my awareness, it freed her—and thus me—from the strict categorizations of my previous attitude. My former "naive" assumptions about authority figures were exposed as particularly un-naive. They were suddenly revealed as what Husserl called sedimentation (Harvey, 1989), in this case, ideas about authority and infallibility layered and reinforced until tacitly supposed. Of course, such sediment does not easily spread to the winds. My prejudices were not—are not—completely banished. But they were suddenly made visible to me as prejudices, and there was something funny and liberating about that revelation.

Thus, "funny" relies not just on an unexpected stimulus, but on one's orientation to the original "expectation." Suppositions of the natural attitude are paradoxically both enabling and constricting. We identify people and things by what we "expect" of them. Because our perspective is always a personal one, identification occurs relative to self. Thus, in defining other things, we define ourselves. It is a two-sided yoke that, although convenient and unavoidable, does sometimes chafe. Humor thwarts, and thus reveals, prejudices of the natural attitude. When the prejudice is a defining one, its disputation is sometimes funny. Funny is a sensation of pleasant liberation—liberation from the confines of one's own "expectations."

Furthermore, at times we may be poised to have our "expectations" disputed. For instance, I sometimes get tickled at funerals—but not at just anyone's funeral. It happens (rather regrettably) when I am profoundly, overwhelmingly moved by the occasion. Then the slightest event will seem hilarious. I find myself, quite literally, laughing to keep from crying. At those times, it is important to me to decommit somewhat from my somber orientation. The slightest excuse to do so offers profound relief. It is hilarious.

A similar effect can be noted at comedy clubs where a warm-up performer primes the audience to laugh. The performer helps to induce a certain orientation, one in which members of the audience are poised to consider as comically absurd their everyday assumptions. It is as if we sometimes line our prejudices like tin cans atop a fence rail, hoping they will be knocked askew. To find something funny is to experience respite from serious consideration of it. It is sometimes a relief to perceive that a restricting prejudice can be toppled like a flimsy tin. It is comic relief, and for that reason laughter is commonly considered good medicine.

Constituting a thing as funny therefore requires three steps. Step 1 is the antecedent condition that we harbor some "expectation." It further requires that we encounter a surprising deviation (Step 2), and perceive a pleasurable liberation relative to it (Step 3). Without "expectations" (even tacitly held ones), there can be no "unexpected." The following passage examines surprise as a necessary (but insufficient) element of funny.

The Surprise/The Reaction

Jokes and funny occurrences are alike in that both present a surprise, something unexpected. "Timing is everything" because we must neither guess the punch line in advance, nor fail to understand the set-up. A joke must be told neither too slowly nor too quickly. However, surprise is not sufficient for funny. We are surprised when we wreck the car, but it is not funny. In this section, I continue the argument that the funniness of an unexpected occurrence depends essentially on one's orientation and commitment to the original "expectation." In addition, it is revealed that the perceived profundity of a surprise affects how funny it is. Seen this way, it is immediately obvious that there can be no real division between Steps 2 and 3, encountering the unexpected, and perceiving it.

Funny things are given to us through many modes. When something is surprising or inappropriate in the way it looks, sounds, smells, tastes, or feels we often perceive it as funny. Moreover, our thoughts and memories stir a funny feeling as often as anything else. But we must go beyond what is given to experience a thing as funny.

A thing is funny only in relation to something else. For instance, imagine that you are the guest of a foreign tribe who sit you before their campfire and proceed to leap and whirl about. You have no sense of what is appropriate in this setting. They could be performing a holy rite or treating you to a bit of buffoonery. You may think their actions are funny compared to those to which you are accustomed. But if you do not share their intersubjective sense of appropriateness, you cannot, without cues, know what they think is funny. It is difficult to grasp or create humor in another culture without a sense of that culture's expectations.

Commitments and Violations

How funny a thing seems is affected by one's orientation, and the degree to which an "expectation" is violated. I submit that—within certain boundaries—a thing is funny in degrees relative to the feeling of liberation it affords. The fallen teacher episode has remained salient for me because it was such a profound liberation. It concerned power issues central to my identity. One's level of commitment may also explain why jokes tend to go stale sooner than funny memories. In this section I argue that there is an essential link between how funny a thing is and how committed we are to the assumptions it challenges.

A joke typically contrives a scene, then turns it on its ear. In the rope joke I am surprised at the unexpected play on words, and perhaps the sudden reversal when a character personified with human characteristics is suddenly identified again with rope characteristics (a knot). To find it funny, I must apply the "expectations" of my natural attitude to the joke (with allowances for its fantasy theme). But I do not experience the "expectations" as profound or as being profoundly violated. My commitment is mild and I find the joke mildly funny. Like most jokes, it challenges the expectations of the natural attitude, but only indirectly.

By contrast, situational events often have a particularly salient, ongoing relevance for us. In my experience, they are often funnier and funny longer. Although we usually groan to hear a joke repeated, we are fond of recalling "I laugh every time I think about the time. . . ." By contrast, only the best jokes attain the significance of repeated presentation before the same audience. The reason may be that situational humor more directly relates to "expectations" of our natural attitude, "expectations" to which we are at least moderately committed. Moreover, it arises less from contrived factors, possibly giving its challenge added potency.

Situational "expectations"—because they share the enduring nature of the natural attitude—are not likely to be eradicated. Therefore, memories of a humorous event may continue to play on an existing prejudice. By contrast, the reality of a joke—once banished—may be effectively dispelled. Although we also apply the "expectations" of the natural attitude to a joke, its contrived nature may establish it as less immediate, less relevant than situational occurrences. I submit that the rare punch line that is twice funny probably taps into a particularly salient life attitude.

Thresholds

We may conclude that the funniest episodes are those that dispel profound "expectations." But this is only true when we find liberation from those "expectations" to be pleasurable. There is an upper and lower threshold beyond which a surprise is not funny.

We may react with aversion when a cherished and strongly held assumption is challenged. When you are the one who falls on your behind, for instance, it may not seem funny. Likewise, you may feel incensed by an off-color joke about an issue to which you are particularly sensitive.

Conversely, if you are indifferent or only weakly committed to a prejudice, its disputation may be of minimal consequence to you. Children enjoy word plays and riddles that, for adults, are trivial and unfunny. (No doubt, adults' fascination with sex-related jokes is equally baffling to children!)

In fact, I think the topics of humor reveal what a society finds most disconcerting. Consider the prevalence of jokes about AIDS, sex, Helen Keller, and race. Humor provides a liberation from our commitment to these topics as serious, threatening issues. They may be seen (at least for a moment) as ridiculous, not menacing. In humor we experience a temporary liberation from our fears.

SURPRISE LIBERATION THEORY COMPARED TO OTHERS

Although there are several existing theories of humor, no one of them fully captures the essence of funny phenomena. Most theorists have taken a stimulus–response perspective, analyzing the message more than the way it is perceived. Among them, these theories advance the ideas that humor relies on disparagement, superiority, disposition, a dual process of exposure and social cuing, incongruence, and arousal relief. A brief examination of these theories in light of the preceding phenomenology suggests that a unifying theory of humor is possible.

Disparagement and Superiority

Disparagement and superiority theories (Wolff, Smith, & Murray, 1934) posit that people have a natural inclination to protect themselves from ridicule, and to belittle things not associated with self. Laughter is a triumphant response to the denigration of objects, concepts, or persons unaffiliated with self. This is used to explain the heady effect of laughing at one's problems or at members of a threatening minority. To do so is to assert one's superiority. These theories, however, cannot explain instances in which it is pleasurable to laugh at oneself.

Phenomenological analysis suggests that *liberation* may be a better word than *superiority*. It is often funny when something threatening is revealed in a different light. But superiority theory overlooks the enabling/restricting aspect of self-image. Expectations related to self and associates may themselves be threatening or constricting. Laughing at one's self can ease the burden of self-related expectations as surely as it eases the expectations associated with unaffiliated threats. Consequently, a surprise liberation may be funny whether or not it concerns self.

Disposition

Disposition theory (Zillmann, 1983) goes beyond superiority/disparagement theories to specify that enjoyment of disparaging humor depends on an individual's attitude toward the "butt of the joke" and the degree of negativity expressed by the humor. An employee on good terms with his or her supervisor, for instance, will probably be less amused to hear "the one about the boss" than his or her colleagues who harbor harder feelings.

This theory was based on research findings that jokes in which the underdog bests the bully are rated funnier than those of the reverse scenario (Gutman & Priest, 1969; Wicker, Barron, & Willis, 1980). But even well-placed aggression does not make a predictable punch line funny, and beyond a certain point brutal slander is not funny.

Disposition theory, like others, explains only part of the humor process. It does not explain why extreme levels of disparagement are not funny. Neither does it account for episodes in which there is no clear butt of the joke. One's disposition, or attitude, is treated as an enduring mental state. From a phenomenological perspective, *disposition* is defined as commitment—a commitment that may vary according to one's perspective. This notion recognizes people's conscious ability to adopt different perspectives, thus to have multiple and changing "attitudes" about the butt of the joke. We may find something funny from one angle, but not from another, irrespective of our supposedly singular, enduring attitude about it.

Moreover, the butt of the joke may have less to do with the funniness than the underlying expectations that are challenged. For instance, we may find "farmer's daughter" stories funny regardless of our disposition toward female rural residents. Overall, disposition theory, like disparagement/superiority, fails to address the presence of humor thresholds. In actuality, the funniness of a thing may be more accurately described in light of one's commitment to underlying expectations, and be bounded by upper and lower thresholds.

Dual Process

Dual process theory stresses the effects of environmental cues and self-perception on one's perception of humor. The presence of other people laughing, for instance, is predicted to enhance the humorousness of a stimulus. Humor appreciation, like laughter, is apparently contagious (Cupchik & Leventhal, 1974; Leventhal & Cupchik, 1975). This effect is by no means constant, however. Researchers observe that susceptibility to "funny cues" may differ according to gender (Cupchik & Leventhal, 1974; Leventhal & Cupchik, 1975) and self-consciousness (Lammers, 1991; Porterfield et al., 1988).

Thus dual process is plagued by evidence that environmental cues have an unpredictable, not strictly causal, effect on humor perception. This is remedied if we adopt the phenomenological perspective that it is our awareness of factors—not their presumedly separate exist-ence—which affects how we think and feel. I suggest that social cues matter not at all if we are unaware of them, or if we are unwilling to adopt a perspective that is hospitable to them.

In the studies mentioned, humor is measured by amounts of laughter. We must first ask: If cues indeed incite more laughter are they also indicative of funnier perceptions? I am hesitant to make that assump-tion, but I do think it plausible that one's orientation to a phenomenon is influenced by awareness of environmental factors. Return for a moment to the comedy show. From the perspective of the natural attitude, we laugh at the show, and because other people are laughing, and because we came expecting to laugh. More essentially, however, we laugh because—in the way that we are oriented to the phenomenon—the surprises within it are pleasurably liberating. Our orientation probably is affected by our perceptions of self, others, and the situation. But it is possible to sit through the show and be bored, oblivious, or depressed. Social cues may enhance humor perception, but it is ultimately the perception, and not the cues, that are funny. Consequently, social cues as separate entities are neither necessary nor sufficient to explain humor.

In summary, dual process theory makes an important point. We are influenced by our perceptions of the social world. Indeed, we ourselves are identified in relation to those perceptions. But the theory's suppo-sition that cues exist as entities makes it susceptible to unpredictability. A more essential statement of the theory would be that our orientation to phenomena is affected by our perceptions of self and others, and that orientation may make us more apt to find things funny.

Incongruence

The theory of incongruence suggests that stimuli that trigger smiles and laughter "involve some kind of contrast between something to be taken seriously and something trivial, or between something befitting a ra-tional adult and something worthy of only a child" (Berlyne, 1960, p. 256). Among the examples Berlyne gave are a dignified person slipping on a banana peel, or the startled amusement of one who prepares to lift a heavy suitcase and finds it empty.

Incongruence theory identifies the unexpected as an essential element of humor—a thesis in keeping with the current analysis. However, the theory stops short of explaining what distinguishes a funny surprise from a simply pleasant (or unpleasant) surprise. The weakness of this theory is that it rests on the idea that "funniness" resides in the *stimulus*, not (as I would argue) in the *interpretation* of the stimulus. As asserted previously, not all surprises are funny. I submit, again, that the funniness of a surprise varies according to the profundity of the surprise and one's commitment to the original expectation. This is a more essential and thorough explanation than that offered by incongruence theory.

Arousal Relief

Berlyne's (1969) later theory of arousal relief succeeds in overcoming many shortfalls of incongruence theory. The later theory holds that emotional arousal (unless extreme) is pleasurable and laughter provoking. The relief component suggests further that a resolution or reduction in arousal should inspire even greater mirth. As researchers have interpreted it, we might find cartoons funnier in the presence of a sexually provocative experimenter (Davis & Farina, 1970), the threat of shock (Hom, 1966), test anxiety (Byrne, 1958), or fear (Shurcliff, 1968). Empirical research has not provided encouraging support of the theory, however.

If we interpret arousal to mean a heightened sense of expectancy, arousal relief shares many properties with the current phenomenological analysis. The more vivid our expectations, the more profound is their challenge. Phenomenological analysis may also explain why empirical research has failed to demonstrate a relief component to humor. Experimental studies have generally introduced humorous stimuli unrelated to the cause of the participants' main arousal. For instance, they showed cartoons or a Bill Cosby monologue to people judged to be sexually excited, fearful, or anxious. The current analysis suggests that funny relies on one's commitment to the original expectation. Challenges to less salient expectations may be amusing, but not of a magnitude relative to the main arousal. In other words, if the joke is not pertinent to the source of the arousal, the theory may not be directly applicable.

CONCLUSIONS

In conclusion, eidetic reduction reveals that funny is essentially a constituent of awareness and perception. This is not well addressed by existing theories of humor, which are largely handicapped by the suppositions of stimulus–response thinking. I propose an alternative, unifying theory of humor I call Surprise Liberation. It holds that, to consider something funny, we must begin with an expectation, perceive a surprising deviation from that expectation, and experience the deviation as pleasurable and liberating.

According to the Surprise Liberation Theory, whether a thing is funny or not lies more with our perceptions than with the thing itself. Humor is given in relation to a preconceived idea. Funniness depends essentially on one's commitment to an "expected" outcome, and one's willingness to see that "expectation" thwarted. Sudden anomaly can be liberating, threatening, trivial, or funny depending on one's perceived stake in the expected outcome.

In conclusion, I suggest that funny is essentially irreverent to the natural attitude. Funny is a feeling of liberation that restores a certain naivete. It arises from the pleasurable realization that things are different than we had assumed them to be.

Chapter 8

▼

Funny in Relation
to Health Care

Examining funny at its most essential, conscious level does not help in an empirical way to distinguish between what is funny and what is not. Funny, after all, is not a directly observable phenomenon. But by considering funny to be a pleasant surprise it is easier to initiate and understand humor in medical settings. To be more specific, there are implications that humor may be particularly easy to achieve, and particularly apt at reducing anxiety in medical settings. These ideas are explored here.

First, it is relatively easy to experience funniness in a regimented (uptight) situation like most medical settings. Just as the slightest incident in church can set off waves of giggles, the smallest surprise in an otherwise rigid medical routine often seems very unexpected and comical. Thus, a medical professional who wishes to initiate humor may do something minimally surprising or unexpected. Indeed, joking around in medical settings often takes the form of puns, silly faces, comical poses, exaggerations, absurdities, and outlandish statements. I have noticed that, particularly when people are tense, the slightest deviation is often treated as funny. One nurse got a big laugh by calling out "Room Service!" as she tapped on a patient's door.[1]

---

[1]Funny is unavailable for direct scrutiny. Thus the most we can say is that the participants treated this episode as a funny one. For more on this see Part V.

Second, the liberation of laughing at a threatening phenomenon may be a valuable means of relieving the stress of a medical situation. This analysis suggests that when expectations are particularly threatening, the unexpected is often a profound and exhilarating relief; it is funny. To joke about the taste of a barium swallow may provide at least a temporary respite from fearful consideration of the brain scan to follow.

My observations support that humor is a particularly persuasive signal that things are "not so bad." For example, I once observed an elderly male patient and his wife, sitting together in his hospital room gripping each other's hands. The man had "coded" earlier in the day. That is, his heart had stopped beating and emergency measures were taken to revive him. The couple appeared badly shaken. Each time a nurse walked into the room they scanned his or her face, apparently looking for cues about the severity of the situation. Repeatedly, nurses told the couple in very serious tones that the patient was okay. The couple heard the words, but they reacted to the nurses' expressions. The nurses looked and sounded serious, and so did they. The couple did not visibly relax until one nurse quipped, "Mr. Cameron, if you don't stop causing so much trouble 'round here, we're gonna send you home!" The couple suddenly laughed out loud and relaxed their posture. (I wonder, looking back, if the couple would have responded so well if the nurse had told a rehearsed joke. My sense is that they would have considered the joke to be a diversion, but not as powerful a commentary on the situation as was the nurse's situation-oriented quip.)

The idea of funny thresholds is relevant as well. It suggests that when people are extremely or only minimally upset they may not find incidents to be very funny. Interestingly, in my observations, this seems to apply more to caregivers than to patients. While observing the hospital care of several AIDS patients in their last days of life, I noticed that caregivers seemed more serious than usual in their presence. But the patients, if they were alert enough to converse, made more dramatic efforts than usual to be funny. Although the caregivers responded to the patients' attempts, they generally seemed too wary of offending the patient, or too committed to their own feelings of seriousness, to initiate much humor themselves.

In summary, the assertions of this analysis and the tenets of arousal-relief theory suggest that the high emotion usually associated with medical settings makes them an apt arena for humor. Particularly when the humor seems spontaneous and situational, it may be taken as a sign that things are not so bad as they seem. Thus, conventional wisdom that says that medical settings are not funny may, paradoxically, make incidents in those settings seem funnier. Furthermore, when fears and anxiety are within a certain threshold, relief may be particularly profound and exhilarating. All this suggests that humor may have therapeutic properties pertinent to medical care.

III

Tones, Functions, and Topics
of Medical Setting Humor

Chapter 9

▼

The Ethnographic Approach

Ethnography provides a vivid means of depicting humor in different health care settings. Through descriptive language, the reader may get a sense of the hectic atmosphere of a physical therapy department, where therapists amuse patients by quoting funny country music lyrics ("I got tears in my ears cause I'm lying on my back cryin' over you"). With its macroscopic focus, ethnography also helps to explain how the topics of humor (e.g., torture, breast size) and the way it is delivered (loud and bold or subtle and timid) shape and reflect the cultural expectations of people in each setting.

In this chapter, I describe the ethnographic perspective, including its assumptions about culture and knowledge, the means of collecting and analyzing data, and the advantages and limitations of ethnography relevant to this study. Chapters 10, 11, and 12 discuss three ethnographic studies of humor in health care settings: "Torture by Hickey Machine," a study of the bold humor in a physical therapy department; an analysis of "Discreet Humor in a Breast Care Center" and "Empathic Humor in a Doctor's Office."

ASSUMPTIONS OF ETHNOGRAPHY

An "ethnography of speaking" was first proposed by Hymes (1962). Drawing on his background in anthropology, Hymes advanced the assumption that communication is affected by rules of cultural appropriateness. His idea was to meld linguistics and anthropology in recognition that speech is governed, not only by the arbitrary rules of grammar, but also by cultural mores (Hymes, 1962, 1967). With a particularly memorable illustration, Hymes (1967) challenged readers to imagine a culturally void individual: "A child capable of any and all grammatical utterances, but not knowing which to use, not knowing even when to talk and when to stop, would be a cultural monstrosity" (p. 26). Hymes (1972) proposed a taxonomy of description. This taxonomy, or discovery model, presents a flexible system of categories meant to organize the observations of researchers in diverse cultures. It is built on the idea that cultures differ in key ways. For instance, they differ in expectations about silence, who speaks to whom and when, and what utterances are appropriate in different situations.

I adapted Sherzer and Darnell's (1972) version of Hymes' model, tailoring it to a focus on humor (see Appendix C). The model is extensive and a complete answer to any one question could probably fill a book. But the questions do call attention to easily overlooked aspects of culture and communication. By using the questions as guideposts, I am better able to compare and contrast different communities—with illuminating results.

A third assumption of ethnography is that members of a speech community share an underlying set of assumptions about what behavior is "good" and "appropriate" in different situations. Although these assumptions are often known only tacitly by community members, they are identifiable by the consistency with which members behave and the negative sanctions imposed on people who violate cultural expectancies. It bears emphasizing that cultural codes of conduct are necessarily malleable and open to interpretation. They must be weighed and mutually managed based on a complex array of factors including participants' relationships to each other, their goals, and their situations.

Epistemologically, ethnographers hold that an understanding of cultural rules is attainable if one becomes familiar with the everyday activities of cultural members. This requires extensive observation of people in their everyday environments. To minimize the degree to which researchers' observations are colored by their expectations, ethnographers usually approach a study without hypotheses (Lincoln & Guba, 1985). The researcher must become so familiar with the culture that he or she understands the rules of competence, but sufficiently removed from the situation to recognize the rules as remarkable.

Finally, ethnographers assume that transferability is a more productive goal than generalizability. Lincoln and Guba (1985) challenged what they called the "naive realism" (p. 297) of statistical generalizations.

Such generalizations, they said, assume that a specified population is homogeneous without regard to time or contextual factors. In reality, Lincoln and Guba argued, researchers generalize to populations they have not studied and know little about. Rather than assume a *generalizability* of this sort, ethnographers strive to make *transferability* possible. Transferability is accomplished when the researcher provides sufficient contextual information to allow the *reader* to judge the applicability of the research data to situations with which he or she is familiar.

In summary, ethnographers assume that communication is governed (in part) by rules of cultural appropriateness. They hold that these rules can be identified by an observer who is knowledgeable about cultural mores, but attentive to the structural processes behind them. Culture and relationships are the units of analysis rather than individuals, and the focus is on everyday activities. Ethnographers typically insist on inductive, post hoc analysis to minimize the distortion of prior expectations. They do not presume that their results are generalizable, but strive to make their transferability clear with accurate contextual descriptions. Furthermore, communication ethnographers following Hymes' lead assume that cultures differ in key ways, and by comparing and contrasting them along those lines, believe it is possible to build a cohesive corpus of ethnographic data.

Ethnography is particularly well suited to my study of medical settings because it allows access to what Rosenblatt (1981) called "patterns of conceptually related characteristics" (p. 196) as they naturally occur. In this way, natural influences on human action—controlled or distorted by other measures—are made available for inspection. I can examine humor as it occurs in different health care settings without inconveniencing the participants or imposing the artificial constraints of a contrived setting such as a laboratory. Ethnographic researchers such as Todd (1993), Danziger (1980), Zola (1983), and Firth (1977) offer thick descriptions of patienthood, the exam room culture, and the connection between culture and medical symptoms. Their studies support the concept that medical settings are microcultures characterized by particular rules of appropriateness. Thus, for theoretical and methodological reasons, I believe ethnography is a particularly valuable means of examining the forms and functions of humor, and the rules that determine its appropriateness in medical settings. My methods of data collection are described in chapter 5. Following is a brief account of how I analyze the data here using the constant comparative method.

CONSTANT COMPARATIVE METHOD

I approached the medical settings with research questions, but no hypotheses. Sometimes the transition from one setting to another was so drastic that I felt quite disoriented at first. As data began to accumulate, however, I began to be aware of patterns. In the hospital, for instance, I became aware of subtle distinctions between attention-getting humor and rapport-building humor. Often, I got a feel for a phenomenon even before I realized it. For example, after watching the same nurse for several days I realized that I predictably poised my pencil to write seconds before she said something humorous. Thus, it sometimes seemed that my hand knew more about the situation than my head did. Realizing that, I set about unraveling my intuition to see what subtle cues triggered it.

During this process I organized my perceptions based on the constant comparative method (described by Glaser & Strauss, 1967; Schatzman & Strauss, 1973; Schwartz & Jacobs, 1979). Using that method of analysis, as data accumulated I was sensitive to aspects of the phenomena that seemed to resemble each other. For instance, I noticed that humor in the physical therapy center fell into two main categories: quips about "torture," and comical sarcasm about the "luxuries" of therapy. Identifying the resemblance was the basis for forming tentative categories—in this case, common topics of humorous utterances.

Following the constant comparative method, I continually tested my early inferences against new observations—refining, combining, and expanding categories as warranted by the data. I think this flexibility and reliance on grounded data is an important strength of ethnographic research. Following are other points in favor of an ethnographic analysis of humor in health care settings.

ADVANTAGES OF ETHNOGRAPHY

One advantage of ethnography is its proximity to real life. Because communication is examined within a natural setting, it is minimally affected by research manipulation.

Ethnography also offers the benefit of transferability. That is, readers may judge the relevance of the data for themselves. Some of the settings described may seem quite similar to those you know, others quite different and foreign. Either way, you have more than a list of numbers to go by. Rosenblatt (1981) wrote that field studies are especially meaningful because they are more vivid and less ambiguous than quantitative research.

Ethnographic data also offer useful information for practical application and continued research. Spradley (1979) advised: "In our world-become-spaceship, where knowledge is power, ethnographers must consider the potential uses of their research" (p. 13). I hope the information in this book is useful in shaping and understanding health communication. Although many medical students and practitioners do not have the time nor the opportunity to carefully observe their peers, they may learn indirectly from them through studies such as this one. Grounded data of this sort may also be used to test theories and suggest phenomena for future studies.

Finally, ethnographers consider the influence of context and relationships. This allows them to admit the complexity of everyday transactions.

LIMITATIONS OF ETHNOGRAPHY

On the other hand, ethnography is limited in some respects. The reader should be aware there are certain goals ethnography is not designed to address.

First, ethnographic research is not directed toward causal explanations. Because natural settings are comprised of complex factors, researchers cannot isolate or control variables. For instance, I can report that breast center caregivers use diversionary humor but I cannot isolate the separate factors which contribute to their use of this humor. The most I can do is report a range of apparent influences and presume that—in some combination—they affect the participants' behavior. (Some theorists, such as Dubin, 1978, question whether any method is qualified to assert specific causal links.)

Ethnographies are also time consuming. Becoming familiar with a culture can take months or years. Danziger (1980) observed 250 interactions before offering her analysis of pregnancy care patterns. I have spent years conducting part-time field studies of medical situations.

Ethnography is also threatened by two possibilities: a researcher's observations will be significantly distorted by his or her biases, and the researcher's presence will affect the transactions he or she observes.

All in all, I consider *imprecision, inefficiency,* and *nongeneralizability* to be unavoidable limitations of ethnography. Furthermore, I think they are counterbalanced by related advantages. Stated in positive terms, ethnographies are *contextual, thorough,* and *transferable.* However, I take it very seriously that an ethnography can be compromised by a researcher's bias and his or her influence on the situation. Therefore, I would like to specify how I minimize these threats to my own research. Here, I describe the methods I have used to minimize the effects of researcher bias and research influence.

OFFSETTING THE LIMITATIONS

Unobtrusiveness

I attempted to minimize my influence on the people observed. For example, I tried to be as unobtrusive as possible by placing myself out of the patient and caregiver's direct line of vision. I was also sensitive to cues that my presence made any participant uncomfortable, and instructed everyone involved that I would leave the room any time they wished me to. I emphasized to caregivers that I did not wish to observe patients who showed any discomfort or reluctance to participate. (I maintain a vehement conviction that I would rather compromise my research than compromise the success of a medical transaction.) I refrained from taking part in patient–caregiver conversations as much as possible, responding only when politeness demanded it, and in those instances, extricating myself as quickly as possible from the conversation. (When I did speak to participants to gather information, I did so after exams were complete.)

There are several indications that I was as unobtrusive as I wished to be. First of all, circumstances were in my favor. Student observations are a regular part of medical training, and patients and caregivers often seemed to regard me as just another student. The presence of an observer was part of their regular routine. Although I informed participants that I was a communication observer many seemed to forget that fact, and often treated me as a nurse or technician in training. My "naive student" status seemed to put most people at ease, and offered me the unforeseen benefit of a mini medical education. I was happy to soak up the terminology and tips of the trade so often offered me.

Second, the nature of the medical transactions seemed to supersede participants' concern about my presence. They were often so busy or so intent that they would look at me and exclaim, "Oh, you're still here!" or "Nearly forgot about you."

Third, patients and caregivers seemed quite willing to be observed. As I mentioned, fewer than six people have said no in 3 years of observations. And I do not have reason to think people participated reluctantly. When asked if I could sit in on exams, most patients said, "Sure!" or "Won't bother me."

Strategic Ambiguity

As mentioned, I did not divulge my interest in humor until the study's conclusion. I wished to avoid a halo effect in which people used humor to please me, and the opposite effect, in which humor use was stifled by self-consciousness. If anything, I suspect that I saw conservative amounts and types of humor. Caregivers tended to loosen up after I had been observing them for several hours, and humor use generally become more venturesome and prevalent.

Building Trust

I approached each caregiver with assurances that I was not trying to evaluate him or her—and I wasn't. I assured caregivers that I would protect their anonymity and that of their patients. I made an effort not to align myself with management, and made it clear that management would not be privy to my notes or recordings. I promised all participants that I would make the results of my study available to them, and would appreciate their feedback. Above all, I stressed to participants that this was not a study of right and wrong. I was a student there to learn from them, and there was much they could teach me just by letting me watch.

Overall, I believe participants have trusted me. They have confided in me even more than I am willing to divulge to others. I have resisted the opportunity to present fascinating details when I felt they might endanger the anonymity of a participant. Throughout my research I have kept my promises and, I believe, developed mutual trust and respect with those I have studied.

Member Checks

To minimize the distortion of my personal biases, I conducted what Lincoln and Guba (1985) called *member checks*. It might otherwise be said I sought an informal type of intercoder reliability. At opportune moments—usually during break room conversations—I asked members for their perceptions and asked them to comment on the accuracy of what I perceived. I wished not to lead them into answering a certain way, and I did not (at first) want them to deduce my interest in humor. Often, I would ask something such as "How do you handle a patient like Mr. Anderson?" "What do you do if . . ." "I wonder if caregivers are more apt to joke with some patients. What do you think?" I used these member checks to get information and to see if the participants perceived the situations as I did. Throughout this book, I use participants' statements to demonstrate their agreement.

Acknowledging Subjectivity

I also include thick descriptions and transcript excerpts so readers may weigh their perceptions against mine. In this way I hope the effects of my biases will at least be detectable. Following the advice of Glesne and Peshkin (1992), I acknowledge aspects of my own subjectivity—to myself and to the reader. (See Philosophy Statement, Appendix D.) With explicit awareness of my personal biases, both the reader and I may be more sensitive to their effects, and better able to understand and judge the decisions I make within the study.

Following are three ethnographic analyses. The first is about humor in a physical therapy department, the second about humor in a breast care center, and the third about a family physician's office.

Chapter 10

▼

Torture by Hickey Machine:
We're All in This Together

Feet on pedals, slowly revolving, college coeds churn the wheels on a row of stationery bikes. Nearby, other people lie about on a neat row of beds, occasionally talking and joking among themselves. It might be a health club or a dormitory recreation center. It might be, if it weren't for the large white letters on a bulletin board behind them. The letters read "WALL OF PAIN" and are illustrated by photographs and magazine illustrations of people wearing tortured expressions.

I was mildly horrified by the bulletin board when I first saw it. It reminded me that this was no health spa, and these people were indeed in pain. They were physical therapy patients, slowly recovering from reconstructive knee surgeries, sprains, shoulder injuries, dislocated elbows, and a range of other, less prevalent injuries. Although I was no patient—only an observer—I cringed.

Days later I stepped onto the exercise deck, made my way through the stationary bikes and took an up-close look at that bulletin board. I saw then that the photographs were comical caricatures of pain—a therapist posed as if to strike a patient's knee with an enormous rubber mallet, another patient in a comically awkward position with feet above head. This was no shrine to pain. It was a nose-thumbing way to laugh at the grim inevitability of it. By that time, I had noticed verbal humor serving the same function. Joking references to "torture," "pain," and "cruelty" were plentiful, and seemed to help smooth the relational waters. In this environment defined by pain, humor was comic relief and more. That's what this analysis is about—humor and play, and their role in a culture of pain. It seeks to answer several questions:

- How does the setting help define communication?
- What are the various keys, tones, or manners in which humor is delivered?
- What are the recurrent topics of humor?
- What are the ends, goals, and purposes of humor in this setting?

After observing more than 60 patient–caregiver transactions in the physical therapy department, I propose that humor is used there as a face-saving means of socialization. The patients and caregivers—who must work closely together under trying circumstances—use the ambiguity of humor to negotiate the uncertainty of their relationships. Humor allows them to do this without losing face.

FACEWORK

Face is the term used by Goffman (1967) to describe the positive social self that others perceive. For instance, if a caregiver wishes to present a face of benevolence and knowledge, he or she will act in certain ways to project that image. Goffman called this pattern of behaviors the caregiver's *line*. Others' reactions demonstrate their understanding of the line taken, and facework becomes a process of saving or recovering a desired face.

To save face is to maintain a favorable or desired image. But face can be threatened or lost, as Goffman (1967) wrote: "Should he sense that he is in wrong face or out of face, he is likely to feel ashamed and inferior because of what has happened to the activity of his account and because of what may happen to his reputation as a participant" (p. 8). A loss of face causes embarrassment and awkwardness for others as well as for self. Thus, social actors usually try to help others maintain face. This seems particularly true in the patient–caregiver relationship, mutually defined so that a threat to one's face is often a threat to the other's as well. For instance, a patient might exclaim: "This hurts!" Such a statement is potentially threatening to the caregiver's "caring, helpful" face and the patient's "brave, cooperative" face. But if the patient exclaims, with even a wry smile, "This is torture!" the event can be treated (on one level) as "joking around"—an event compatible with both their faces. At another level, the caregiver undoubtedly registers the patient's expression of pain and may react to it. Although both parties know this, the display of social face-saving remains important.

What I wish to show here is that humor marks a statement as intentionally "out of line." A smile or laughter signals that an utterance is not to be taken in the ordinary way. When a patient or caregiver must criticize, complain, boast, or chastise—which they often must—humor excuses the action as an otherwise direct face threat. A humorous exaggeration such as "This is torture!" softens the impropriety of a complaint. It implies, "Although I seem to be acting out of line, I do it with friendly intentions." This idea is illustrated more fully after an explanation of the setting, participants, and nature of humor in the physical therapy unit.

ABOUT THE SETTING

The physical therapy department described here is staffed by two licensed physical therapists who treat patients and supervise the work of several physical therapy students. The students range from senior-level interns to beginning student aides. (In dialogue excerpts I refer to all caregivers as "therapist.")

I primarily observed one of the licensed therapists, a Euro-American male in his late 30s. Like the other caregivers in the unit, he goes by first name and wears no lab coat. Like the others, he dresses casually and neatly, usually in slacks and a crisply ironed shirt.

The center offers only outpatient care, so patients are fairly mobile. Many undergo treatment several times a week for weeks or months. The patients are predominantly Euro-Americans. Most are between 18 and 22 years old, although I did observe several middle-aged and elderly patients.

HOW DOES THE SETTING
HELP DEFINE COMMUNICATION?

The main therapy room is rectangular, with six stations along the longer walls. Each station includes a treatment table, which is an adjustable wooden platform about waist high with a cushion on top. Each station may be enclosed with curtains hanging from runners in the ceiling. The curtains are drawn while patients change into shorts, and during treatments that require them to partially disrobe. Much of the equipment in the room is portable and can be carried or rolled to different stations as needed. Thus, the only physical barriers in the main room are the movable cloth curtains that sometimes enclose treatment tables. The curtains do not muffle sound, however, and conversations often go on between people across the room from each other and between people separated by curtains.

There are often 6 to 10 patients in the department at a time, attended by 5 or 6 caregivers. In an atmosphere in which everyone hears everyone else, transactions are rarely private. Even the physical therapists' desks are located in the main room. Things can seem pretty hectic. In this respect, the department is very social, and as one patient put it, "schizophrenic:"

> It's the most schizophrenic thing I've ever seen from the patient's point of view. They [caregivers] never spend 120 seconds on one thing before someone walks in the door and it's like "Hey Suzy! . . ." It's the most undefined context I've ever been in.

Other patients seem to thrive on the active social transaction of the department. One told me with a laugh: "They know a lotta stuff here. They're friendly. I don't need to come here any more. I come cause I like it here." Another patient said of a mutual friend and former patient: "He just likes ta come in and socialize!"

The open environment contributes to a sense that "we're all in this together." Patients strike up conversations with each other and join in nearby conversations. Humorous statements are often delivered to the room at large, or in a tone of voice apparently meant to be overheard.

For example, one day a patient brought in a chocolate layer cake that was distributed to caregivers and patients throughout the day. Enjoying a slice, one patient playfully called to a therapist across the room, espousing the wisdom of treating her hangover with sweets.

(A) PATIENT 1: Nothin' soaks up alcohol like a big greasy slab a cake!

THERAPIST: ((also eating a slice)) There's no grease in here!

PATIENT 2: No. Just about six sticks a butter!

Everyone in listening range joined in the resulting laughter. This type of conversation, which everyone hears and anyone may join, is common in the physical therapy department.

In a similar way, patients commiserate about treatment successes and hardships. Dealing with injuries unfamiliar to most people, the patients sometimes seem to serve as a loosely formed support group. Once I saw two therapists exclaim in delight when, during a neck massage, they heard the desired crack.

(B) THERAPIST 1: Oooow. I heard it. I heard somethin'.

THERAPIST 2: I heard it too.

The patient being treated said nothing until a nearby patient, hidden by a curtain, exclaimed "I heard it too!" Then they all laughed.

The physical layout of the department contributes to the feeling of being "all in it together." The similarity of most patients and their frequent and extended contact no doubt contribute as well. Whatever the causes, the "togetherness" of the department helps to explain the role humor serves and the bold tones it takes.

WHAT ARE THE KEYS, TONES, OR MANNERS OF HUMOR?

Humor use in the physical therapy department is bold and public. Probably because the patients and caregivers interact so frequently and so closely, they develop elaborate humor rituals. Participants often tease each other with feigned anger, as in the following exchange between a therapist and a regular patient who missed her last appointment.

(C) PATIENT: ——, I'm sorry about Monday.

THERAPIST: Oh! You rolled me!

PATIENT: ((grinning)) I-

THERAPIST: ((severe tone)) You rolled me.

PATIENT: I had one week to do a paper and I got all my materials together and I had two days on my computer.

THERAPIST: ((catching the eye of another patient)) Priorities!

PATIENT: Hah hah you're making me feel bad.

THERAPIST: I said priorities. ((breaking into a smile)) You're here to go to school. One day won't make much of a difference. As —— can tell you.

PATIENT: Yeah.

THERAPIST: ((teasing tone)) But hey. I'm gonna keep you
in here for HOURS today! ((patient laughs))

Sometimes therapists take part in playful banter, with a no-pressure invitation for patients to join in. In the following episode, two therapists working with different patients begin to quote funny country music lyrics.

(D) THERAPIST 1: I heard one. "She doesn't cry about Old
Yeller."

PATIENT: ((laughing)) I heard that one too.

THERAPIST 2: I tell you, it's un-American not to cry at
that movie. ((patient laughs)) How about
"I got tears in my ears cause I'm lying
on my back cryin' over you?" ((all laugh))

Out of context, the bold humor used in the department might seem insensitive. One therapist quipped before a particularly dreaded procedure: "Got any Advil or ibuprofen you wanna take real quick?" Consider also the following exchange.

(E) PATIENT: ((laughing)) Are you goihhng tuhh do aneee
more! I'm serious ((laughs)) Ihh don't think
I can take any mohre. That hurts.

THERAPIST: ((smiling)) You're just still upset about that shot
you thought I was gonna give ya. ((both laugh))

The treatment continued. In such instances, I watched the patients' reactions and could detect no signs of indignation or outrage at the humorous treatment of their pain.

At other times, patients did register their own bold, humor-couched complaints. One patient, grinning, remarked loudly: "Slave drivers around here!" Another patient remarked of his therapist: "After all this, —— owes me. He's tough!"

Probably because of the nature of their transactions and the intensity and longevity of their relationships, physical therapy patients and caregivers are bold in their humor use. They come to know each other better than most patients and caregivers and quickly shed stiff decorum.

In summary, humor is conspicuous in the physical therapy department. It is easily overheard, and often said in tones meant to be overheard. Patients and caregivers often playact mock confrontations.

In this way, humor seems to be a safety valve for the inevitable tension between hurting and helping. Because of the need for rigorous and uncomfortable treatment, humor often has a serious undertone: "Keep on. Even if it hurts." The goals of treatment and the communal nature of the department shape the tone and also the topics of humor, as shown in the next section.

TOPICS

Torture is the metaphor most commonly mentioned in the physical therapy department. Patients and caregivers use the word jokingly, and make references to *pain* and *slavery* as well.

> (F) THERAPIST: I'm gonna show you this before I do it. You tell me how you like it.
>
> PATIENT: ((wry smile)) Huh! I'm shure Ih'll love it hhh human torture. Thank you.

Within the category of *torture*, the most common topic of humorous remarks is the hickey machine. This is a pet name for a profusion therapy instrument about the size of a hair brush. It has a black handle and a clear plastic suction cup about 1 inch in diameter. The therapist places the suction cup on the skin and adjusts it until the skin is sucked upward into the cup. This suction increases blood flow to an area, and it leaves hickeylike bruises wherever it is used. The therapists in this department are enthusiastic about profusion therapy and use it with many patients. Most patients joke about the hickey machine but say it does speed healing.

> (G) THERAPIST: ((to me)) We call this profusion therapy.
>
> PATIENT: No they don't. Don't let him tell you that. They call it the hickey machine!

> (H) PATIENT: Oh. You're gonna hickey me huh?
>
> THERAPIST: ((smiling)) Yeah.

> (I) THERAPIST: ((holding the instrument high, and announcing to the whole room)) Now it's time for the hickey machine! ((the patient and others laugh))

(J) THERAPIST: ((smiling)) Man you're all red.

PATIENT: Well I'll look all bruised in a minute.

THERAPIST: No. You'll just look hickeyed. People will ask if you had a good night last night.

PATIENT: Yeah ((laughs)) me and the hickey machine!

As so often happens with humor, it is also funny to juxtapose a situation with its opposite. Humorous references are sometimes made to the "luxuries" of physical therapy.

(K) PATIENT: I wanta do whirlpool today. I have plenty of time.

THERAPIST: ((from behind a curtain)) And she wants a pedicure an' a piece o' that chocolate cake!

PATIENT: ((grinning)) A pedicure and I don't want a piece a cake.

(L) THERAPIST 1: What am I supposed to do for ___ now?

THERAPIST 2: Your call. Your say. Your professional judgment. ((to patient)) Glass a wine an' a bubble bath? That's what you were supposed to do for yourself.

PATIENT: Well I did the bubble bath.

THERAPIST 2: ((smiling)) I did the wine for you so

Like the bulletin board, humorous treatment of pain seems a way of dealing with it. The superiority theory of humor (Wolff et. al., 1934) supports the idea that it is funny to ridicule that which we fear. In the physical therapy department, where pain is fearful and inevitable, humor seems to be a valuable coping mechanism. As one patient said, "I'm afraid I'm not doing it right if it dudn't hurt. . . . I think that's just the way it is."

WHAT ARE THE ENDS, GOALS, AND PURPOSES OF HUMOR?

In the physical therapy department, patients and caregivers use humor most often to soften or discourage complaints, motivate, boast, and make amends. Those activities are crucial elements of the treatment process, but are generally met with negative sanctions in everyday transactions. No one much admires a person who consciously inflicts pain, complains, boasts, or criticizes. Yet patients and caregivers must do these things to negotiate the terms of their relationships. When couched in humor, these activities lose some of the sting that might generally be associated with them. One can complain without seeming to gripe, and chastise without destroying rapport. In short, one can do what one has to do and still save face.

Patient and caregiver are so interdependent that neither can succeed alone. Yet the two begin as strangers. Moreover, the caregiver must often hurt to help. Negotiating their important and complex relationship requires a great deal of social foot work—or in this case, word work. Because it is excusable and ambiguous, humor is a particularly useful way to test limits. Following is an explanation of the ways patients and caregivers use humor to negotiate what is to be endured and what is to be changed.

Softening Complaints With Humor

It is difficult to interpret pain, especially for inexperienced patients. Pain can be either a side-effect of progress or a sign of damage being done. Having experienced one injury, the patient naturally dreads worsening it or incurring another. Thus, it is important that the patient let the therapist know when a treatment causes pain. Yet complaining is not a desirable line for most people. It threatens the social face they would like to present. One solution adopted by many patients is to complain jokingly. Consider the following examples.

(M)   PATIENT: I had these terrible dreams like my bone was gonna fall apart ((laughs))

THERAPIST: Huh! That's not going to happen.

(N)   PATIENT: Yoweee!

THERAPIST: Pretty hot [ultrasound machine] Gollee. One a those screws is glowin! ((both laugh))

(O)   PATIENT: ——! Ask —— what she wants me ta do now. I'm getting bored. ((tone of mock exasperation))

THERAPIST: ((relaying message to whole room)) ——'s
bored!

In these examples, the patients use exaggerations or playacting tones
to comment on grievances. The caregivers respond playfully, going
along with the exaggeration ("Gollee") or laughing as (or before) they
reassure the patient (Ex. M). By joking around, the patient is able to
communicate about pain (or boredom) without casting him or herself
as a griper. Conversely, the caregiver is not put on the defensive. At a
conversational level, humorous treatment characterizes the line both
have taken as amicable partners in the treatment process. All in all,
joking around seems to provide a way for the patient to make his or her
discomfort/fear/boredom known to the caregiver without either person losing face. (See chapter 21 on laughter-coated complaints for a
more thorough examination of this phenomenon.)

Discouraging Complaints With Humor

One principle of relational communication is that a message is not
meaningful until it has been interpreted. Thus, the receiver—through
feedback—helps to determine the way a statement is ultimately treated.
In this way, caregivers can respond humorously to seriously delivered
complaints. This is particularly useful when the caregiver wishes to
acknowledge the complaint, but not to change the circumstances. To
seriously challenge or deny the complaint would often threaten the face
of both patient and caregiver.

   In the following instances, therapists respond playfully to patients'
exclamations of fear or pain.

(P) THERAPIST: Pull up. Relax. Pull up. Relax.

       PATIENT: No. I feel like it's gonna pop.

     THERAPIST: ((Donald Duck voice)) Oh come awn. I- won'
pawp. But come awn. This is good.

(Q) THERAPIST: I gotta thumb ya.

       PATIENT: ((grimacing)) Oh ho ho.

     THERAPIST: Wanna put a rag in your mouth?

       PATIENT: Oh ho ho.

     THERAPIST: ((teasing voice)) You love it. You know you do.

This is not to suggest that caregivers often do or should ignore the cries of their patients. Indeed, I do not think they do. I believe most caregivers consider the information given, and may act on it in ways apparent or not. Even as he or she laughs, for instance, the caregiver may take steps to assuage or explain the grievance. Thus, humor should not be accepted solely at face value, as "all there is" to the exchange. There are serious undertones to humorous gripes and we may presume that both the patient and the caregiver realize this.

Complaints, whether seriously or humorously delivered, are apparently meant as more than jokes and their underlying meaning must not be overlooked. After all, negative sanctions await the caregiver who does not "get the message" of joking around. The patient may be injured or may resort to a more confrontational approach (such as "I SAID that hurts!"). In my observations, joking around complaints far outnumbered straight-faced complaints—a testament, perhaps, to their usefulness and to unfavorable associations of "griping" and "being accused."

Motivating With Humor

One of the most difficult aspects of the therapists' job is keeping patients motivated. Therapy is often tedious and grueling. For maximum results, many patients must report for treatment several times a week and do exercises at home as well. Healing occurs painfully and gradually and even the most enthusiastic beginner can become discouraged and bored. When that happens healing slows even more. The therapist becomes frustrated, because if patients do not do their homework therapy is of little benefit. Perhaps for this reason therapists are lavish in their praise and encouragement. Often their praise takes the form of humorous proclamations.

(R)   THERAPIST: You're doin' good.

         PATIENT: Thanks.

         THERAPIST: You are. Your knee feels so good I bet you wanta go out and do some hoops!

(S)   THERAPIST 1: ((to whole room)) Watch ____!

         THERAPIST 2: That's great. Goll. That's great ____!

         THERAPIST 1: ((uplifted hands as if a miracle has occurred)) Get rid o' those crutches!

(T)   THERAPIST: You're amazing. That you're doing this when
                   we did the first one a week ago.

     PATIENT: ((laughs)) For a mature woman like me
                   ((laughs))

     THERAPIST: Spring chicken. ((pause)) If I have your health at
                   your age it'll be a godsend. What's your secret,
                   Jack Daniels every night?

     PATIENT: ((laughing)) No. I don't do that ever night. ——
                   Maybe a glass o' wine.

Praise and shared humor accentuate that patient and caregiver are on
the same side. Humor helps align them as cohorts, not adversaries. In
a setting that often requires that the caregiver inflict pain, such repartee
seems especially valuable.

Boasting

Demonstrating good behavior is a tricky business. One must display
success without seeming to brag. Again, humor does the trick. In the
following example, a patient playfully parades her good deed.

(U)   PATIENT: ((proclaimed loudly as she walks in)) You're
                 gonna be so surprised. I did my exercises.

     THERAPIST: Good.

     PATIENT: ((smiling)) I mean hard core did 'em.

Playful boasting is a socially acceptable way for the patient to let the
caregiver know she has done her homework. This is sure to be well
received by the therapist whose success relies on the patient's efforts.

Making Amends

Sometimes a perceived oversight or mistreatment threatens the rapport
shared by a patient and caregiver. In those cases, humor mimics the timid
tail-wagging of a dog who wishes to be forgiven. It is a bid for forgiveness
and friendliness. Consider the following episode that occurred after a
busy therapist forgot about a patient.

(V)   THERAPIST: ——, you still here?

     PATIENT: Yeah.

> THERAPIST: Huh! Bout forgot about you.
>
> PATIENT: I about wenta sleep.
>
> THERAPIST: ((smiling)) It's easy to do in here. Unless we have Urethra. ((gestures to tape player))
>
> PATIENT: ((smiling)) Aretha ((pause)) Franklin.
>
> THERAPIST: ((grinning)) I call her Urethra.

In this case, the caregiver's humor seems an effort to mend the rapport that might have been damaged by his inattentiveness. I noticed similar behavior by patients who initiated humor after sheepishly admitting they had not done their at-home exercises. By bracketing an event with humor, a person may bid for gentle judgment. Humor is a show of friendliness, a social bid for the acceptance implied by shared laughter.

CONCLUSIONS

Taken out of context, the bold humor of the physical therapy department may seem insensitive. But participants showed no signs of being offended. Indeed, many patients made a point of telling me about the friendliness of the staff. And it often seemed to me that therapists joked around most boldly with patients they knew and liked best.

Therapist and patient are much like coach and player. Success is not won without pushing the barriers of comfort. And although neither can afford to splinter the relationship with straightfaced challenges, some degree of interpersonal friction is inevitable. Humor may be a salve and a safety valve for feelings of animosity between the two.

This analysis suggests that humor is a pleasing, face-saving way to accomplish many objectives of the patient–caregiver relationship. Humor offers a way to establish rapport, complain, make amends, and praise. Although the tone and manner of humor may differ across medical settings, those functions are the same in every setting I have studied.

Significantly, humor in this physical therapy department is almost identical to humor I witnessed in a hospital physical rehabilitation unit 600 miles away (Smith-Dupré, 1992). However, as the following chapter demonstrates, this humor is much different in tone and topic than humor of the breast care center and physician office I studied. Following an ethnographic analysis of those settings, I close the section with an overview that compares and contrasts humor used in these different medical settings.

Chapter 11

▼

Discreet Humor
in a Breast Care Center

In contrast to the antiseptic atmosphere of many medical settings, the breast care center is luxuriously intimate. It is decorated with antiques, pastel floral prints, and soothing shades of rose and mint. Entering, one has the feeling of stepping into the private sitting room of an elegant and gracious hostess. The decor conveys mature femininity without girlish bows or frills. The furniture and wall hangings are decorated with polished, carved wood, offset by watercolor prints and cushiony chairs and sofas. Rather than white paper gowns, patients are asked to change into attractive cotton smocks that tie in the front. These details, says the center's director, are the result of careful thought.

Initial plans for this center and several others were overseen by a female benefactor, herself a breast cancer survivor. Her early mission statement is echoed by the current director: Provide a respectful environment where women may maintain dignity while receiving the best medical care possible. Staff members echo this philosophy with remarks such as: "We try to make our clients feel comfortable," and "We want our clients to feel good about themselves for having a mammography."

There is a catch, however. Despite their best efforts, the staff is aware that no one much enjoys a breast exam. To be screened for breast cancer, a woman must stand nude from the waist up while a technician looks at and touches her breasts. To make matters worse, mammography requires that each breast be placed upon a flat x-ray deck and compressed. Greater compression allows better diagnostic images, but causes greater discomfort. Many women attest that mammograms are only uncomfortable, not painful. But fears naturally persist. "I hear a lot of jokes about putting your tittie in the wringer," said one technician.

Added to patients' trepidation about the exam is their fear of a devastating diagnosis. A cancerous lump may lead to the removal of a breast or even death. "Rain is bad for business around here," declares the director. "We start getting calls saying, 'I can't come in.' Everyone's looking for an excuse not to come." That awareness—that a breast exam can be avoided or postponed—contributes to the center's emphasis on polite, pleasant-as-possible care. Staff members say that a woman who has, or hears about, a bad experience may never return to the clinic. Worse yet, she may avoid breast cancer screening altogether.

All in all, caregivers and patients in the breast care center are continually involved in a problematic circumstance that characterizes many medical encounters—one must hurt to help. A breast exam is both intimate, and for most patients, embarrassing, frightening, and physically uncomfortable. But perhaps because most mammograms are undergone voluntarily, by assymptomatic women, the staff treats it as particularly important that exams seem to help more than they hurt. Thus, they have the challenge of being both rigorous and accommodating. Considering the unpleasant nature of an accurate exam, these goals often seem to be oppositional. This analysis explores the function of humor in patient–caregiver transactions of the breast care center.

In the interest of comparability, I address the same questions as in the physical therapy study. I propose that humor is used in the breast care center to offset the embarrassment of the exam, sidestep complaints, and help the patient and caregiver negotiate the relational dialectic between hurting and helping.

ABOUT THE SETTING

The breast care center is privately owned, and located in an affluent section of a large southwestern city in the United States. A staff of three radiology technicians performs mammograms looking for early signs of breast cancer. They also use ultrasound imaging to gather diagnostic data and assist the staff radiologist with needle (nonsurgical) biopsies to collect breast tissue for testing.

All three radiology technicians are women, one in her mid-20s, one in her mid-30s, and another about 50 years old. Each wears a print or solid pastel-colored lab coat and a name badge that indicates her accreditation as a technician. The technicians usually wear comfortable slacks and athletic or nursing shoes.

The only male employee is the staff radiologist who remains largely behind the scenes. According to the center's director (a woman in her late 30s), the presence of a nearly all-female staff is meant to contribute to an understanding, nonthreatening environment.

Like the staff, the center's clientele is almost exclusively female. Most of them are quite well groomed and many appear to be expensively dressed. Appearances and the center's location in an affluent area of town support the impression that the patients are predominantly women of high socioeconomic status. Most are between 40 and 60 years old, although I observed older and younger patients as well. I was aware of one male patient during my study, but did not observe him.

I refer to women who undergo screening at the breast care center interchangeably as *patients* or *clients*. Certainly they would be called patients if they were seeking routine cancer screening (such as a pap smear) at a physician's office. But the breast center staff often refers to the women they see as clients. This word choice is interesting, for it is one of many subtle reminders that women come to the center largely of their own accord.[1] To appreciate the implications of this, imagine a physician who specializes in routine checkups rather than treatment (which, of course, few physicians do). In such a case, business would rely on the number of people who believe it is worth their while to be checked for disease just in case it is present. Obviously, this is a different—and for most people, a less urgent—enterprise than seeking care "because" disease is indicated.

People will presumably seek routine health screening only if they believe it will preserve their health to do so, and if the advantages of screening seem to outweigh the disadvantages. The disadvantages may include the cost, pain, embarrassment, and time required, and the possibility that one will be confronted by a devastating diagnosis. Considering this, the difference between a *patient* (symptom-driven) role

---

[1] A physician referral is required for mammography at this center and others, but women may often choose which breast center to patronize. Furthermore, obtaining a referral requires that a woman first see her doctor. In most cases, women who undergo mammographies have no detectable symptoms of breast cancer. Therefore, the routine screening is particularly easy to put off or avoid. Thus, the breast center must rely for business, first, on the occurrence of women visiting their physicians, and second, on the number of women referred for mammography who seek it, and choose this particular center.

and a *client* (assymptomatic, voluntary) role is appreciably different. As I show here, this difference seems to have a pervasive influence on the way patients and caregivers interact in the breast care center.

HOW DOES THE SETTING HELP DEFINE COMMUNICATION?

Unlike the physical therapy department, patient–caregiver transactions in the breast center are almost always private and dyadic. Examinations are conducted in private rooms, and the patient usually interacts with only one caregiver.

The office is quiet; so too are conversations. Behind the scenes, caregivers work in close quarters, juggling time in the darkroom and small x-ray viewing area, but they keep their voices respectfully low. As one caregiver told me, "You don't want any patient to think you're laughing at her."

Likewise, humor initiated by caregivers is offered very quietly and subtly. Indeed, when I entered the breast center after completing observations in a hospital I wondered for a few days if there was any humor there. There were certainly none of the bold quips I had seen in surgery. As I became acclimated to the subtle undertones of the breast care center, however, I began to be aware of humor used in a very different way. The subtle tones and different topics of this humor, and the objectives it serves, are described on the following pages.

WHAT ARE THE KEYS, TONES, OR MANNERS OF HUMOR?

Caregivers in the breast care center make few bold moves. Their actions and words are gentle and usually well prefaced. Humor is no exception. Technicians offer trifles of humor ambiguously enough that patients can accept them as serious or as humorous. These statements are usually delivered while the technician adjusts instruments, not during direct eye contact.

(X)   TECH: ((to researcher)) It's pretty frustrating to get a double
                exposure. ((slight pause in which she raises her
                eyebrows slightly as she adjusts instruments)) The
                patient doesn't like it much either.

In this instance, the patient chuckled in appreciation of the last comment. It might have passed quite gracefully without a laugh, however. Following are more examples of subtle humor that drew laughs:

(Y)   TECH: Athena is workin' on her doctorate degree in
                      communication. So if I don't communicate
                      with you, jus' let her know. ((both laugh))

(Z)   PATIENT: ((regarding ultrasound)) That's like when you're
                       pregnant and they roll that thing over. And they put that
                       cold gel.
             TECH: It's not cold! We have a warmer for it! ((Both laugh))

(AA)   TECH: It's been warm in here all day. I turned the heat
                      down but I didn't turn the air on, cause I figured
                      that would be overreacting. ((both laugh))

In these instances, the caregiver waits on the patient's interpretation of the utterance before either joining in her laughter or continuing seriously.[2] This suggests that the caregiver is willing (perhaps poised) to laugh, but does so only with the patient's encouragement. Consequently, it is largely the patient's choice how such utterances will be handled. Goffman (1974) made the point that social actors employ sophisticated machinery such as this to avoid misunderstandings: "For us the important point here is not that misunderstandings occur but rather that they occur so infrequently, and behind this the fact that persons ordinarily take precautions in advance to make sure of this infrequency" (p. 328). In summary, caregivers seem to defer to patients in the breast care center. Humor initiated by the technicians is usually subtle and quiet, a vivid contrast to the bold, public quips of physical therapists in the previous study. In a medical culture that grants high value to a sense of decorum and dignity, this timidity seems to help assure that no one is offended.

As described in the next section, patients are often bolder than caregivers in their humor use. Although caregivers choose innocuous

---

[2]In chapter 21, detailed transcripts show how patients and caregivers collaboratively manage ambiguous complaints as laughable utterances.

subjects like technical procedures and room temperature, patients are more direct, often joking about the size of their breasts and the "squeezing" and "skwooshing" aspects of the exam.

TOPICS

I made the argument in chapter 7 that it is often a relief to douse subjects that we fear in laughter. From that perspective, it is no surprise that patients in the breast care center make jokes about their breasts.

When I interviewed the center's director, she remarked that women are particularly self-conscious about their breasts: "Our breasts are the most visible feature that distinguish us from males. It's not where we reproduce, but it is where we nurture." This self-consciousness is no doubt heightened by a cultural emphasis on breast size as a measure of sexual desirability. For these reasons, the director told me, women seem to fear mammography in a way they do not fear other medical exams: "We don't want to be maimed in a way that seems so abhorrent. . . . When we go to the gynecologist for a pap smear, we don't say 'Oh my God. I might have cervical cancer.'" To display one's breasts—or worse, to have them removed because of breast cancer—stirs up particularly vivid fears.

As women stand nude from the waist up, they frequently make humorous remarks about their breasts. Following are a few examples.

  (BB)   PATIENT: There's not very much to put on there
                   ((compression begins)) you're going to squash what
                   I have left! ((laughs))

  (CC)   PATIENT: I'm flat-chested. They aren't very big so-o ((laughs)).

  (DD)   PATIENT: I've watched [the instructional film]. I've played
                   with 'em. I feel a million lumps in there! ((laughs))

  (EE)   PATIENT: About 10 pounds each!

  (FF)   PATIENT: ((regarding my presence)) Won't bother me if she
                   can stand to look at these big boobs. ((smile))

(GG)   PATIENT: Last time I had 'em [breasts] checked, they told me it
                   was mostly fat! ((laughs))

(HH)   PATIENT: ((regarding breast implants)) I went to Dr. —. He
                   wanted to take 'em out and leave 'em out. I said,
                   Unn-uhh I'm single. We're not gonna have that.
                   I'm not goin' around like Papoose Granny! ((both
                   laugh))
                   . . .

          PATIENT: I started [with implants] in '67. The first ones
                   were pretty but not as pretty as the ones in '72.

          TECH: You wanted the new model, huh? ((both laugh))

One 70-year-old patient spoke animatedly of her breast reduction surgery, grinning and laughing:

(II)   When they were big, I had to get special things to put
                   'em in. ((cups hands with breasts)) Now they're so small,
                   hard to get 'em out there. They took too much really!

Other (fewer) humorous quips focused on the exam itself.

(JJ)   TECH: Need your arm outa your right sleeve.

          PATIENT: Sorry. I'm just standin' here waitin' for mother ta
                   tell me what to do! ((both laugh))

(KK)   TECH: I need your left sleeve off this time.

          PATIENT: I feel like we're doin the hokey pokey!

(LL)   PATIENT: ((regarding another patient)) I told 'er she's gointa
                   get squeezed! I told 'er I don' wanta hear 'er yell!
                   ((laughs))

These quips sound very much like the "torture" humor of the physical
therapy department, suggesting that physical discomfort and awkwardness are key sources of concern for participants in both settings. In
addition, patients of the breast care center give attention to their physical
appearance, a topic predictably more salient when partial nudity is
involved. The next section examines what functions this type of humor
serves.

WHAT ARE THE ENDS, GOALS, AND PURPOSES OF HUMOR?

I propose that patients and caregivers in the breast care center capitalize on the ambiguity of humor. Patients use this ambiguity to solicit feedback about the legitimacy of their fears, and caregivers use it to reframe potential complaints in positive terms. Additionally, both use humor to campaign for a less somber relational climate.

Fearful But Funny

In the breast care center (like the physical therapy unit), patients use humor to comment ambiguously about a source of fear or discomfort. In the following examples, patients express their apprehension even as they laugh and speak in comically exaggerated tones.

(MM)   PATIENT: I'm just really nervous that you're going to burst my [breast] implants huh huh ((in tone of mock horror)) I'm going to have silicone leaking into my system!

TECH: No! huh we won't do that. Deal with implants all the time.

(NN)   TECH: This machine has automatic compression it=

PATIENT: =does itself and doesn't stop 'til it gets there, huh?! I don't know that that's such a good idea! ((both laugh))

By presenting two messages at once (e.g., "I'm really nervous" and "I'm laughing") the patient allows the caregiver a choice of responses. In the first example, the caregiver might laugh, endorsing that it is a funny exaggeration to imagine silicone leaking into one's system as a result of mammography. In this case, she exhales a laughter breath (huh) but reassures the patient in serious tones that she need not be afraid.

In the second example, the caregiver elects to laugh along with the patient rather than seriously rebut her statement. The difference, presumably, is that the "silicone" fears are taken more seriously than the "machine-that-won't-stop" fears as something about which the patient might legitimately and seriously worry. Hazardous silicone leakage was the subject of much news coverage at the time of my observations. Several times, caregivers showed me x-rays in which silicone could be detected in the breast tissue of a patient. (In no instance was the leakage caused by mammography.) By contrast, there is little to support the threat of an out-of-control mammography machine, and the patient's laughter was apparently persuasive enough to convince the technician that the utterance might be treated as a jest.

In summary, humor permits patients to voice their apprehensions in a way that requires active interpretation by the caregiver. Whether the caregiver responds in a playful or a serious manner suggests how she views the threat and how she will respond to it. We might imagine a scenario in which the caregiver in Ex. NN remarks seriously that "This machine HAS been acting up" or "Is this too tight for you?" The patient's serious/funny utterance makes it acceptable for her to respond this way. Likewise, the caregiver in Ex. MM might have merely laughed. Thus, by making several reactions available to the caregiver, the patient can express fears and solicit feedback about them. In this way, the patient gains information and sidesteps the face-threatening possibility that—by seriously presenting her fears—she will seem weak, uncooperative, or disagreeable. If the fear is laughed away by the caregiver, the patient too may treat it as laughable without noticeably changing her line.

Bidding for a Lighter Tone

Although many patients seem to initiate humor in reference to their own unease or embarrassment, in several instances patients seemed more concerned about putting the caregiver at ease. For instance, some women who did not seem self-conscious made funny remarks about their breasts.

The former breast reduction patient (Ex. II) took off her smock on entering the exam room and left it off even when the technician left the room for several minutes. (Most patients remove only one arm at a time and cover themselves during even brief pauses in the exam.) This patient's humor seemed to dispel her own self-consciousness and an overriding sense of weirdness or untenable somberness about the encounter. It was as if she said: "I won't take the fact of my nudity very seriously and you needn't either. Let's laugh and lighten up a bit."

At other times, patients use humor to "forgive" the technician when she seems hesitant or apologetic. For instance, when a technician informed one patient (quoted in Ex. HH) that she needed to take more x-rays, the patient exclaimed:

(OO)   PATIENT: That's alright. I get my money's worth. I'm glad you're takin' pictures of my titties instead of my face!

Humor earns obvious results in situations such as these. The tone of a transaction typically becomes more relaxed and conversational. The caregiver often becomes more adventuresome in her use of humor. I noticed more eye contact between patient and caregiver, and they seemed to speak in more lilting, less formal, tones of voice. (The relational persuasiveness of humor is discussed more thoroughly in Part V.) Overall, humor seems an effective and often-used method of breaking the ice and establishing a more comfortable intimacy between participants. (This effect is noted as well in Smith-Dupré, 1992.)

Sidestepping Complaints With Humor

The breast center staff uses humorous statements to acknowledge patients' feelings, at the same time keying or rekeying their experiences as "not so bad." *Keying* is a term used by Goffman (1974) to describe the conventions with which interactants display how a sequence should be interpreted. He wrote that keying and rekeying often have the effect of radically transforming the participants' sense of what "is really going on" (p. 45).[3] In the breast center, caregivers sometimes key an experience with an advance interpretation of it, as in the following examples. The first statement was used by one technician with a variety of patients.

(PP) TECH: This bottom corner is goin' ta poke you in the ribs, and this top corner is goin' ta poke you up under your arm. It's not really comfortable 'cause we're not built like corners. ((Sometimes adding: "It keeps your mind off the compression!"))

(QQ) TECH: Do ya remember about compression? I don't like ta surprise people with that!

(RR) TECH: See how easy it is for me to tell you to relax? ((patient laughs))

(SS) TECH: Are ya havin' fun yet?
      PATIENT: ((sudden grin)) Well ((pause)) no.

---

[3]See chapter 19 for a more thorough explanation and analysis of keying and framing.

(TT)   TECH: We told you to wipe your deodorant off and we got
                     goop all over you. Don't you feel lovely now?
                     ((both laugh))

With these statements, caregivers acknowledge in advance that they
understand the patient's situation. Thus, the patient may be discouraged
from voicing negative reactions, knowing explicitly that her feelings have
already been acknowledged. Furthermore, she is presumably aware that
the experience has been keyed or preinterpreted by the caregiver as
uncomfortable but bearable for those who approach it in a good-natured
way.

   Another approach is to respond to patients' utterances with humorous rejoinders that reframe grievances as accomplishments.

(UU)   PATIENT: I don't remember this [part of the exam].

              TECH: You were problee havin' so much fun!

(VV)   PATIENT: This one didn't hurt near so much as that one two
                        years ago.

              TECH: You're just havin' more fun today is all. ((both laugh))

(WW)   PATIENT: It's hot in here.

              TECH: Worked up a sweat on that one, huh?

In this way, the caregiver responds to a potential complaint with a
compliment. In these instances, patients allowed the caregiver's interpretation to stand. That is, they smiled or laughed and did not reiterate
their grievances. Consequently, in the overall scheme of the conversation, the patient's utterance takes on a different cast than it might have.
It seems, in retrospect, more like a collaborative contribution to a
pleasant exchange than a bald-faced complaint. Potential complaints are
turned into humorously congratulatory remarks insinuating that the
patient felt discomfort because she did so well.

   In summary, the ambiguity of humor allows a caregiver to acknowledge a grievance and to treat it as a topic for good-natured kidding
around. By foreseeing a complaint or responding immediately to one,
the caregiver can respectfully key the experience in a less grievous, even
a congratulatory way. Thus, humor is a particularly useful means of
managing the delicate balance between hurting and helping.

CONCLUSIONS

To summarize, I propose that humor is a potent, yet subtle means of negotiation between patients and caregivers in the breast care center. Using humor, participants can solicit information and bid for a less somber, more affiliative relational tone. For example, by presenting their feelings in funny/serious ways, patients seek informative feedback from their caregivers. Whether a caregiver reacts in a serious or playful way may suggest how she views the patient's utterance. Serious treatment of a patient's fear (as in the "leaking silicone" conversation) may suggest that the fear is a reasonable one that merits serious assurances. In other instances, ambiguously stated fears may be treated as laughables if cues (such as comical exaggerations) suggest they are meant in jest, laughter is judged an appropriate way to emphasize that the cause of the fear (e.g., a malevolent machine) is so inconsequential as to be laughable, or the caregiver uses humor (e.g., "Are ya havin' fun yet?") to soften her insistence that the grievous circumstance be carried out.

It bears emphasizing here that—beyond the moral orders of the culture—none of these responses are inherently right or wrong. We might, from a different cultural perspective, feel indignant that a patient's fear is "laughed off" by a caregiver. Within the climate of the breast care center, however, such "laughing off" is morally justified if it helps the patient attain a less fearful, more realistic perspective. Indeed, we might wonder what goes through a patient's mind when a fear that she expects to have laughed off is treated seriously. Burton (1986) quoted a patient who said, "if they don't use humor, then I *really* worry that something is the matter!" (p. 166). Furthermore, patients participate in the humor by wording their feelings in ambiguously humorous ways[4] and by joining in their caregivers' laughter.

Additionally, patients and caregivers use humor to dispel the embarrassment and solemnity of breast exams. Humor offers a way for caregivers to suggest in advance that a grievance be born good-naturedly. It also allows the caregiver to rekey grievous circumstances in complimentary terms (e.g., "Worked up a sweat on that one, huh?"). In a similar way, patients use humor to make their feelings known without seeming to be weak or bitchy. In these ways, the ambiguity of humor makes it a particularly useful tool of interpersonal negotiation. In the breast care center, it seems to help patients and caregivers negotiate the dialectic between hurting and helping.

---

[4]Embedded laughter is not always an invitation to laugh. See chapter 21 for an explanation of "brave laughter" in troubles talk as described by Jefferson (1986b).

Chapter 12

▼

Empathic Humor
in a Doctor's Office

Were it not for the stethoscope around her neck, it might be hard to distinguish Dr. Lane (not her real name) from the majority of her patients. Most fit the same description—early 30s, female, casually but neatly dressed. Like her, they refer frequently to the experiences of motherhood. They go by first names and know many of the same people. These similarities are emphasized in exam room conversations, during which the physician expresses empathy for her patients' concerns and lets them know she shares many of the same experiences. Many examples of this are included in the analysis that follows.

Humor is less visible in Dr. Lane's family practice office than in the physical therapy unit or the breast center. In the doctor's office, laughter is used in many instances that do not seem particularly humorous. For instance, patients often "huh huh" while describing their concerns and hardships. The physician does not typically treat such utterances as funny, however. Instead, she responds to them with seriousness and empathy. Where shared humor *does* surface, it usually serves the same purpose—to accentuate an expression of empathy or concern. Following a description of this setting, I present evidence that Dr. Lane and her patients use humor to express their identification with each other. Furthermore, in contrast to the other settings under study, participants in this setting often make humorous remarks about topics not directly related to the medical exam. They joke around about changing diapers and getting older—conditions not precipitated by the medical encounter.

This provides an interesting contrast to the "breast size" and "discomfort" humor of the breast center and the "torture" humor of the physical therapy department.

ABOUT THE SETTING

Dr. Lane's office is traditional in appearance. Patients sit in a brightly lit waiting room, flipping through magazines. Once summoned behind the scenes, they are directed first to a nurse's station in a small alcove, then to one of three private examination rooms where they await the physician.

Between exams, Dr. Lane returns patients' phone calls at a desk she shares with a medical partner. It is piled high with patient charts and pharmaceutical giveaways (mugs, pens, note pads, brochures). The bookcase behind the desk is a testament to the diverse demands of family practice medicine. It displays volumes on gynecology, pediatrics, pharmacology, principles of surgery, pathological bases of disease, family practice, internal medicine, skin diseases, psychiatry, and orthopedics. During a break I ask the doctor if it is difficult to treat such an extensive variety of maladies. She responds that the variety "keeps things interesting" and points out that her schedule is often routinized by seasonal illnesses like flu and sinus infections. Her favorite medical service, she says, is delivering babies. A mother of three young children at the time of this study (now four), she showed a particular enthusiasm for obstetric and pediatric care.

Dr. Lane is an attractive Euro-American woman in her early 30s. She does not wear a lab coat nor a name badge. During the warm days of autumn while I was there, she typically wore colorful skirts and blouses with sandals and a small black beeper attached to her waistband. Many patients refer to her familiarly by first name. Several patients are neighbors of hers and some know her socially through school-related events involving Dr. Lane's children and their own.

During my observations, Dr. Lane saw patients ranging from 2 weeks to 69 years of age. Most were women and children. I only observed two adult male patients, and male pediatric patients were almost always accompanied by their mothers. A large majority of patients are Euro-American.

Many patients come to Dr. Lane seeking help with depression. Her caseload also includes pediatric patients typically in for coughs, colds, and checkups; adolescents concerned about minor illnesses, injuries, or excess weight; women in for gynecological and obstetrical care; and elderly and middle-aged patients suffering from respiratory ailments, arthritis, insomnia, migraines, allergies, and other conditions.

EXAMINATION PROCEDURE

Each patient is summoned from the waiting room by a female nurse, who checks the patient's weight, blood pressure, and temperature and collects information about his or her health concerns and health history. She notes this information on the patient's chart and orally briefs the physician about the patient before most exams. (It often seems that patients disclose concerns to the nurse that they do not immediately disclose to the doctor. Several times I heard the nurse tell Dr. Lane something such as, "She's in for a sore throat but I believe this may be a depression case," or "He sort of hinted about a former drug problem.")

It is Dr. Lane's policy to interview adolescent patients by themselves, before inviting their parents into the exam room. As she told one 11-year-old girl, "If you ever have any questions that are private, that you don't want to talk about in front of your parents, I'll always let you come back here alone first."

If an exam requires that a patient disrobe—particularly if this is the patient's first visit—Dr. Lane makes a point of talking with the patient first, then leaving the room while he or she disrobes. She explained to me, "I just think it would be horrible to have to meet someone when you were undressed."

For most patients, the doctor's visit is comprised mostly of talk. After talking with the patient, Dr. Lane may propose a physical exam such as "checking your tummy" or "looking at your throat" or "listening to your heart." Most patients do not display that these procedures are particularly embarrassing or uncomfortable. One striking exception is the gynecological exam, in which (as I show) conversational work to offset embarrassment and discomfort is usually quite evident.

Like most physicians, Dr. Lane does not administer injections herself. That task is left to the nurse. This arrangement may serve the interest of efficiency. But it has another effect as well; it excuses the doctor from inflicting pain. This does not entirely extricate the doctor from the hurting–helping dialect so evident in the breast center and physical therapy unit. After all, the physician must still perform some "grievous" procedures such as pelvic exams, and she may prescribe unpleasant treatment routines (although, unlike the physical therapist, she is not usually present when these routines are carried out). For the most part, however, the physician is not the perpetrator of discomforts. This role falls to the nurse, as is evident in the following exchange when Dr. Lane inquires about a pediatric patient the nurse has just vaccinated.

(XX)   DOCTOR: Ooh. Is Kelly okay?
           NURSE: Yeah. She didn't hold a grudge like Rodney.
                    Rodney sees me in the grocery store and starts
                    crying. ((both laugh))

Patients—particularly children—are perhaps more likely to "hold a grudge" against the nurse than the doctor. In interactions with older patients, this "grudge holding" may be less evident, but I propose that the doctor's role as mostly a helper (not a hurter) has significant effects on the types of complaints she hears and the way she deals with those complaints.

HOW DOES THE SETTING HELP DEFINE COMMUNICATION?

This doctor's office is much like the breast care center in that conversations are usually conducted dyadically and in private. Patients' contact with caregivers is constrained by closed doors. The patient does not have license to seek out the physician or to summon her attention out of turn. (Indeed, it is sometimes hard for the nurse to find the physician behind so many closed doors!) Rather, the patient must wait until the doctor comes to him or her, and must accept that the doctor's exit from the exam room is instrumentally the end of the exchange.

This is a different situation than the physical therapy unit, where caregivers are visibly and audibly available to patients for an extended time. In that setting, patients may summon a caregiver at almost any point, and may even join in transactions involving other patients (with the consequence that a patient must sometimes compete for the caregiver's attention). Perhaps because the doctor's office limits patient–caregiver interaction and renders it dyadic and private, humor there has the same mild tone as humor in the breast care center.

WHAT ARE THE KEYS, TONES, OR MANNERS OF HUMOR?

Dialogue quoted throughout this section supports that Dr. Lane and her patients joke around in a mild way much like participants in the breast center. But they use laughter in an additional way as well. One hears a great deal of what Jefferson (1986b) called "brave laughter." Jefferson noted that people often embed laughter particles in serious statements of woe, but conversational partners do not join in the laughter; instead they treat the utterances as serious ones. Presumably, laughter in these instances is meant to imply that the speaker is being brave, not being funny.

In Dr. Lane's office, patients talking about their troubles sometimes laugh as if to imply "I've suffered but I'm not complaining." The following excerpt is an example.

(YY)   PATIENT: This was a lousy decade madame huh huh huh
                   brain surgery, hip replacement, breast cancer.
         DOCTOR: Go:sh.

If this is humor, it is certainly very wry. Although the unusual word choice of "madame" and the embedded laughter in the patient's utterance might signal it as something meant to be funny, the content of the utterance suggests otherwise. The doctor responds to the patient with a sympathetic rejoinder. In examples such as these, laughter is not treated collaboratively as a sign of humor.

Following are more examples of what we might term *wry, humorless,* or *brave laughter.*

(ZZ)   PATIENT: ((regarding obesity)) Well you know I wasn't
                   expectin there to be anything wrong with me. My
                   m- I think my mom really wants there to be
                   something wrong with me huh huh y'know.
         DOCTOR: Yeah.

(AAA)   PATIENT: ((regarding relationship with another
                   physician)) We've been through thin and thin
                   together! ((laughs))

(BBB)   PATIENT: I just want to eliminate AIDS huh huh
         DOCTOR: You don't have any other symptoms. You look healthy.

The presence of shared laughter is noticeably absent in these excerpts as compared to dialogue in the other settings. This may be because the imperative to make light of the situation is not so strong for Dr. Lane as for the radiology technicians and physical therapists. In those settings, the patients' complaints were often directed toward actions of the caregiver and events of the exam. To openly treat those events as grievous threatened the caregiver's face as well as the patient's. In Dr. Lane's situation, however, she is ostensibly not to blame for the sources of the patients' complaints. Consequently, although patients in Dr. Lane's office (like patients in the other settings) may use laughter to avoid the negative sanctions of griping, her patients' "gripes" do not directly implicate her. That is, they do not usually threaten her face as a benevolent caregiver. Shielded from this risk, she takes the line of a sincere and sympathetic listener—displaying that she hears the serious messages in the patients' utterances, and further, that she sympathizes (thus does not consider them to be weak or bitchy).[1]

TOPICS

Topics of humor in the doctor's office also contrast somewhat with topics in other settings. In the other settings, participants often make light of issues concerning the exam itself—breast size, skwooshing, torture, the hickey machine. Humor in Dr. Lane's office is apt to concern topics more extraneous to the exam. And perhaps because she sees a wide variety of cases, the topics are more diverse. Following are examples of humorous statements made about issues outside the exam context.

(CCC)   DOCTOR: ((to child)) Can you just play a lotta quiet games? Like maybe watch some movies?

         MOTHER: Yeah he's good at that. ((doctor and mother laugh))

(DDD)   PATIENT: My sister told me I'm goin to have twins and my dad said so too.

         DOCTOR: Now why?

         PATIENT: They said "cause you deserve it!" ((both laugh))

---

[1]Other differences between seriously managed complaints and laughter-coated complaints are discussed in chapter 21.

(EEE)   DOCTOR: Is she blowin yuckie stuff out of her nose?

          MOTHER: Every time she sneezes it comes out everywhere
                   but 'er ears! ((both laugh))

(FFF)   PATIENT: ((regarding adoption of an older child)) It's
                    wonderful. And I didn't even have to change
                    diapers either! ((patient and doctor laugh))

Interestingly, when an intimate procedure such as a gynecological exam is
conducted, humor does focus on aspects of the exam, as in the following
examples.

(GGG)   DOCTOR: Okay. Here let me get these lovely stirrups out.

          PATIENT: Huh huh huh are they ever going to improve this?
                    And when do I get to stop having this done? What
                    age limit is there on this?

          DOCTOR: Boy! Never! huh huh I know ((pause)) ((smiling))
                   you're stuck with this for life.

(HHH)   PATIENT: Is everybody this awkward on this tuhable huhhuh

          DOCTOR: ((smiling voice)) Oh ye:ah. Everybody is!

(III)   DOCTOR: ((regarding paper gown)) Now let me just give you
                   these lovely drapes! ((both laugh))

In summary, Dr. Lane and her patients laugh together about a variety of
topics. It is interesting that their humor seems to focus on the exam only
when it is particularly problematic. During gynecological exams, for
instance, participants in the doctor's office (like participants in other
settings) often joke around about issues of awkwardness and unpleasantness. This strengthens the proposition that humor is used in medical
settings to mitigate embarrassment and discomfort. Following is a discussion of another function served by humor.

WHAT ARE THE ENDS, GOALS,
AND PURPOSES OF HUMOR?

Dr. Lane and her patients use humor to display a sense of mutual identification. This is often done through expressions of empathy, as when one
participant conveys in a humorously exaggerated way that she understands
the other's situation.

(JJJ) PATIENT: I have a spastic colon and a spastic stomach.

DOCTOR: Oh boy. No fun! ((both laugh))

PATIENT: It's all from the job. ((both laugh))

(KKK) MOTHER: I lost twenny in the hospital.

DOCTOR: That's great. I think I only lost five and then I had all this weight to lose! ((both laugh))

(LLL) DOCTOR: Boy I bet you were flippin out when they said sixty dollars for that test! ((both laugh))

(MMM) DOCTOR: ((regarding anesthesia during labor)) A lot of people hit six or seven centimeters and say forget this. ((all laugh)) Me I hit about two! ((more laughs))

(NNN) DOCTOR: Gosh ——, you've got poison ivy? ((child nods, doctor laughs)) I do too!

In these examples, humor seems to emphasize commonalities between Dr. Lane and her patients. By insinuating that the speaker understands the other's plight ("No fun!") and has experienced something similar ("Me too!"), humor calls attention to commonalities between the conversants. The same effect was noted by Beck and Ragan (1992) in their study of gynecological exams conducted by a female nurse practitioner. Displays of mutual identification may be especially attainable in this study (and in Beck and Ragan's) because the caregivers and patients have so much in common (same gender, similar ages and concerns).

Humor may also be used to make a favorable comparison ("I only lost five") or help shape the other person's expectations about a future event ("me I hit about two!"). During my study of hospital communication, an obstetrical nurse told me how and why she uses humor to prepare couples for childbirth:

> We tell the dad that his wife—this sweet, precious little flower—may tell him to get the hell out of her face [during labor]. But he shouldn't take it personally. . . . It lightens things up. It's a way to prepare them and let them know it happens. Knowing that going in alleviates a lot of postpartum guilt and the husband wondering, "Why didn't she even want me in there?"

In summary, humor in Dr. Lane's office seems to convey a sense of empathy between participants. Judging by existing literature (see chapter 2), this effort to minimize the status difference between a patient and physician is atypical. But the status-bridging function of humor is especially consequential in light of indications that patients prefer doctors who are affiliative (Buller & Buller, 1987; Street & Wiemann, 1987), courteous and good listeners (Burgoon et al., 1987; Comstock, et al., 1982), and involved and expressive (Street & Wiemann, 1987). The implication is that, by sharing a laugh about a common experience, a physician and his or her patient may remove some obstacles to effective communication.

CONCLUSIONS

Humor use between Dr. Lane and her patients seems to foster/reflect a sense of empathy and mutual identification. As proposed (chapter 4), the relationship between identification and communication seems to be circular and reflexive. From one angle, similarities in the participants' ages, gender, and family lives seem to enhance empathic communication. From another angle, empathic communication seems to foster a sense of semblance, as similarities between Dr. Lane and her patients are made available and noteworthy through such communication. For example, by joking around about changing diapers and undergoing pelvic exams, the doctor and her patients display that they have common experiences and feelings about those activities.

Perhaps more than most physicians, Dr. Lane is willing to disclose to patients how she feels about concerns similar to theirs. This presents a different scenario than the traditional "objective medical professional" who asks intimate questions but does not reciprocate with self-disclosive statements of his or her own. Thus, we see in Dr. Lane's transactions a greater relational equilibrium than in most patient–physician encounters described in the literature. Judging by research on patient cooperation and satisfaction, this equilibrium may minimize the barriers of status difference, embarrassment, disparate goals, and communication reticence that jeopardize the effectiveness of medical communication.

Another phenomenon of interest in Dr. Lane's office is the prevalence of wry or brave laughter embedded in troubles talk. Such laughter is generally offered by the patient—perhaps to avoid the negative sanctions of griping—but is not taken up by the physician, who reacts instead with seriousness and empathy. I suggest that Dr. Lane is less apt to endorse a humorous treatment of complaints because she is not usually implicated as the cause of them.

Humor use in Dr. Lane's office is typically mild, and may include a range of topics, many of which are extraneous to the exam itself. This is not true, however, during gynecological exams, when the the majority of humor does focus on aspects of the exam and the patient's discomfort.

Chapter 13

▼

Overview and Significance of Humor in Medical Settings

While observing humor in different medical settings I am continually amazed at its prevalence and versatility. Although it may take different topics and tones, humor is almost always present. Furthermore, "joking around" seems to serve the same functions in a variety of settings. Overall, there are subtle differences and striking similarities between humor use in the the physical therapy department, breast care center, and doctor's office. Following is a synopsis of the differences and similarities and comments about the significance of this analysis to health care practice and research.

CONTRASTS AND COMPARISONS

As described, humor in the breast center and doctor's office is gentle and mild—a contrast to the bold, public humor of the physical therapy department. Several explanations for this difference are presented here.

Humor use in the breast care center seems to be influenced by several factors. First, the center is unusually luxurious and more oriented than many medical centers to pampering the patient. The breast center staff is committed to providing what they call a "respectful environment." Second, practically all the caregivers are female and the center caters to an affluent all-female clientele (average age of 50). Third, a moderate degree of informality is encouraged. Caregivers and patients go by first names, but caregivers wear name badges and lab coats. Fourth, most patients embody "client" roles in that they are assymptomatic, voluntary consumers of the medical service offered. Most of them come in no more than once a year. Contact with caregivers is brief and private.

There are contrasts and similarities between the breast center and the doctor's office studied. For instance, Dr. Lane's office is less luxurious, more traditionally "medical," than the breast center. A contrast is also available in the patient role played by Dr. Lane's clientele. Most people who come to her are seeking treatment or diagnosis for current symptoms; and even those in for routine checkups are referred to as patients, not as clients. Dr. Lane's office is similar to the breast center in that patients and caregivers in both settings are predominantly upper and middle-class females. Dr. Lane encourages some degree of informality by addressing patients by first name and by dressing in street clothes rather than a white lab coat. Many (but not all) patients refer to her by first name.[1] Like caregivers in the breast center, Dr. Lane interacts with patients one on one in a quiet, private atmosphere.

The physical therapy department is the least formal and least private of the settings studied. There is little to communicate a status difference between patients and caregivers. The patients and many of the caregivers are college students. Patients and caregivers go by first names. Caregivers do not wear lab coats, and few of them wear name badges. Furthermore, patient–caregiver contact is intense and long term. Successful treatment requires a close working relationship and frequently a great deal of discomfort. Treatment is conducted in a communal, not a private, atmosphere.

Based on these contrasts and comparisons, it seems likely that patient–caregiver communication is affected by such factors as the length and nature of treatment, status differences, goals, and privacy. Considering length of treatment, it is understandable that physical therapy participants seem the most familiar with each other. Given more time and incentive to become acquainted, they are usually bolder in their transactions. It is likewise understandable why breast center patients and caregivers—who interact only for a few minutes—treat each other more as strangers or acquaintances than as friends. Familiarity effects are also detectable in Dr. Lane's office, where communication is bolder and

---

[1]Although Dr. Lane apparently makes an effort to minimize perceived status differences between herself and her patients, members of the North American culture in which she practices typically display great reverence for physicians. Thus, it is difficult to say how much status differential patients actually perceive.

more relaxed when the doctor and patient have a lot in common and/or know each other well. Likewise, the perceived status difference between patients and caregivers is apparently least in the physical therapy department, where caregivers display fewer status symbols (name badges, medical garb) and are relatively similar to patients in age and education. As we might expect, communication is more playful and less formal than in the other two settings, where status differences are moderately displayed. The privacy offered by the breast center and doctor's office may also help to explain why communication is quieter and more often dyadic in those settings. By contrast, in the communal set-up of the physical therapy unit, louder, bold humor may be a particularly useful way of getting and keeping another person's attention.

It is also interesting to note that participants in every setting use humor to lighten the tone and become more casual, but who initiates the humor is different. Caregivers are more apt to initiate rapport-building humor in the physical therapy department, but patients are more likely to initiate such humor in the breast center and doctor's office. This may reflect the therapists' need to quickly socialize and motivate patients versus the technicians'/doctor's mission of being respectful and nonassuming.

HUMOR ACROSS SETTINGS

There is reason to believe that participants in the breast center, doctor's office, and physical therapy department are not unique in the way they use humor. In many ways, they resemble each other and participants in other settings like them. In each setting, humor seems to represent an acceptable way to mitigate embarrassment, soften or sidestep complaints, display identification, solicit feedback, and good-naturedly insist on compliance with unpleasant routines. Many of these functions are substantiated by existing literature (see chapter 3).

Moreover, humor in the physical therapy unit described here is nearly identical to humor in another physical therapy center I have studied (Smith-Dupré, 1992), although the two are 600 miles apart. In both settings, humor use is bold and public. It is initiated by both patients and caregivers (although more by caregivers) and often involves elaborate playacting scenes where one participant feigns anger or indifference toward another. Likewise, the mild "embarrassment" humor of the breast center is mirrored during gynecological exams in the doctor's office. In both situations, the humor is typically initiated by the patient to comment upon some aspect of her own nudity or awkwardness. These comparisons suggest that humor is more than an idiosyncratic occurrence. To the contrary, similar types of humor seem to arise in similar situations.

Interestingly, humor in the doctor's office most resembles humor in the breast center when the doctor is performing gynecological exams. During those instances, gynecological patients (like breast center patients) make frequent quips about embarrassing and uncomfortable aspects of the exam, and the doctor (like the other caregivers) responds in ways that display that she empathizes, and sometimes that the situation is funny or absurd rather than somber and threatening.

However, in other situations—as when Dr. Lane treats a patient for sinus trouble or depression—humor looks very different. Her patients, like patients in other settings, use laughter to avoid the negative sanctions of "griping." But Dr. Lane, unlike caregivers in the other settings, does not join in their laughter. I suggest that this reflects her different position on the dialectic between helping and hurting. Except for gynecological exams and the like, where her actions cause the patient discomfort, Dr. Lane is generally not to blame for the patient's complaints. In that way, her relationship with patients is less problematic than that of caregivers in the breast center and physical therapy unit. If, as I propose, humor is a method of negotiating a helping–hurting dialectic, it is understandable that Dr. Lane would use less humor. She simply has less need for the services it provides.

One implication of this analysis is that the traditionally stoic view of medical professionalism may be an unfair and undesirable standard. I urge the reader (and future researchers) to be cautious about out-of-context judgments. Writing this, I am continually frustrated by the inability of language, particularly the written word, to fully capture the phenomena under study. For instance, it is phonetically difficult to depict the difference between a merry peal of laughter and a polite chuckle, although the difference is seemingly detectable and important to the participants themselves. Largely because of this, there is always the risk that humor quoted out of context will seem offensive or unfunny, although it did not seem that way when it was delivered. As I write, I wonder if the reader will label the bold humor of the physical therapy department unprofessional. I doubt that this type of humor (or humor at all) is included in health care textbooks. Yet I believe that humor in the physical therapy center is effective. And I believe it is no less appropriate in its setting than the breast care humor is in its.

IV

Humor and Appropriateness

Chapter 14

▼

The Rules of the Humor Game

During field studies in different locations, I was interested in the ways humor seemed to reflect/affect cultural assumptions of the interactants. This section takes ethnographic observations to a higher level of abstraction. In the way the preceding chapters describe the playing field and activities of the game, this section explains the rules participants follow. I describe two codes—The Code of Dignity and the Code of Compassion. A code, as I explain more fully, is a collection of maxims or moral orders that guides the behavior of participants within a speech community. For instance, Philipsen (1992) uses the Code of Dignity to describe mainstream America's reverence for individuality and uniqueness.

In chapter 15, I show how participants in the breast care center and doctor's office uphold the Code of Dignity in the way they use humor to maintain individuality and dignity in potentially embarrassing situations. In accordance with the code, caregivers cater to the patients' wishes as much as possible. They are careful not to ridicule patients and make great efforts to encourage and congratulate them.

An interesting contrast is provided by transactions in the physical therapy unit and hospital settings (described in chapter 16). In those settings, communication is consistent with a different set of moral orders that I call the Code of Compassion. (The two codes are not completely different. They share some of the same goals. But the central assumptions are different.) In accordance with the Code of Compassion, caregivers may consider it compassionate to (good-humoredly) challenge a patient's behavior if it means that the patient becomes more cooperative, attentive, or communicative. In short, they act from the

117

assumption that it is sometimes justified—indeed it is compassionate—to provoke or "rile up" a patient for his or her own good.

Following is an explanation of codes and their theoretical significance, and a more thorough analysis of the Code of Dignity and the Code of Compassion in chapters 15 and 16.

ABOUT CODES

From an ethnographic viewpoint, members of a speech community are seen to uphold a working agreement about "correct" or "appropriate" ways to behave. Unwritten codes or maxims determine what is considered acceptable and unacceptable within the community. Maintaining the code is not a straightforward practice of acting in rigidly prescribed ways, however. Different rules of appropriateness apply to different situations within the same culture. For instance, a person might be shunned as rude or crazy for reciting T. S. Eliot aloud during the silence of a prayer at Christmas mass. But if that person were a zany character in a movie, audiences might find his outburst hilarious. An inherent presumption is that "codes" are not "laws." There are few or no absolutes. What is appropriate depends a great deal on goals and situational factors, what Geertz (1973) dubbed "webs of significance."

Implicit in the idea of sanctioned behaviors are shared values, such that there is a moral imperative to uphold the code, and negative sanctions are imposed on people who violate its maxims. Philipsen (1992) wrote that codes

> are not only about communication, but are as well about what it means to be a person, how persons are and can be united in social relationships, and how communication can be and is used to link persons as social beings. Thus, they provide, for their users, a distinctive way of being, saying, and hearing. (p. 102)

Humor, one soon learns, is not to be understood in isolation from the overall objectives of speech. Understanding humor in medical settings becomes a process of understanding the problematic character of patient–caregiver transactions, where humor is often used to imply that things are not so serious or so institutional as they might seem.

In this way, we may say that codes serve a persuasive function. They suggest how members should behave and how certain behaviors should be interpreted. For example, Wieder (1974) identified a persuasive function of the convict code used in an East Los Angeles halfway house.

"'Telling the code' was persuasive not by virtue of what was merely said as such, but by virtue of the kind of interactional event that 'telling the code' was" (p. 177). In his words, the code provided a "guide to perception" (p. 131) and a means of rationalizing situations. I suggest that humor functions in much the same way, to lend a rational sense to medical interactions and to bid that a tense scene be treated as "not so bad." Use of humor is persuasive in the way it suggests that participants perceive (or at least outwardly treat) a situation in a certain way.[1] Components of the social reality enhanced by the Code of Dignity suggest: "I respect you," "You're doing well," "This isn't so bad," and "This is normal." The Code of Compassion suggests: "I like you," "Open up to me," "Listen carefully," "Relax."

IDENTIFYING THE CODE

Ethnographers do not assume that people are conscious of their goal work or of the cultural maxims they uphold. If that were the case, identifying the code would be a simple matter of asking an honest society member. Although open-ended interviewing is an ethnographic technique, members' responses usually illuminate the code only indirectly. For example, a community member can attest that a certain behavior "simply is not done" without seeing that as a code at work. Other behaviors are so taken for granted or so utterly forbidden that members may be unaware of them. Typically, ethnographers attain a cultural understanding by abstracting a sense of the code from consistencies in members' statements and actions. Spradley (1979) wrote: "The ethnographer observes behavior, but goes beyond it to inquire about the meaning of that behavior. The ethnographer sees artifacts and natural objects but goes beyond them to discover what meanings people assign to those objects" (p. 6). Sometimes the most obvious sign of consistency is the fuss made over a rare inconsistency. In his study of Teamsterville, for instance, Philipsen (1975) was quickly derided as being homosexual after he violated that culture's expectations about masculine behavior. When Philipsen remarked in a hypothetical way that he would probably not hit a man who insulted his girlfriend, the Teamsterville boys he was chaperoning cut their field trip short. Philipsen wrote that: "The boys' definition of the situation had been radically altered by the conversation in the car. The closer they got to Old Town (where,

---

[1]Indeed, humor displays may be particularly persuasive considering that one who does not "laugh along" or "get the joke" may often be seen as rude or inexperienced.

they would reason, they might need an adult for security), the uneasier they became" (p. 16). After that, Philipsen (1992) recalled, it was nearly impossible for him to fulfill his duties at the Teamsterville youth center until he rather elaborately demonstrated his adherence to the Teamsterville code of masculine behavior.

As I became familiar with the speech codes in medical settings, I could perceive a practical and consistent method to humor use. (I might as truthfully say, as I became familiar with humor use, I could more clearly perceive the code. The processes were interrelated.) For example, the Code of Dignity explains what a technician might have been about when she responded to a patient's statement, "It's hot in here," by saying with a smile, "Worked up a sweat on that one, huh?" I took her to mean: "Perhaps. But that is a small matter really, compared to this experience of an exam, at which you are doing so well." Of course it's impossible to know if the patient perceived it just that way. But the outward effect of such remarks was demonstrated to me many times. Patients smiled more and complained less. Indeed, it was largely by attending to these results that I was able to understand why the caregivers might take such a line. Put simply, the means sometimes became apparent in light of the end.

IMPLICATIONS FOR THIS STUDY

The position that humor is regulated by unspoken agreements about appropriateness is advanced by Goffman and Emerson. Interaction rituals described by Goffman (1967) are characterized by agreed on, although usually unspoken, codes of conduct. Competent use of humor relies heavily on its perceived appropriateness. Effective use of humor requires the consideration of many factors. Glib treatment of overly sensitive topics can result—not in laughter—but in hurt feelings (Burton, 1986; Emerson, 1969; White & Howse, 1993; Wooten, 1995; Ziv, 1984).

This view of communication assumes that people are teleological and adaptive, selecting strategies that maximize goal achievement without violating cultural expectancies. Moreover, depending on the situation and the tolerance of others, rules of appropriateness can be negotiated or even breached. Humor and verbal play represent one form of rule-breaking. The unexpected or inappropriate is sometimes funny (see chapter 7). But in those cases as well, I argue that there are maxims at work. Based on my observations, I describe tacit rules that seem to affect how and when humor is permitted in the medical settings studied.

Chapter 15

▼

Humor and the Code of Dignity

As mentioned in chapter 14, Philipsen (1992) coined the term *Code of Dignity* to characterize Nacirema's emphasis on individuality. *Nacirema* (American spelled backward) is the term he uses for mainstream America.[1] In drafting this analysis, I originally described the breast care center within what I termed a *Code of Respect*. Later I was struck by a similar code underlying behavior in Dr. Lane's office. Although I was well acquainted with Philipsen's work, I did not immediately realize how similar his Code of Dignity was to my Code of Respect. In the interest of comparison and continuity, I adopt his terminology and respectfully offer the following analysis as further explication of the Code of Dignity. The categorization—although it was certainly informed by Philipsen's work—was not fashioned a priori. It reflects, rather, the useful applicability of the Code of Dignity to diverse settings.

The Code of Dignity, as described by Philipsen (1992) "does not merely deemphasize a person's social roles but also positively emphasizes the uniqueness and legitimacy of each person's cognitive and affective world" (p. 114). He reflected that users of the code respect social differences and self-expression. They downplay inequality and social precedent, and see life as an ongoing process of developing and changing one's identity. Within the Code of Dignity "society is less valuable than the individual" (p. 114). Good communicators are empathic. Interpersonally, they engage in "close, supportive, flexible

---

[1]The reverse spelling is used to make the point that "mainstream America" is more a theoretical construct than a stable phenomenon.

speech" (p. 97). Such standards closely mirror those of the breast center and Dr. Lane's office, where caregivers strive to be sensitive to each patient's unique concerns and expectations.

Philipsen (1992) submitted that a speech code "can provide individuals with a kind of practical knowledge about what to feel and what to do" (p. 127). My observations support this idea. Humor seems to facilitate quick and persuasive communication. Within the breast care center and doctor's office this entails an acute sensitivity to, and respect for, each patient's mood and situation. Dr. Lane and the caregivers in the breast care center often speak of fulfilling patients' expectations and acting "as the patient would wish." Caregivers address patients by first name and usually go by first names themselves. Participants in these settings do not always embody the code in precisely the same ways, but I show here that their actions are consistent with the same underlying assumptions. In the following analysis, I illustrate what Saville-Troike (1982) called "salient features of the code" and explain how caregivers use humor to achieve the goals prescribed by it.

FEATURES OF THE CODE

The Code of Dignity, as it is characterized in the breast center and doctor's office, consists of several maxims or rules. Humor plays a role in the embodiment of each maxim, as I illustrate here. To my knowledge, the maxims I identify here have never been written down. Their existence became apparent to me over time, during observation and conversations with staff members.

Create a Nonthreatening Environment. The breast care center was designed with women's input to be comfortable and feminine. The privacy of patients is protected with curtains and closed doors, and they are allowed to wear attractive cotton smocks rather than paper gowns. According to the center's director, the presence of an all-female staff is also meant to contribute to an understanding, nonthreatening atmosphere.

Through gentle use of humor, caregivers often communicate a feeling of empathy and camaraderie with patients.

(OOO)   TECH: ((to patient)) The only man we have in the office is a radiologist. And we don't let him in! ((laughs))

(PPP)   TECH: ((to patient)) I hate ta tell you but I forgot to put a
                      film in there. I'm not telling you this. I'm supposed
                      to make you feel secure. I'm supposed to say you
                      breathed or something and lay the fault on you!
                      ((both laugh))

(RR)   TECH: ((to patient)) See how easy it is for me to tell
                      you to relax?

(QQQ)   TECH: Here's some warm gel. ((both laugh softly))

          PATIENT: You expect it to be cold.

               TECH: Yeah, we don't like to have you jumpin' outa
                      your pants here. ((both laugh more loudly))

(RRR)   TECH: Breathing causes motion and it might get blurry.
                      Most women tell me they can't breathe anyway
                      when you're in there like that. ((patient and tech
                      laugh))

Dr. Lane seeks to create a nonthreatening environment by visiting with
patients before they disrobe and by allowing adolescents time to talk with
her alone, out of their parents' presence. She also guards patients' privacy
behind closed doors. Like participants in the breast center, Dr. Lane and
her patients use laughter to show that they empathize with each other.

(LLL)   DOCTOR: Boy I bet you were flippin out when they said sixty
                        dollars for that test! ((both laugh))

(MMM)   DOCTOR: ((regarding anesthesia during labor)) A lot of people
                        hit six or seven centimeters and say forget this. ((all
                        laugh)) Me I hit about two! ((more laughs))

(NNN)   DOCTOR: Gosh ———, you've got poison ivy? ((child
                        nods, doctor laughs)) I do too!

Often, Dr. Lane's statements imply that the patient's situation is understandable, nothing to be embarrassed about. This presumably lessens
the threatening aspect of discussing that issue with the doctor.

In summary, caregivers in both settings strive to make patients feel comfortable and accepted. Through decor and routines, they try to reduce the threatening aspects of a medical exam, and they demonstrate through humor that they understand and empathize with the patient's situation.

Avoid Technical Jargon and Clinical Terms.   In the breast center, staff members avoid words like *pain* and *x-rays* and *radiation*, referring instead to *discomfort* and *pictures* or *films*. They vigorously deny that mammograms are especially painful, reiterating that the procedure entails only moderate discomfort.

> (PP)   TECH: This bottom corner is goin' ta poke you in the ribs,
>   and this top corner is goin' ta poke you up under
>   your arm. It's not really comfortable 'cause we're
>   not built like corners.[2]

Dr. Lane also makes an effort to speak in a language the patient can understand, using words like "yuckie stuff" instead of "mucus" and referring in vernacular terms to "squished discs" and the like.

> (EEE)   DOCTOR: Is she blowin yuckie stuff out of her nose?
>   MOTHER: Every time she sneezes it comes out everywhere
>   but 'er ears! ((both laugh))

> (OOO)   DOCTOR: They call it conjunctivitis. Everybody thinks that's
>   just the biggest thing. And actually it's just a real
>   mild infection on the lining of the eyes.

> (PPP)   DOCTOR: The GOOD news is that I don't I I seriously doubt
>   whether this is like a squished disc or anything.

In summary, caregivers in both settings attempt to accommodate their language to make it understandable and nonthreatening to the patients.

---

[2]There is an interesting contrast between the way caregivers talk about mammograms backstage and the way they describe them to patients. Among themselves, they often share exaggerated, gallows-type humor much bolder and franker than anything they say around patients. For instance, when I told one caregiver that I would leave an exam room anytime she signaled for me to, she said laughing, "I'll announce, 'Will the woman who DOESN'T have her breast in a vise please leave the room!'" Likewise, a poem on the break room bulletin board satirizes the patient's experience: "My skin was stretched 'n stretched/From way up by my chin/And my poor tit was being squashed/To Swedish pancake thin!"

The technicians' avoidance of words like *pain* and *radiation* seems a persuasive effort to depict the transaction as a helpful and healthy one. One implication is that the caregiver is cast as benevolent and kind—not in league with the sadistic, white-starched nurse characterized on get-well cards and in slapstick movies.

Do Not Become an Adversary. As mentioned in chapter 11, caregivers in the breast center are faced with a particularly problematic dilemma. To uphold the Code of Dignity, they must convincingly justify that the benefits of a breast exam outweigh the discomforts involved in getting a good diagnostic image. ("I'm hurting but I'm helping more.") In the breast center, complaints are taken as a sign that the code has failed, and caregivers head off grumbling with humorous remarks that acknowledge, but reframe, the problem. For instance, one technician frequently assures patients, "You just tell me if you can't stand this for more than a second or two." The statement implies that the patient is in control, but sanctions a "chin up" attitude through what is, explicitly, a momentary discomfort.

In the following exchanges, the caregiver sidesteps an adversarial role by reframing the patient's grievance as the result of her own hard work or exemplary efforts. In this way, the caregiver is able to take the stance of an encouraging partner or fan, while neatly deflecting any implication that she has acted cruelly or disrespectfully toward the patient.

(UU)   PATIENT: I don't remember this [part of the exam].
         TECH: You were problee havin' so much fun!

(VV)   PATIENT: This one didn't hurt near so much as that one two years ago.
         TECH: You're just havin' more fun today is all. ((both laugh))

(WW)   PATIENT: It's hot in here.
         TECH: Worked up a sweat on that one, huh?

Within a code that emphasizes consideration and personal attention, caregivers use humor to offset the hurtful nature of institutional procedures. By using mild humor to be empathic and congratulatory, the caregiver is able to imply that she understands the patient's situation while minimizing the violation as "not so bad." (The patients also have a stake in avoiding an adversarial role with the caregiver, and they almost always word complaints in humorous, nonaccusatory ways.[3]

As previously mentioned (chapter 12), Dr. Lane's role as caregiver is perhaps less adversarial than the radiology technicians' because it is not usually necessary for her to subject patients to painful or embarrassing procedures. Within these different circumstances, she upholds the Code of Dignity in another way. Whereas breast center caregivers try to downgrade or reframe grievous episodes into affiliatory ones, Dr. Lane often upgrades the patient's complaint in an apparent effort to demonstrate her empathy and make the patient feel okay about "complaining." Following are a few examples.

(QQQ) PATIENT: It's so sore, I don't know why . . .

DOCTOR: This you know this happened to me right after I had my last baby. This low back pain. And I never it gave me such a new appreciation for how patients feel

PATIENT: uh huh huh

DOCTOR: because it-it-it's just horrible

PATIENT: if you never had it, I mean I never had see?

DOCTOR: you wouldn't understand how bad it is. ((laughs))

(RRR) PATIENT: An' I don't share that with him because he thinks there's nothin' wrong with me. . . . . Cause I don't feel good.

DOCTOR: So that's making it even harder when you don't feel good. It's that much worse by havin' him not be very sympathetic about it.

In both instances, the patients nonverbally suggest that their conditions are worse than their verbal accounts of them. For instance, the woman describing lower back pain grimaces and stiffens as the doctor touches her back, although she describes the sensation in relatively mild terms as "so sore." The patient quoted in the second excerpt appears very depressed, with slumped posture and slack facial muscles.

In both instances, the doctor verbally upgrades the patient's complaint. She elevates the patient's account of a back that is "so sore" to a

---

[3]See chapters 10 and 11 for a more thorough examination of humorous "gripes" and chapter 21 for more on complaints managed as candidate laughables.

condition that is "just horrible" and displays that she is in a position to know, having experienced the same pain herself. In the second example, Dr. Lane elevates the patient's statement of "I don't feel good" to a situation that is "even harder" and "that much worse." By upgrading the patients' statements, Dr. Lane displays that they are justified in complaining—indeed, she suggests that they are putting on brave faces by minimizing their discomforts. In this way, she affords them the dignity of brave soldiers doing their best under particularly trying circumstances. Interestingly, this is basically the same message implied by the breast center caregivers when they reframe "complaints" in congratulatory tones.

To appreciate the different situational imperatives at work in each setting, it is interesting to scramble the dialogue. For instance, imagine that a breast center patient comments about the discomfort of the exam and her caregiver upgrades the statement by saying, "It's just horrible. If you'd never had one you wouldn't understand how bad it is." This does not seem a particularly helpful or kind comment considering that the patient must nevertheless undergo the exam, and for her own good must continue to seek such exams. In as much as realities are cultivated by words, upgrading the hurtful reality of the exam does not seem to help either the patient or the caregiver.

Likewise, imagine that a patient complains to Dr. Lane that her back is sore and the doctor responds, "You were problee havin' so much fun!" Such teasing may do momentarily, but if the doctor persists in reframing the patient's condition in positive, congratulatory terms we might expect an adversarial role to develop in which the patient sees the doctor's behavior as belittling or unkind. After all, the goal of transactions in Dr. Lane's office is to alleviate discomforts. The goal in the breast center is to achieve a diagnostic image, and discomfort is but a brief and necessary means to that end. Considering this, it makes sense that participants in each setting would frame "discomfort" in different ways.

In summary, I propose that caregivers in both settings uphold the Code of Dignity. In different ways, they display that the patient is brave and dignified, either because she is willingly undergoing a difficult exam or because she is bearing (even minimizing) life's discomforts.

Cater to the Patient's Wishes as Much as Possible. In accordance with this maxim, humor is used tentatively to avoid offending. Technicians in the breast care center say they look for clues about "how the patient is" before they attempt humor. Such clues include smiles, greetings, and eye contact. "If you can't get them to give you any eye contact, you know they're going to be a problem," said one technician. They also declare that, at a certain level of anxiety, humor is unwelcome: "Someone comes in here who's 29 and she's got a lump in her breast. She doesn't want to have any kind of laughs."

In most cases, humor is advanced so ambiguously that it might naturally pass without a laugh. Patients who respond readily to humor, however, pick up on it. This subtle negotiation sets the tone for an exam. Following are a few particularly ambiguous lines that drew laughter.

(X)   TECH: ((to researcher)) It's pretty frustrating to get a double exposure. ((slight pause in which she raises her eyebrows slightly as she adjusts instruments)) The patient doesn't like it much either.

(Y)   TECH: Athena is workin' on her doctorate degree in communication. So if I don't communicate with you, jus' let her know. ((both laugh))

Ambiguity and attention to subtle cues help caregivers judge which type of presentation will be most pleasing to the patient. A similar sensitivity helps them judge when the patient's statements are intended to be humorous. In this way, the caregiver (and the patient) adjusts her style to suit the other's expectations.

Dr. Lane often caters to the patient's wishes by inviting him or her to comment on the diagnosis and treatment advice.

(QQQ)   DOCTOR: Well the first thing to get you the quickest relief honestly would be to put you into a physical therapist . . . um does that sound reasonable?

            PATIENT: We:ll ah huh huh my boss is gone that's the only thing about taking off.

(RRR)   DOCTOR: At this point that's what I'd recommend. Putting you on an antidepressant. Are you comfortable with that?

            PATIENT: Sort of.

            DOCTOR: You feel a little nervous about it?

            PATIENT: Yeah.

            DOCTOR: Tell me what your concerns are.

By encouraging participatory decision making, Dr. Lane implies that the patient plays an informed and responsible role in maintaining his or her own health. This show of respect for the patient's feelings and preferences illuminates adherence to a code that honors individuality.

In summary, in the way the exam is carried out and decisions are made, participants in the breast center and doctor's office display that the patients' individual expectations are as important, or more important, than adherence to strict medical routines. In accordance with the Code of Dignity, individuality is given preference over conformity.

Make Light of Face-Threatening Situations.   Caregivers carefully avoid making jokes about breast size or body weight. "You don't want the patient to think you're laughing at her," explained one technician. For patients, however, there seems an impulse to joke about both subjects. Making light of a threatening situation often seems more comfortable than stoically enduring it, and no one has a stake in preserving the patients' dignity as much as the patients themselves. Following are examples from both settings in which patients seek comic relief from face-threatening situations.

(SSS)   TECH: We gotta get this tummy back a little bit.
             PATIENT: I'm workin' on that! ((laughs))

(TTT)   PATIENT: ((after receiving an injection to numb her
                       breast for a biopsy)) That's much better than
                       getting a shot somewhere else. I'm going to
                       recommend that they always shoot me there.
                       ((playacting tone)) "Can you take blood out of
                       my left breast please?"

(UUU)   PATIENT: ((during gynecological exam)) This is my year to get
                       me in shape. I've done eyes this and now it's to the
                       dentist. ((laughing)) I've gone from top to bottom
                       ((laughs as she looks down)) or maybe bottom to
                       top ((laughs and winks))

In summary, humor often seems to be patients' way of maintaining dignity in an embarrassing exam—a reminder that patients participate in the Code of Dignity as much as their caregivers. In the language of Long and Graesser (1988), wit often signals "decomittment" to something unpleasant. By joking about her body and the exam, a patient implies: "Let's not maintain our straight faces. I'm more comfortable laughing at this strange situation." The result is predictably more eye contact between patient and caregiver, more smiles, and lighter, more lilting tones of voice. If interactants perceive this as a pleasing result—and they seem to—humor's role in communication is especially intriguing. Within the Code of Dignity, humor may be a way of humanizing an impersonal transaction.

Congratulate Patients for Taking Care of Themselves and for Performing Well in the Exam.   Caregivers adept at using humor often attain several goals with one statement. They may, for instance, turn a complaint into a trophy by insinuating that the patient experienced discomfort because he or she did so well or was so amiable. In other ways as well, they honor the patient for maintaining his or her health. In the breast center, each patient is given a fresh flower as she leaves, with the verbal message: "This is for taking care of yourself." A congratulatory tone is presumably meant to make patients feel special and pleased with themselves. Following are other examples from both settings.

(VVV)   TECH: You're such a good patient, we'll do you again!
                    ((patient and tech laugh))

(WWW)   DOCTOR: ((to smoking cessation patient)) This is just the best
                    I've heard of anyone doing!

(XXX)   DOCTOR: Well you're just to be applauded for getting in here
                    and getting your regular checkup. I've gotta get mine.

With remarks such as these, caregivers give credit to the patient, not to medication. With this emphasis on personal health accomplishments, the caregivers emphasize that they respect and support the patients' efforts to take care of themselves. The patient is not depicted as a passive recipient of medical care, but as a proactive agent whose efforts are praiseworthy.

CONCLUSIONS

This analysis suggests that communication between participants in the breast center and in the doctor's office is guided by several maxims that uphold a Code of Dignity. The six maxims identified are:

1. Create a nonthreatening environment.
2. Avoid technical jargon and clinical terms.
3. Do not become an adversary.
4. Cater to the patient's wishes as much as possible.
5. Make light of face-threatening situations.
6. Congratulate patients for taking care of themselves and for performing well in the exams.

Together, adherence to these maxims affects/reflects the cultural assumption that individuality is more important than conformity to collectivistic goals.

Of course it should not be assumed that all medical settings, or even all breast care centers or doctors' offices, subscribe to the Code of Dignity described here. These centers' allegiance to the code is presumably influenced by many factors. The clientele, the nearly all-female populations, the nature of the exams, the personalities of those involved, and the decor and routines seem to contribute to the overall feel of these settings. No doubt they are also influenced by the Nacirema culture in which they operate, and women's identity in that culture.

The utility of Philipsen's Code of Dignity deserves credit for illuminating, in a wider sense, the cultural nuances that make patient-caregiver interactions in these settings culturally similar to mother–child discussions in Nacirema:

> She tries to help her children "feel good about themselves"—she listens to them, answers all their questions, and provides detailed explanations and information. . . . It is important to her not to have any "hassles" with her children. . . . (Katriel & Philipsen, 1981, p. 304)

The tricky business of respecting individuality in a medical setting presents, I believe, an interesting application of the Code of Dignity.

If the Code of Dignity seems an utterly natural and assumable one, the reader will perhaps be surprised at the contrasts it presents to the code upheld by participants in an outpatient physical therapy unit and four hospital settings. Participants in those settings uphold a different code, one I call the *Code of Compassion*. I urge the reader to consider it as distinctly different—not better or worse—than the Code of Dignity.

Chapter 16

▼

Humor and the
Code of Compassion

A caregiver at the breast care center once remarked to me, "We don't use a lot of humor because patients don't expect it." This was a characteristic statement, quite explicable within the Code of Dignity. (Cater to patients, do *not* provoke them.) What astonished me was its direct contrast to remarks made by hospital caregivers I had observed. Many times, in different ways, they explained their humor use by saying something such as: "We try to use a lot of humor because most people expect a hospital stay to be really serious." This is a statement pulled from my memory and not from my notes, for it was so often repeated to me that I accepted it as obvious, not worth note. In the following section, I briefly describe the settings under study, and contrast humor use within the Code of Compassion to humor use in the breast center and doctor's office.

ABOUT THE SETTINGS

The outpatient physical therapy unit considered here is the same one described in chapter 10. The hospital settings include an inpatient physical rehabilitation unit, surgery, pediatrics, and an orthopedics/general medicine unit where I conducted observations in the early 1990s. For purposes of this analysis, I focus on the commonalities between these hospital units and between them and the outpatient physical therapy department. This is admittedly a gloss that underrepresents the distinct features of each unit. (For a more thorough analysis and comparison of the hospital settings, see Smith-Dupré, 1992.) However, as I explain here, I do not think it is misleading to characterize all these units in terms of one overarching similarity—their adherence to the Code of Compassion.

The humor used in the inpatient and the outpatient physical therapy units is so similar I had a perpetual sense of dejà vu during my observations in the later location. In both settings, treatment routines are carried out in an open area where patients and caregivers freely interact. Humor is bold and public and may involve many people at one time. Therapists often joke around among themselves, inviting patients to join in or implicating patients in their remarks, as when a hospital nurse told one patient, "You tell [the therapist] to hurry up. You don't have all day to wait on him!" and the therapist playfully retorted, "You tell [nurse] to just get back to work. She's not supposed to be in here." This type of patient-inclusive joking around by caregivers is prevalent in both settings. Also common in both settings are elaborate rituals in which patients and caregivers playfully pretend to be angry or indifferent toward each other. I saw this type of playacting routine in other areas of the hospital as well, where patients were well acquainted with their caregivers.

TERMINOLOGY

In dialogue excerpts I distinguish between the different settings as follows:

PT–OutPt—outpatent physical therapy unit.
PT–Hosp—inpatient physical therapy department.
Surgery—hospital surgical unit (mostly pre-op).
Pediatrics—hospital pediatric department.
Ortho/Gen—hospital orthopedics/general medicine floor.

Within the text, however, I often speak in terms of the commonality between these settings, referring to participants in the hospital and outpatient therapy units as "long-term caregivers" and "long-term patients." Not all hospital personnel had well-defined relationships with patients; contact was sometimes as brief as 5 or 10 minutes in the surgical preparation area. But I believe that, overall, the extended contact between patients and caregivers is a significant component of most hospital and physical therapy transactions, and is a principle difference between these settings and the breast center and the doctor's office previously described. Because they are typically in contact for extended periods of time, patients and caregivers become more familiar with each other and they often share the responsibility of carrying out treatment routines.

FEATURES OF THE CODE

Communication in the long-term settings reflects the Code of Compassion, characterized by a bold and persuasive use of humor. On the following pages, I discuss the way the code is embodied in these settings and the assumptions it actualizes.

Encourage Patients to Cooperate.   Unlike the breast center, where technicians try to accommodate patients' wishes as much as possible, long-term caregivers frequently try to enlist the patients' cooperation with prescribed treatments and routines. Thus, their goals are more collectivistic than individualistic. Individuality is not completely suppressed, but long-term caregivers display a greater imperative to secure cooperativeness and to acclimate patients to the unique environment that surrounds them.

For instance, one (outpatient) physical therapist challenged a patient to work harder by proclaiming in a tone of exaggerated sorrow, "I would hate for him [the patient] to have to sell his Goldwing [motorcycle] to me cause he couldn't ride it." Within the breast center, this type of playful "threat" would be considered too provocative or potentially offensive. Within the Code of Compassion, however, one is morally justified in provoking a patient for his or her own good. Following are other examples of humor used to engender a more cooperative stance on the patient's part.

(YYY, Ortho/Gen)

> NURSE: ((warning patient to smile, or else)) I'm gonna
> walk in, hurt you, walk out, don't smile!
> ((patient grins))

(ZZZ, Surgery)

    NURSE: ((encouraging patient to squeeze her hands))
              Tight, tight, tight. Hurt me!

(AAAA, PT-Outpt)

    THERAPIST: How 's your ( ) joint?

    PATIENT: I don't know but my back is sore from doin'
             those superman crunches.

    THERAPIST: Good for you! You're doin' em!

    PATIENT: Well it hurts.

    THERAPIST: Is it muscle pain or joint pain?

    PATIENT: It's like I can't tense my butt huh huh huh

    THERAPIST: ((grinning)) Oh you big weenie!

This type of bold, motivational humor may be particularly useful in long-term settings, where progress is often slow and patients become bored and discouraged. One outpatient therapy patient told me: "I had this dream that I was on a trip and my things kep' being stole. My watch, then something else. I think that's how I feel. Like I'm in therapy three days a week and it's stealing all my time." Another said to me: "I'm outa food in my apartment. With the crutches I can't get groceries. I can't load 'em in my car. I'm so disgusted." Compared to weeks and months of painful physical rehabilitation, it may be fairly simple to motivate a patient to respond cooperatively during a brief mammogram. Particularly in the hospital, patients may also be less responsive because of serious illness or brain damage (many hospital physical therapy patients are recovering from strokes or head injuries). For these reasons, it is understandable that long-term caregivers are particularly bold and persuasive in the way they encourage patients' efforts and seek their cooperation.

Furthermore, caregivers in a clinic or doctor's office are not typically on hand to see that patients follow treatment advice. By contrast, hospital personnel and physical therapists pick up where the doctor leaves off. Their job is not so much to diagnose as to speed healing, and they are accountable both to the patient and to the doctor. This provides an added imperative for securing the patient's cooperation. They have a personal (and professional) stake in seeing treatment routines carried out, and they become well acquainted with the patient in the process. These factors probably contribute as well to the bold use of motivational humor.

Display a Sense of Intimacy or Familiarity.   In long-term care situations I have often observed signs of an instant or accelerated intimacy between patients and caregivers. Even when patient–caregiver contact is brief, it often concerns a big event such as surgery or diagnostic testing. Emotions seem to run high and participants are often more disclosive than in everyday situations. For instance, I once observed a hospital orderly as he arrived in a male patient's room to wheel him to surgery:

(BBBB, Surgery)

> ORDERLY: You wanna leave your robe here?
>
> PATIENT: That's all I got on except this gown.
>
> ORDERLY: ((smiling)) That ain't nothin' where you're goin!
> ((both laugh))

Joking about nudity is strictly out of bounds for Dr. Lane and for breast center caregivers (although their patients can and do initiate it). But there is a greater latitude between hospital patients and caregivers I have observed. They often allude to more personal or intimate matters, and their humor use often has a flirtatious tone as in the following examples.

(CCCC, PT–Hosp)

> NURSE: ((to elderly amputee)) You didn't go get on a horse or nothin' this week, did you? I heard you went to the track. I don't trust you no farther than I can see you!

(DDDD, PT-Outpt)

> THERAPIST: Yeah if you'll go wash my car it'll help your elbow.
>
> PATIENT: ((grinning)) No:!
>
> THERAPIST: Yes. Yes it will.

(EEEE, PT–Outpt)

> THERAPIST: You like these [curtains] open.
>
> PATIENT: Well yeah ((pause)) although I problee look like the livin' dead here on your table.
>
> THERAPIST: ((smiling, teasing tone)) Well you do kinda but

(FFFF, PT–Hosp)

> NURSE: ((to patient)) Tell him [the therapist] to hurry
> with your therapy because you've got a
> boyfriend to go back to and you can't be playing around!

In summary, within the Code of Compassion it is more permissible to take interpersonal liberties. There is a less formal decorum and less hesitancy than in the breast center or Dr. Lane's office. It sometimes seems that long-term caregivers quickly take on the roles of surrogate friends and relatives. They tease and flirt in a way that implies interpersonal attraction and familiarity. (I have heard it said that patients fall in love with their caregivers but I did not see any evidence of this firsthand.) I believe the exaggerated displays serve to balance somewhat the institutionality of long-term care. Hospital patients often find themselves isolated from their social networks in an environment that thrusts them into intimate contact with relative strangers (caregivers). Perhaps acting like close acquaintances makes the situation more sensible, human, and comforting. In short, displaying interpersonal familiarity may be a more compassionate line to take. Acting like an intimate may also offset the hurtful role caregivers have to play in enforcing uncomfortable routines and procedures.

Campaign for Attention and Individuality.   When caregivers do not display a sense of intimacy or familiarity, patients often campaign for more personal treatment by initiating joking around sequences themselves. For example, I observed the following exchange in the surgical preparation area.

(GGGG, Surgery)

> DOCTOR: When we finish you can have a cup of coffee.
>
> PATIENT: You can send that home to my pig.
>
> DOCTOR: Your pig!?
>
> PATIENT: ((grinning)) Yeah, I don't like the stuff! ((doctor laughs))

The physician, who was looking at the patient's chart as he rather absentmindedly spoke of the coffee, looked up when the patient made the surprising comment about his pig. It seemed to me that the impersonal routine of filling out the presurgical checklist was personalized by the patient's comical declaration. It might not be important in a medical sense that the patient dislikes coffee and owns a pig (and is willing to joke around with the doctor), but knowing these things, the physician may regard the patient in a more personal, less dispassionate way. In a setting that sanctions adherence to institutional routines, patients often use humor to campaign for more individualized consideration.

Following are more examples of humor that earned the attention of distracted caregivers.

(HHHH, PT–OutPt)

> PATIENT: What's that called?
>
> THERAPIST: Echomosis. Copious echomosis.
>
> PATIENT: Yeah echomosis. I don't have copious echomosis now. What DO I have? What do you call it if it's not copious? ((smiling)) Dubious?
>
> THERAPIST: Huh! ((smiling)) dubious instead of copious!

(IIII, Surgery)

> NURSE: Did they take any blood from you today, sir?
>
> PATIENT: Oh yes. If they take any more I'll be fresh out! ((both smile))

In these instances, humor seems to humanize the transaction. The participants make eye contact and laugh or smile together. Typically the tone of the transaction following humor is more personal than before.[1]

In sum, if we perceive a dialectic between individualism and collectivity, we might expect to see negotiations between these two extremes. Humor seems one way of displaying interpersonal connectedness in a medical arena that tends to be collectivistic. Thus, it represents a persuasive means of negotiating for individual consideration. A long-term caregiver must usually attend to many factors at one time, and may be in charge of six or seven patients, each with serious but different conditions. The attention-getting function of humor may be especially important when the caregiver seems distant or distracted or when the patient must compete for the caregiver's attention, as in an open-air physical therapy unit or a busy hospital floor.

Keep the Patient's Spirits Up.   In instances in which the Code of Dignity might sanction respectful acceptance of a patient's mood or emotion, the Code of Compassion suggests that it is often kinder to

---

[1]See chapter 19 for more about the Gestalt effect of humor.

actively promote a positive mind-set. For instance, when patients display that they are anxious or uncomfortable, long-term caregivers often take a provocative stance, seeking to lift the patients' spirits or "bring them around." In areas such as physical rehabilitation, where patients work closely with caregivers for weeks or months, elaborate humor rituals are observable. Even in areas of low continuity, however, caregivers typically take an active role—not simply respecting—but actively seeking to influence patients' expressed attitudes. For instance, one anesthesiologist regularly made fun of the music played in the preoperative (holding) room: "Rod Stewart! Is this holding or a torture chamber?" I took this as an effort to relieve the tension of people in the room.

Following are more examples of humor apparently meant to improve another person's spirits.

(JJJJ, Surgery)

> NURSE: ((to patient's wife)) You don't have to leave just yet.
> ... Oh, I see, you want to get in as many kisses as you can!

(KKKK, Pediatrics)

> NURSE: ((to child about to receive a shot)) Look at the Band-Aid, Miss ——. Look at the Band-Aid!

(LLLL, Ortho/Gen)

> NURSE: ((to patient disappointed because he wasn't discharged)) You don't want to go home today. I told your wife, when you leave here, to drive you straight back to work!

In an interesting turnabout, patients sometimes initiate humor to brighten up their caregivers. A hospital rehabilitation nurse told me this story:

> We have an 83-year-old woman who had been suffering severe depression for 2 weeks. Sunday she had some nausea and she experienced some more Monday. Tuesday morning, me and the doctor were standing by her bed discussing her condition. He felt maybe it was the medication that was causing this [nausea]. She looked at us and said, "Well, I can tell you I'm not pregnant!"

If the patient's words were meant to wipe away the worried looks of her caregivers, they worked. The nurse told me, "We laughed and laughed. And I knew then that she was going to be okay."

In summary, within the Code of Compassion long-term caregivers often seem to provoke patients into a assuming a "better" frame of mind. Of course this maxim has limits; caregivers are noticeably more hesitant and less jovial around seriously ill or very anxious patients. (Interestingly, cancer patients were reputed in this hospital to be among the most jovial, perhaps in an effort to soothe those around them.) Caregivers have told me that patients who are anxious complain more and cooperate less. Brightening the patient's (or the caregiver's) outlook may make it easier to work together, foster a more pleasant work environment, and may speed healing. Considering the interdependent, extended contact between many hospital and physical therapy caregivers and their patients, participants may feel that a lot rides on improving the emotional climate in which they interact.

CONCLUSIONS

The Code of Compassion is suggested by adherence to four maxims I identify as follows:

1. Encourage patients to cooperate.
2. Display a sense of intimacy or familiarity.
3. Campaign for attention and individuality.
4. Keep the patient's spirits up.

The duration of a hospital stay or physical therapy treatment usually allows patients and their caregivers to become well acquainted. They often work together for extended periods of time, and treatment success requires their interdependence. Underlying the Code of Compassion is an awareness that patients may be overwhelmed by the situation in which they find themselves, and may need help coping with it. This, combined with interpersonal familiarity, sanctions the use of bolder more adventuresome use of humor.

It is also important to realize that, although long-term caregivers do not wish to offend patients, they acknowledge that people who do not feel well often complain. Mild complaints generally do not carry the same sanctions as in the breast care center. Long-term caregivers seem aware that a patient's short-term grumbling is often replaced by long-term gratitude for the caregiver who helped them get better. This realization facilitates bolder, more proactive use of humor strategies. Caregivers are less hesitant to provoke a patient for long-term gain.

Chapter 17

▼

Overview and Significance
of Humor and Appropriateness

If I have been successful in describing the sense of these medical settings, the reader will realize that the breast center caregivers would usually be out of line if they borrowed quips from their counterparts in the long-term care facilities. Caregivers' references to nudity, torture, or imaginary boyfriends would violate the decorum of Dr. Lane's office. Conversely, hospital caregivers may find little goal fulfillment with the subtle, ambiguous humor of the breast center or doctor's office.

Humor's role in medical settings seems largely a matter of cultural appropriateness. Overall, the Code of Dignity is characterized by an individualistic orientation. There is a moral imperative for caregivers to cater to patients and to avoid offending them. Within the Code of Compassion, greater emphasis is placed on securing the patient's cooperation with prescribed routines, and caregivers may sometimes provoke patients "for their own good."

However, I do not wish to suggest that the Code of Dignity is purely individualistic and the Code of Compassion purely collectivistic. Indeed, from my perspective, both codes are addressed to the dialectic between collectivism and individualism. Maintaining that dialectic requires that each code has provisions for drawing a transaction toward either pole. For instance, within the comparatively collectivistic code of the hospital and physical therapy unit, humor is available as a means to display and campaign for individualized attention. Conversely, the means of managing complaints in the breast center is collectivistic in the way it encourages compliance with medical routines. Thus the codes are not opposites. Indeed they differ only as a matter of degree—one lying closer to one pole (individualism) and one closer to the other (collectivism).

Methodologically, this chapter underscores the informativeness of cultural contrasts. The Code of Compassion seemed completely unremarkable to me when I first encountered it during hospital observations. At the time I could not imagine a different code, so persuasive was its internal logic. (I was later to feel the same way about the Code of Dignity, and it is only with a mental effort that I am able to make the Gestalt switch from consideration of one code to consideration of the other.) Had I been exposed to only one code I think it would still seem as invisible and unremarkable to me as it is to the participants. My attitude, like theirs, was: "Of course things are done that way, how else?" Only after exposure to both codes was I able to fully appreciate the different social realities created by each. In this way, I have found Hymes' discovery model particularly advantageous. In my experience, by asking the same questions in a variety of settings, phenomena are revealed that might otherwise be overlooked.

V

Humor Makes Sense
of Problematic Situations

Chapter 18

▼

Ethnomethodological Approach

It is to be expected that patients in medical encounters experience a feeling of nakedness—physical and emotional. In giving up our clothing and/or intimate details of our lives, we violate many features of social reality. The everyday world as we commonly recognize it rarely includes this type of activity with nonintimate acquaintances.

From a common sense perspective, how does a woman act when she stands bare-chested before a mammography machine? How does a person gracefully discuss urine output or sexual habits, or prepare to receive an injection? If, as Bogden and Taylor (1975) asserted, "people abstract rules and common sense understandings in order to make activities appear routine, explicable, and unambiguous" (p. 16), they often have a hard time doing so in the intimidating atmosphere of a hospital or clinic. In some cases, the situation is so fearful or unique that it eludes one's repertoire of appropriate responses. Otherwise, one may struggle with a discrepancy between what is expected, and what one would prefer or expect to do. Although the motions of a medical exam or hospital stay become familiar and routine to some, for most there remain activities that are fearful and unfamiliar.

This section is about dilemmas such as these, and the way people deal with those dilemmas. The thesis that people use humor to make sense of problematic situations is illustrated with examples from medical encounters. In these situations, actors are more called on than usual to make their interpretations and intentions available to each other so they may achieve a working sense of order.

In chapter 20, I describe several health care transactions in detail, specifically showing humor's placement in the exam sequence, its wording, and the way it marginalizes the effects of anxiety and embarrassment. In this way, I propose to analyze the use of humor as an observable, rational means of organizing and interpreting a health care experience. The reader is able to see—not only that humor embodies a certain topic or tone—but what leads up to that humor, and what follows it. Emphasis is on members' ongoing efforts to manage health care transactions in the most comfortable, sensible way.

Ethnomethodology (EM), as described by Garfinkel (1967), is concerned with the pragmatic ways that people abstract a sense of order and predictability from the occurrences of daily life. Following is a discussion of the basic tenets of ethnomethodology and their relevance to the proposed study.

As stated, EM focuses on the means by which people organize and make sense of everyday situations. The accomplishment of "life as usual" is considered to be based on a socially approved body of practical knowledge—what Schutz (1962/1967) called "common sense." I interpret Schutz to mean that common sense is a set of reliable expectations that social actors hold to be true for all practical purposes. In other words, social actors perceive the world in terms of a common understanding of what *ought* to happen or *usually* happens. I emphasize ought and should to say that the social world is reasonably predictable, but not completely so. A social occurrence is interpretable only within a sequence of events and an array of situational factors. How is it then, that social actors recognize the humorous ambiguity of sarcasm, irony, and verbal play? I show that social actors rely on situational cues and shared (commonsense) understandings to create and interpret humor. Taking the argument one step further, I show how patients and caregivers treat humor as a persuasive bid to treat the situation as "not serious" or "not so bad."

My analysis is informed by the work of Garfinkel, and indirectly by the scholars who have influenced him. As the founder of EM, Garfinkel has drawn on the writings of Schutz, Gurwitsch, Merleau-Ponty, and others (Heritage, 1984). Similar to Schutz, Garfinkel (1967) described a body of "socially-sanctioned-facts-of-life" which every "bona-fide-member-of-the-society-knows" and assumes that others know as well (p. 76). I take Garfinkel to mean that these facts of life represent a working agreement about what is typically meant and typically expected within the society. But as Garfinkel (1967, especially chapter 3) pointed out, social situations are always changing and information about them is constantly made more or less available. Therefore, interpretations are continually revised and refined.

In summary, EM is based on several assumptions. First, it assumes that social transaction is orderly and that orderliness is an ongoing accomplishment—something made to happen, not something that just happens. Second, ethnomethodologists hold that people are largely unaware of their everyday expectancies about life as usual. EM does not rely on members' explanations, nor attempt to account for their cognitive states. Ethnomethodologists assume that the methods of accomplishing everyday activities are detectable and observable by those who suspend, or are strangers to, the assumptions of the natural attitude.

On the following pages I describe the methods of analysis and the advantages and limitations of applying EM to a study of humor use in medical settings.

DATA ANALYSIS

How does one apprehend what Garfinkel (1967) called the "formal properties of common sense activities" (p. viii)? I submit that the investigator must first focus on everyday activities, viewing the mundane as something more than chance. Sacks (1986b) expressed this point well in his essay, "On Doing Being Ordinary":

> The world you live in is much more finely organized than you would imagine..an initial shift is *not* [to] think of "an ordinary person" as some person, but as somebody having as one's job, as one's constant preoccupation, doing "being ordinary." It is not that somebody *is* ordinary; it is perhaps that that is what one's business is, and it takes work, as any other business does. (p. 414)

To a *bona-fide-member-of-the-society* (Garfinkel's term), the business of being ordinary is almost entirely unremarkable. Common sense expectancies are characterized by their taken-for-granted nature. These background expectancies become visible only when they seem problematic or strange (Garfinkel, 1967). Thus, an ethnomethodologist may create a problematic situation and observe members' attempts to make sense of it, as with Garfinkel's (1967) "unpredictable analyst" experiment in which subjects repeatedly struggled to make sense of a series of random replies. Garfinkel has also asked students to thwart normal expectations by openly cheating at ticktacktoe and by asking friends to clarify commonplace remarks (Heritage, 1984). (So noted are Garfinkel's breaching experiments that the verb *Garfinkeling* has become a popular label for them.)

Garfinkel (1967) wrote that there are "demonstratably rational properties" (p. 34) in the organization of everyday activities. I take him to mean that we subtly make our interpretations and intentions available to others in the process of achieving a practical understanding with them. Members' engagement in this process is available to others and also to the researcher—although the engagement is usually known only tacitly by the social actors involved. With a process similar to phenomenological reduction, I attempt to suspend assumptions and examine medical situations as a stranger might—seeing the patient–caregiver transaction as a situated accomplishment organized by the participants. My task is made somewhat easier by the unfamiliar and problematic nature of many medical transactions. Members' efforts to achieve understanding and order are often particularly elaborate.

I present intact sequences of conversation so the reader may appreciate humor's place in a transaction and the ways the transaction changes after humor has become a part of it. This is an enterprise rather different than reductionistic approaches, with good reason. Social transaction naturally occurs as a constant, cumulative stream of situations, settings, and utterances whose meaning is tied into present, past, and future interpretations. As Barnlund (1981) put it, "every act is both prologue and epilogue; a consequence of all preceding events and antecedent to all subsequent ones" (p. 96). He admonished that "the continuous flow of human acts is something we seem more sensitive to as people than as scientists" (p. 96).

It is also informative to examine humor using conversation analysis (see chapter 21). The following advantages and limitations of EM apply to conversation analysis (CA) as well.

ADVANTAGES

First, the focus on naturally occurring activities helps to assure that the phenomenon is likely to occur as it naturally does, undistorted by research manipulation. Because EM/CA data is usually collected with observation and/or a taperecorder, the research is only minimally obtrusive. Unlike survey instruments or experimental procedures that embody their own sense of order, naturally occurring transaction may be studied with its context and sequential order intact.

Two more advantages are the flexibility and coherence of EM/CA. It is possible to collect data in a range of situations without inconveniencing the participants. I have collected data in seven health care settings, observing several hundred medical transactions. The flexibility of EM/CA has allowed me to collect diverse data and also to analyze it in a coherent and comparable way.

Fourth, the data of EM/CA are uniquely available so the reader can compare his or her own conclusions with the researcher's. In CA, for instance, analyses are presented along with the transcript excerpts on which they are based. In this way, conversational data can be subjected to repeated and rigorous review. The reproducibility of taped conversations facilitates an active dialogue between scholars. Although the data of EM are usually less tangible, the assertions are (dis)confirmable by any member of the described community. Because EM describes folk methods and folk reasoning, members of the community are capable of judging the relevance of research conclusions. Although members may not initially be aware of folk methods, those methods, once explicated, should stand up to the scrutiny of common sense.

A final advantage is that EM/CA—more than most methods—recognizes the interactive nature of the social world. Because it examines transactions, not survey answers or singular utterances, EM/CA can say something about collaborative methods of social transaction, such as the way people introduce new topics into conversation or make puzzling situations sensible.

In summary, EM/CA is compelling because it makes few assumptions beyond what social actors explicitly provide. Put another way, as social actors communicate their understanding to each other (which they must), it is likewise displayed to the analyst as a competent communicator in that society.

LIMITATIONS

Of course, there are also boundaries to what EM/CA can accomplish. Following are the limitations of examining medical dialogue from this perspective.

First, attention to the microstructure of social transaction means that macrocontextual issues are largely ignored. In focusing on one aspect of a phenomenon, other aspects are marginalized. Conversation analysis as designed by Sacks, Schegloff, and Jefferson (1978) focuses singularly on the structure of conversation, ignoring situational factors. I submit this as a limitation of EM/CA, not a weakness. Others have argued, and I agree, that a narrow focus is necessary to conduct the detailed investigations of EM/CA. There is also some evidence that the microstructure of social transaction occurs, to a great extent, independently of context (i.e., cross-cultural procedures for turn-taking). Still, the reader should be aware that CA, particularly, is characterized by a very specific focus.

Second, EM/CA is not directed toward causal speculation. It is impossible for researchers to isolate the complex influences in a natural setting. Frankel (1984), for instance, observed that patients typically yield the floor to doctors, but he did not determine which factors specifically contribute to their acquiescence.

In summary, as with any other method, EM/CA is not qualified to explain everything about a situation, nor to explain anything that applies to all situations. The most serious charge against EM and CA is that they overlook many situational factors. To offset that, I have analyzed, the data from an ethnographic perspective as well (see Parts III and IV of this volume)—using observation and fieldnotes to examine the presence of situational factors and cultural codes.

Several conceptualizations are useful in examining humor from an ethnomethodological perspective. This analysis is particularly influenced by ideas about Gestalt psychology developed by Gurwitsch and by Bateson's and Goffman's work on frame analysis. Together these ideas form the framework for the analysis that follows.

Chapter 19

▼

Candid Camera
and Gestalt Psychology

One might ask why humor—with all its ambiguities—is a useful communication tool in an already problematic situation. It is not immediately apparent why social actors who so carefully cultivate a shared sense of reality derive pleasure from the unexpected, rule-thwarting nature of humor. A statement is often funny precisely because it traipses on forbidden ground (see chapter 7).

Perhaps the answer lies in the persuasive suggestion that an occurrence characterized by mirth cannot, after all, be "all that bad." Such a notion is evident in the folk adage about "laughing your cares away." Similarly, the rueful idiom, "I'll laugh at this someday," implies: "When I can take the situation less seriously I will have a different sense of it. What is distressing now will then seem funny." That conviction might be persuasive in present tense as well: "I'm laughing, so it must not be so bad." By implying "this isn't really serious" humor often seems to change the "sense" of a problematic situation (giving additional significance to the term *sense of humor*).

The persuasiveness of humor is apparent in the way that a novel utterance or action (a punch line or funny face, for instance) often changes the overall appearance of a situation. Consider the television program in which the announcement "You're on *Candid Camera!*" repeatedly turns the consternation of practical joke victims into displays of hilarity. A hoodwinked participant—who is quite visibly perturbed or puzzled one instant—is suddenly overcome with "understanding" and an accompanying sense of mirth when he or she realizes he or she has been good-naturedly set-up.[1] By reframing an occurrence as humorous, we suddenly see that it was not supposed to make sense in the way we thought. Humor snatches us from the disturbing glare of anomaly. What was a crisis is reframed in the acceptable countenance of something not serious and we are saved from a painful sense of inexplicable disorder, of having acted badly or out of line. Humor marks an action as intentionally out of line (see Part V, this volume).

Although Gurwitsch did not specifically address humor in his writing about Gestalt psychology, his ideas help to explain the way that a simple humorous utterance might change the complexion of an experience (sometimes called a *Gestalt switch*). As I interpret Gurwitsch (1964), experience is not understood as a collection of random or isolated components, but as a system of organized and integrated constituents, whose overall meaning is interpreted in light of their relation to each other. To illustrate, a person in a doctor's office probably does not perceive that he or she is standing on carpet, by one wall here, there another wall, in visible range of a person who wears a white jacket and is now saying "hi" and is now saying "move this way" *ad infinitum*. Rather, he or she experiences the situation of a medical exam, within four walls whose relation to each other supports the idea of a room, and a particular type of room at that. Within that context, the white jacket suggests that the other person is a medical professional, and the patient's own actions are correspondingly interpretable as those of a patient.[2]

Depending on how relevant they seem, constituents of a situation may have slight or considerable influence on our overall perceptions. As Gurwitsch (1964) put it, aspects may seem thematic, relevant to the theme, or merely marginal. To return to my earlier example, we might consider a crack of thunder overhead to be of marginal relevance to the exam underway, but quite relevant to the drive home that awaits us.[3] On

---

[1] The reaction is surely less positive among participants who feel the set-up was not so "good-natured." Even allowing for the film editor's prerogative not to include those segments in the broadcasts, it is still quite remarkable how frequently participants are willing to instantly accept the transformation of a troublesome situation into a hilarious one.

[2] Here the reader would like to interrupt, am I right? "Of course this is so! Why be so simplistic! Why go on so?" The practices of contextual perception are familiar. These practices are so familiar, in fact, that we are prone to forget that we practice them until they are explicitly described for us. Faced with them in this way you might casually brush them aside as "mere" common sense, or (like me) be fascinated by the sophisticated machinery that enables us to regard common sense as something "mere" and "automatic." This machinery—I find—is what makes social transaction easy and social science hard!

[3] That items or occurrences may be perceived as irrelevant to the overall theme underscores the idea of a perceived *theme*, without which there could be no "relevant" or "irrelevant."

the other hand, a pleasant remark treated as relevant to the theme of the exam may change overall perceptions of it. In this Gestalt concept of contexture, the introduction of something novel may alter the entire feel of an experience (even dramatically change the tone of the occurrence as in the *Candid Camera* examples). I once saw a hospital transaction transformed when a nurse teased an irate patient: "You don't want to go home! I told your wife, when you leave here take you straight to work." The patient's expression changed. He and his wife laughed, and they began joking around with the nurse.

In my observations, the introduction of humor into the thematic field of a medical exam often seems to change the overall complexion of the transaction in observable ways. There is often a sudden increase in eye contact, smiles, and laughter, and the sharing of personal anecdotes. In short, the formal style of an institutional exam is often transformed into the more relaxed, familiar style of friendly conversation. In the way that Gurwitsch described Gestalt theory, humor may be viewed as a constituent whose presence affects the overall character of an experience. I use dialogue from medical encounters to support that—when lightheartedness is taken as relevant to the theme of an exam—other impressions such as embarrassment and anger often seem to be marginalized. Overall, it seems that humor is a means of making sense of an uncommonly weird and emotionally charged situation.

I could continue here with many examples, but I believe it is more revealing to save them for later, after a discussion of framing and keying devices. At that point, the reader may better appreciate—not only that contexts are established and transformed—but also the collaborative apparatuses available for social actors to organize their experiences in just those ways.

ABOUT FRAME ANALYSIS

It is not a great stretch to think of Gurwitsch's idea about themes in association with Bateson's and Goffman's ideas about framing. According to Bateson (1972), social actors "frame" their activities for the same reason that artists frame pictures. A picture frame serves as a boundary—to separate, for instance, the painting from the wallpaper. According to Bateson, "The frame around a picture, if we consider this frame as a message intended to order or organize the perception of the viewer, says 'attend to what is within and do not attend to what is outside'"

(p. 187). In a similar way, a social frame characterizes a situation and distinguishes it from the broader context in which it is embedded. In Gestalt terms, the frame suggests what is to be considered figure and what to be treated as mere ground. Depending on the frame, participants may attend to or ignore certain aspects of the context in which they find themselves. The frame may also suggest when a situation begins and ends. As I see it, a frame makes it possible for participants to organize/classify their actions as overtures within a certain type of "happening"[4] or goings on. The idea that social actors continually orient themselves as participants in framed happenings, which they use as the basis for action and interpretation, is central to ethnomethodology. Goffman (1974) put it this way:

> I assume that when individuals attend to any current situation, they face the question: "What is going on here?" Whether asked explicitly as in times of confusion and doubt, or tacitly during occasions of useful certitude, the question is put and the answer to it is presumed by the way the individuals then proceed to get on with the affairs at hand. (p. 8)

In the current analysis, we might say that participants conduct themselves within the frame of a medical transaction.[5] As I use the words, a frame encompasses (among other things) an organized collection of "doings" (e.g., doing direction-giving, doing telling, doing leave-taking) that are treated as frame-relevant, that is, relevant to the medical transaction.

This view proves to be an exceptionally useful way of understanding medical transactions. But, however clearly organizational phenomena present themselves for *analysis*, they seem to escape the awareness of *participants*. Goffman wrote of the typical social actor[6] that "he is likely

---

[4]The connotation of a *happening* as a rather random, unexpected occurrence ("Shit happens!") may be consistent with members' perceptions. But, on close examination, social transaction is much more organized and predictable than most members realize. I use the word *happening* to connote a collection of events, actions, utterances, and so forth, that members treat in a cohesive way, as contributing to an overall situation or occurrence. Thus we might say that an interview, an exam, getting undressed and dressed all are part of a broader happening called a doctor's visit.

[5]This is arguably an oversimplification in that participants may experience one episode within many layers of frames. For instance, they may be fulfilling an obligation, getting an exam, filling time, and any number of other things. But in this data, members' words and actions support that the medical transaction is a principal consideration.

[6]In light of Goffman's many foresights, which have made his work important for more than 20 years, he can perhaps be forgiven for employing the gender language of his time. Because I quote so heavily from his work, I find it more distracting than helpful to continually "gender neutralize" his words. I present them as is and beg the reader to respectfully consider the historical context in which they were written.

to be unaware of such organized features as the framework has and be unable to describe the framework with any completeness if asked, yet these handicaps are no bar to his easily and fully applying it" (p. 21).

KEYING

To Bateson's concept of *frame*, Goffman (1974) contributed the complementary concept of *keying*. As I interpret it, a "key" is a convention with which participants display that a sequence should be interpreted in a certain way (e.g., playfully, seriously). Cues suggest how a sequence should be interpreted and when it begins and ends.[7] For example, in a circumstance I describe here, a patient signals that he is distressed by deeply inhaling air and audibly exhaling it through his mouth.

Thus, the implication of a keying is that an event is interpreted in a certain way, whether its instrumental appearance changes or not. "The systematic transformation that a particular keying introduces may alter only slightly the activity thus transformed, but it utterly changes what it is a participant would say was going on" (Goffman, 1974, p. 45). The frame usually survives, "else there would be no content to the keying" (p. 8), but activities within the frame are conducted as within another key.

This may explain why playfulness does not seem to prolong or disrupt medical exams (Beck & Ragan, 1992). In sharing humor, participants may not irreparably break the frame of a medical transaction. They may remain within frame, only conduct the same activities in a different key, or break frame only momentarily, in which case resuming frame-relevant activity seems to be a simple matter.

FLOODING OUT

My observations suggest that displays of medical setting humor are akin to what Goffman (1974) called *flooding out*. He used this term to refer to participants' sudden dissolve into laughter, tears, rage, and so on which extend their conduct beyond frame relevancy. As Goffman at-

---

[7]Relevant to this idea is Bateson's (1972) work on "metacommunicative cues," which suggest how an utterance/action should be interpreted. For an overview see Bateson (1972, especially pp. 173-193).

tested, "even a moment's release from the prior frame may allow everyone psychologically to fit back into the frame and be more at ease than before" (p. 381). He elaborated that "a surging of feeling" may sweep participants into "decreased or increased distance from the framed activity" (p. 359).

In the analysis of the next chapter, it is often hard to say whether humor represents a flooding out or a rekeying.[8] Semantics aside, there are (as mentioned) noticeable changes in the transaction. Humor does not seem to greatly disrupt the flow of events, but it often seems to change the tone of what follows it. Examples demonstrate this more clearly.

---

[8]It is much easier to speak of momentary frame breaks in theory than in practice. To consider that humor "breaks frame" I must be more confident than I can be about what participants consider frame-relevant. All I can reliably report is that laughter is not treated as radically tangential to the medical transaction, judging by the ease with which participants continue or resume medical activity.

Chapter 20

▼

Playful Management
of Three Dilemmas

SEQUENCE 1:
"GETTIN' A LITTLE QUEASY"

The way that Goffman described it, an unkeyed event is a rather straightforward one. It is organized in a basic, routine way. The following passages describe an actual transaction in the outpatient physical therapy unit that began as an unkeyed event.[1]

> A new patient arrives for treatment. He is a male Euro-American about 20 years old. After being shown to a treatment table, he sits atop it and is soon approached by a physical therapist who inquires about his condition. The patient says he recently strained his shoulder, and also describes a knot on his elbow that has been bothering him for about 1 year. The therapist reaches out to physically examine the elbow.

For the physical therapist at least, this is a familiar sequence of events, of the unproblematic, standardized nature Garfinkel (1967) called "practical accomplishments" (p. 10). But, in this case, a keying is soon suggested by the patient.

---

[1] In this chapter I forego the Jeffersonian method of conversation transcription so that I may better integrate contextual details surrounding participants' utterances. The purpose of the vignette-style of presentation I use here is to emphasize "doings" rather than "sayings" or utterances.

As the therapist reaches for the elbow, the patient blanches and exhales a slow breath through puffed cheeks. "I'm gettin' a little queasy, but it's okay," he says.

From the caregiver's perspective, this is ostensibly an unexpected (but surely not an unprecedented) shift of events. Her next actions are oriented to the patient's anxiety. Consequently, what began rather straightforwardly as *doing an exam* is soon layered with something else, which we might call *doing comforting*.

> The therapist asks the patient if he would like to lie down or have some water. "I'm just a big baby," says the patient with a wan smile. The therapist helps him recline on the bed and asks a student aide to get him something cool to drink. Once he is settled, the therapist asks, "Is it painful when you touch it? Is that it?" The patient answers, "It's all psychological. I'm just scared to death."

Interestingly, as comforting is being done, the patient offers more clues on how his condition might be interpreted. He accepts the accommodations, but by declaring that he is *"just* a big baby" and *"just* scared," acknowledges that he is more bothered than the situation might merit. The therapist receives this information and bids for more with a sequence of questions about the painfulness of the elbow. Apparently assured that the patient suffers more from anxiety than from agony, the therapist continues with the exam, layering it with a mixture of sympathy and humor.

> The therapist responds, "That's okay. It's okay. I'd feel that way too," as she very gently begins to examine the elbow. Soon another therapist (who seems to have overheard the transaction) approaches the treatment table, exclaiming, "Okay! This is MY patient." The first therapist playfully retorts, "Too bad. We already got him covered." Suddenly laughing, the patient exclaims, "All this attention!"

With this sequence of events it becomes apparent that the initial frame of a medical examination has been preserved, or at least reinstated. The therapist is apparently oriented to doing-comforting-in-order-to-do-an-exam.[2] Goffman (1974) might call this a keying or a lamination of the basic framework.

Playful management of the situation presumably provides a welcome diversion for the patient, who can attend to the therapists' banter rather

---

[2] This opposed to abandoning the examination, which would represent a dramatic instance of breaking frame.

than the dreaded, ongoing examination of his elbow. It also seems to cast him as a sought-after patient—not, as he might fear, a "problem patient" to be disdained or avoided. This playful key prevails throughout his visit, which lasts roughly an hour.

> A few minutes later, as the patient describes how he hurt his shoulder executing a tricky basketball maneuver, the second therapist teases him, "Hook? As in Lew Alcindor?" The patient replies, laughing, "No. As in should have been Lew Alcindor—more like Bart Simpson!" By this time, the patient is smiling and sitting up, apparently much more at ease.

> Later he seems relatively relaxed when a student aide approaches him to shave his elbow so he can apply electrodes to it. The patient laughs and offers his elbow as the aide tells him a funny story about a hairy man who lost a patch of hair when someone yanked electrodes off his chest.

In summary, we might say that—within the frame of a physical therapy session—a straightforward exam has been keyed as a distressful episode and then rekeyed as a playful transaction. Cues are available to suggest each keying and to signal its uptake and management. Applying Gurwitsch's terminology, we might say that humor— as a "constituent of the thematic field"—seemed to soften the institutional atmosphere of the exam. The participants cooperate in keying a straightforward exam as a distressing situation, then rekeying it as a playful episode. When a playful key is introduced, the patient laughs and seems to physically relax. Within the sequence-as-transformed he not only overcomes his queasiness, but laughs, sits up, and willingly offers his elbow for treatment.

This may sound like a fantastic example, to be filed doubtfully under "Humor Saves the Day" or "Happily Ever After." Lest I seem to be overstating an argument, I would like to emphasize that keyings and transformations are everywhere around us. Throughout *Frame Analysis*, Goffman (1974) made the point that social actors quite commonly experience that situations are transformed before their eyes—as when a menacing shadow turns out to be a shrub, a practical joke is revealed, or a theater star steps from the stage and into her or his real-life persona. I might also make the point (Goffman-style) that this text itself demonstrates what a simple affair it is to key back and forth between "narrative segments" and "analysis segments" by using the conventional device of displaying narrative segments in indented block format. The marvel, I think, is that social actors so adroitly manage the complications thrown their way, and do so in ways that seem to satisfy and involve a complex array of characters.

If I had space to fully analyze all the transactions I have witnessed, I am confident that each would reveal a preeminently rational organization. As it is, I hope the reader will be game for the analysis of two more sequences.

SEQUENCE 2:
"THEY TOOK TOO MUCH REALLY"

As mentioned, I have often studied the actions of people required to behave in ways they would ordinarily avoid. Some—very few—remain committed to the normalcy of the transaction. They approach it with a sense of serious decorum. Very few maintain a deadpan countenance, however. The urge seems stronger to laugh, to make fun of, some aspect of their situation. Consider the following example.

> It is a busy afternoon and the radiology technician seems preoccupied. She sighs several times, fiddles with instruments, and makes little eye contact with the patient, a 70-year-old African-American woman in for a routine mammography. Reviewing the woman's chart, the technician asks the patient if she has experienced any problems since undergoing breast reduction surgery several years ago. "Oh no," the woman says, waving her hand through the air as if to brush aside the surgery as long ago and "no big deal."

> When the technician asks the patient to remove one arm from her smock, the patient takes it completely off, apparently sanguine about baring her chest in this way. With an animated grin and raised eyebrows, the patient declares, "When they were big, I had to get special things to put 'em in!" Cupping her breasts with her hands, she winks and continues, "Now they're so small, hard to get 'em out there. They took too much really!"

By commenting on her body in this playful way, the patient draws a laugh from the caregiver, enticing her away from the impersonal, distracted state she has so far displayed. The patient also adopts something of a commentator role. Her breasts are "they's" whose size is a matter of unself-conscious amusement. There is nothing somber in the patient's demeanor to suggest that she sincerely believes or regrets that "they took too much."

The patient may, at some level, have an emotional investment in her breast size that is not apparent. But more to the point, she presents herself in this case as a someone who is not self-conscious or truly upset. In this way, it seems that humorous self-commentary allows a person to project a persona not directly attributable to what we might call the "naked I." Goffman (1974) expressed it this way: "Instead of stating a view outright, the individual tends to attribute it to a character who happens to be himself, but one he has been careful to withdraw from in one regard or another" (p. 551). The patient's exuberant grin and wink suggest that she is "hamming it up," being purposefully animated rather than serious and sincere. This type of animation may be a gloss that diminishes a participant's vulnerability to embarrassing episodes. Through use of such animation, participants may rekey these episodes as funny instead of threatening. This may explain why patients so frequently joke about their breasts when they are forced to bare them. Humorous animation essentially distances them from the situation. As Goffman (1956) wrote, "banter is a way of saying that what occurs now is not serious or real" (p. 270).

Interestingly, after the patient introduces humor into the exchange, the caregiver becomes more attentive, several times making humorous quips herself.

> During the exam, the technician stops to prepare another film, but quickly has it ready. Apparently surprised by her alacrity, the patient remarks, "I thought I was goin' ta get a chance ta sit down." The technician responds in a teasing tone, "Oh no. If I have ta stand, you do too!" They both laugh.
>
> Later, after muttering to herself for a moment, the technician draws a laugh by asking, "Can you tell I'm arguing with myself?"

In summary, it seems that the introduction of humor often keys an exchange as a nonthreatening one. Moreover, one instance of shared humor is often followed by others, evidence of an enduring interpretive suggestion to organize/interpret the exchange in a playful way. Humor seems to serve as a persuasive bid to treat the situation as nonserious or nonthreatening. This may be a particularly appealing key when one is (literally and figuratively) standing nude before a stranger.

SEQUENCE 3:
WHO WILL TIE THE SHOE?

Humor can also be used to camouflage or excuse conflict. This is evident when a patient or caregiver resists a suggestion made by the other, doing so in a way that bids for playful interpretation of the resistance (and perhaps the suggestion as well). Consider the following real-life example.

A local college football player reports to the physical therapy department to be fitted with a knee brace. He changes into shorts for the fitting, then a physical therapist draws the curtains around his treatment table so the patient can put his blue jeans on over the brace. The patient is treated by the staff as something of a celebrity, and several employees gather round to talk to him when he reopens the curtains.

As they are talking, the patient realizes that it will be difficult to get his left shoe back on. The brace—now hidden beneath his pants leg—holds his leg straight. The brace cannot be adjusted or removed without again removing the pants, and it would require great flexibility for the patient to put on his left shoe without bending his left knee. While "talking football" to one therapist, the patient holds his shoe out to a nearby student aide—who is also male, about the same age as the patient, and a student at the same university. The patient does not make eye contact with the aide, nor does he say anything, but his manner suggests rather impatiently that the aide put his shoe on. The student aide stands as if frozen, looking at the shoe and the football player, apparently unsure whether or not he will oblige.

The aide's apparent confusion and indecision are perhaps understandable. Throughout the patient's visit there has been little pretense of conventional patient–caregiver transaction. The medical frame has been but loosely upheld. Talk has centered much more around the young man's exploits on the football field, casting him in a celebrity role he seems pleased to accept. The aide (who is not among the fans to have gathered around) may be unsure which line to take. Framed one way, it is his job to help patients. Framed another way, the football player is a peer (and a rather threatening one at that). His unspoken assumption that the aide will obey his wish may seem presumptuous and insulting, especially considering that the patient does not acknowledge the aide beyond waving a shoe at him, and does so in front of the aide's co-workers. The episode continues.

> After several seconds in which the aide stands immobile, the patient turns to him and says in a teasing tone, "Gotta do your job man."

In this way, the patient displays that he is aware of the aide's reluctance, and by way of seeking compliance with his "request," suggests that the situation be regarded within the frame of a health care transaction. The implication is that, within that frame, the aide is obligated to assist.

> The aide accepts the shoe and puts it on the patient's foot, but does not tie it. (By this time the other employees have wandered away.) Laughing,

the aide says to the patient, "I think it'd be more comfortable *untied*." Now there is another moment of hesitation, while the patient looks at his shoe and then at the aide, apparently unsure how to proceed.

The aide's declaration that he is preserving the patient's comfort is marked by playful tones as not necessarily a justification. Considering the obvious discomfort of hobbling with a knee brace and an untied shoe, the utterance is more vividly available as *not* a true justification.[3] It ostensibly serves another purpose—perhaps to buffer the appearance of what might seem to be bald-faced defiance. The presence of humor admits ambiguity about whether the two men are locked in a serious battle of wills or "just" playing.

At this point, having once asserted (in teasing tones) that the aide is obliged to assist him, the patient has gained partial compliance. That line has taken him just so far, and it is unclear for the moment whether he will acquiesce or take a harder line.

After a few moments, the patient leans over from a standing position to try to tie the shoe himself. The student aide immediately approaches him. "Lemme help you there," he says laughing, jostling the patient as if to knock him over (but carefully keeping him from falling). Then the student aide squats before the patient and ties his shoe. The two exchange a friendly sounding good-bye and the patient exits.

As shown, something interesting happens when the patient begins to tie his own shoe. The student aide, who has seemed reluctant to help, suddenly jumps to assist him. A different kind of doing is underway. Actions that previously had the character of obeying can now be performed in the key of voluntary assistance. The aide's playful jostling of the patient and his humorous "lemme help you" (humorous because spoken during the jostling, and not the tieing) soften the transition.

To elaborate, although the participants' actions have changed, this final playful utterance is in keeping with the other utterances. Interestingly, the verbal track of this encounter consists of only three utterances, all of them delivered in playful tones: (a) "Gotta do your job man," (b), "I think it'd be more comfortable untied," and (c) "Lemme help you there." These may be contrasted with constituents of the nonverbal

---

[3] It is easy to imagine the therapist asserting (truthfully or not) that he is professionally obliged *not* to help the patient so that he may master such affairs by himself. This justification would display that the aide is upholding a medical frame by withholding assistance, and in that different light, the sequence might look quite different.

track, filled with hesitations, delayed responses, and half-filled requests. The contrast is probably not incidental. I have many times seen humor used as a hedge when other elements of the transaction seem potentially threatening or volatile. In this way, humor is an important organizational/interpretive tool. It provides a suggestion of camaraderie and is ambiguous enough to be admissible in many situations. Moreover, this ambiguity allows the social actor a wide choice of next moves, any of which might be made to seem consistent with the line he or she has taken in play. So it is that the patient can attempt to tie his own shoe—and the student aide can jump to help—without either seeming to do an about-face.

In summary, I do not wish by careful scrutiny to overstate the significance of this transaction for the participants. The entire sequence lasted just a few minutes, and both participants may have soon forgotten it. But it seems to me that even brief episodes such as this demonstrate that a remarkable number of framing conventions are available to (and employed by) social actors. There are recognizable ways to request, insist, resist, and comply—even without words, even within a very few moments, even between strangers. Moreover, we can "resist" in one way and "play" in another, mixing signals in such a way that the transaction is strategically ambiguous and negotiable.[4]

OVERVIEW AND SIGNIFICANCE

In conclusion, a close look reveals that the social world is infinitely more calibrated than most people imagine. Even brief encounters are organized with an identifiable collection of framing and keying mechanisms. As shown, the presence of these mechanisms is evident in the way they are introduced and acted on. Even seemingly minor introductions to the thematic field of a medical exam may have a considerable effect on the way the encounter is carried out. A distressful episode is sometimes rekeyed as a playful one, making it less problematic to carry out dreaded routines. Additionally, by adopting animated personae, members may be able to comfortably distance themselves from embarrassing or threatening situations.

---

[4] The potential for an exchange to be displayed as both playful and serious led Bateson (1972) to call play a *paradoxical frame* (p. 184).

I suggest that, in the way that a code organizes the activities of members at a macroscopic level (see Part IV, this volume), frames and keys organize and explain episodes. To an extent, the latitude granted members of a speech community is realized in the ways they cooperatively frame and key specific episodes.

In the health care transactions described here, humor seems to be a particularly persuasive keying device. It is often followed by more humor and by a more relaxed, familiar exchange between participants. For both patients and caregivers, humor seems to soften the repercussions of participating in threatening or disagreeable activities. Even when the activity is maintained, the presence of humor seems to rekey the event as "not so bad" or "not so serious." In summary, play may seem a welcome (and perhaps a cathartic) contrast to the threatening, impersonal nature of many medical events.

Chapter 21

▼

Laughter-Coated Complaints

ABOUT CONVERSATION ANALYSIS

Conversation analysis (CA) was conceptualized in the 1960s, primarily by Sacks, Schegloff, and Jefferson. They shared Garfinkel's interest in the structures of everyday, practical experience. As in ethnomethodology (EM), the goal of CA "is to describe methods persons use in doing social life" (Sacks, 1986a, p. 21). Conversation analysts similarly assume that there is a basic orderliness to social interaction, and that that orderliness is displayed in structures of everyday talk. Following is a brief discussion of the epistemological assumptions of conversation analysis.

First, CA is based on the premise that researchers need not be mind readers, because people are not mind readers. To accomplish a conversation, the people involved must *demonstrate* to other people what they expect and what they wish others to know. Schegloff and Sacks (1973) put it this way:

> If the materials (records of natural conversations) were orderly, they were so because they had been methodically produced by members of the society for one another, and it was a feature of the conversation that we treated as data that they were produced as to allow the display by the co-participants to each other of their orderliness, and to allow the participants to display to each other their analysis, appreciation, and use of that orderliness. (p. 290)

In other words, conversation requires one to display understandings and expectations. The displays made available to conversational partners are consequently available to the researcher as well.

Furthermore, one would not be a more effective analyst if one were a mind reader! Like ethnomethodologists, conversation analysts do not assume that people are conscious of the methods they use. Indeed, conversation analysts are purposefully indifferent to the internal motivations of the individuals whose conversations they describe. From their perspective, it is more important how an utterance is taken up in conversation than how it was meant by the speaker. As Goodwin (1990) wrote: "In essence, the question is not *why* some particular understanding is performed but how conversational events are accomplished as the systematic products of orderly procedures" (p. 5). Goodwin's words bring up a third assumption: Conversation is an interactive accomplishment. One utterance is insufficient for CA, which focuses on the sequential and interactive nature of dialogue. Utterances are viewed as embedded within sequences that help establish their relevance and importance. Nofsinger (1991) explained: "Talk is designed to reflect back on prior turns and project ahead to future ones, and we interpret talk as if it is tied in some way to prior and future turns" (p. 3). Moreover, one conversational partner is considered to accomplish nothing without the collaboration of another. Pick-up, negotiation, and mutual effort are necessary. Sacks et al.'s (1978) well-known essay on turn-taking describes the intricate ways that conversations are locally managed.

In summary, CA shares many assumptions with EM. It is based on the premise that social actors interactively accomplish orderliness in observable and rational ways. That conversation analysts focus on spoken dialogue is a pragmatic matter, not a theoretical one, according to Sacks (1986a). "Conversation is something that we can get the actual happenings of on tape and that we can get more or less transcribed; that is, conversation is simply something to begin with" (p. 26).

CA is valuable to this study because it offers a way to examine more precisely how humor is accomplished and what effect it has on conversational sequences. After analyzing the breast center data, I am particularly interested in a phenomenon I call *laughter-coated complaints*. These are frequent, identifiable episodes in which a "complaint" is mutually managed as something to laugh about. When the methods of CA are used to examine complaints, cues emerge about why some are managed as serious and some as laughables. The advantages and limitations of CA were discussed in chapter 18. Here, I describe the methods of conversational data analysis.

Data Analysis

Audio and audio-videotapes of naturally occurring conversation are the data of CA. The focus is on mundane interaction, that is, the naturally occurring dialogue of daily life. Researchers make detailed transcripts and study both the tapes and transcripts to examine (among other things) turn-taking, topic shifts, interruptions, pauses, presequences, and shared laughter. Considering factors such as these, the analyst is able to examine the specific ways in which a conversation is collaboratively managed.

The transcription method developed by Jefferson (see Transcription Guide, Appendix B) provides a uniform way of depicting many details of conversation. For instance, transcription symbols indicate speech overlaps, pauses, extended sounds, audible breaths, and inflections. Symbols (not included here) are even available to indicate gaze direction and other nonverbal cues.

Using audiotapes and detailed transcripts, I examined breast center dialogue to see how members initiate and take up "complaints" as either serious or laughable. Analysis of the data suggests that patients and caregivers manage complaints in terms of (a) the content of the utterances, (b) their placement in the conversation, and (c) responses to them.

REAL-LIFE EXAMPLES

This analysis reveals a phenomenon called *laughter-coated complaints*. That is, it examines statements of apparent disgruntlement that include and/or are followed by laughter. This playful treatment of misfortune may seem insensitive or unusual, and is not used in every situation. Nevertheless, there do seem to be frequent, identifiable episodes in which a "complaint" is mutually managed as a laughable utterance. Conversations audiotaped in a breast care center include the following exam room "complaints":

> (MMMM) Goina skwoosh what I have left?
>
> (NNNN) Are you sure you have the camera on for my exam?
>
> (OOOO) An' you're going to mash the other un?
>
> (PPPP) You feel like you can't breathe once you get all (.2) sma::shed inta that. huhhhh You're stuck.
>
> (QQQQ) Boy this isn't particularly COMfortable is it?

Of these, all but the last one were managed as playful exchanges involving laughter and/or "playing along" comments such as "Oh yeah!" This may puzzle the reader familiar with Jefferson's (1986b) study of laughter in troubles talk. She found that people frequently include a type of "troubles-resistant" laughter in their tales of woe, but recipients react with serious attention to the troubles.[1] As this analysis progresses, key differences between laughable complaints and the serious uptake of troubles talk are revealed.

The "complaints" listed, isolated from the conversations in which they occur, do little to explain why one might be treated as playful and another serious, or what effect either treatment has on conversation. As their context is restored for consideration, however, clues emerge in the content of the utterances, their placement in the conversations, and recipients' responses to them. The following analysis describes each of these foci to conclude that laughter-coated complaints are marked by ambiguous or idiosyncratic word choices and delayed placement relative to the cause of complaint.

Why This Setting

That the samples provided here were gathered in the breast care center is perhaps irrelevant to the type of structures under study. I chose that corpus because it was readily available to me, without any prior interest in laughter-coated complaints. Perhaps because this setting (like many medical settings) involves what one might call "benevolent hurting" or "for your own good" discomforts, it gives rise to many complaining-with-out-*really*-complaining behaviors. Although patients often make a point of their discomforts, they rarely say "That hurts." They are more likely to exclaim something such as "Goina skwoosh what I have left" to which the response is often laughter and a play-along "Oh yeah!" The same types of playful complaining might be found in a range of life situations. Their prevalence in this data rather incidentally attracted my notice and a closer look reveals what I consider to be useful insights into a little understood conversational art form.

Knowing that it is dialogue from a breast care center, the reader may be better able to understand what participants are talking about ("them" is usually "breasts") and what actions result from spoken instructions to

---

[1]Episodes of laughter embedded in troubles talk are available in the data from Dr. Lane's office (chapter 12).

"lean forward" and "move closer." To conduct a mammogram, a woman's breast is placed on a flat x-ray deck that is part of a larger machine; the technician adjusts the machine to compress the breast tissue, and an x-ray image is taken. Repositioning is necessary to get a range of angles.

Terminology

I introduce the phrase *laughter-coated complaints* because I have not found a preexisting term that better describes the phenomenon under examination. The reader will notice that "complaint" is quoted. That is to make the point that the utterance resembles a complaint but is received and acted on as a laughable utterance. I observed few very seriously managed complaints in the breast care center, but laughter-coated complaints were prevalent in nearly every exam. I soon became convinced that laughter-coated complaints served a distinct and important function in the conversations I witnessed.

To illustrate, the technicians described one patient—a "real sour puss"—who never smiled and frequently complained. In describing her stolid demeanor, they made a point of justifying their actions: "I mean, we have to get a good image. It's not the most comfortable thing in the world, but we only compress because we want to help." The caregivers were defensive—not because the patient complained—but because of how she complained. "We'd try to make a joke and she'd just look at us," declared the receptionist. When asked what the woman had complained about, the caregivers could not recall many specifics, but their vague references echoed the same "complaints" I had heard laughingly expressed by others: The compression was uncomfortable, the position awkward. In the caregivers' estimation, those patients were not complainers, but the "sour puss" was. Laughter, it seemed, changed the overall complexion of "complaints" that were otherwise very similar. An utterance received as sour and accusatory without laughter was treated as justified and nonthreatening with laughter.

Laughter-coated complaints are mutually managed in the sense that they emerge, not as fully "done" by one party, but managed or negotiated by both. For instance, the overall function of the "complaint" is often determined by factors subsequent to its initial presentation. The recipient's uptake and complainer's reaction to that uptake affect how the "complaint" will ultimately be treated. "Complaints" that come to be laughter-coated are not always, or even often, presented with preliminary laughter.

(MMMM)
                    ((machine noise))
    PATIENT: Goina skwoosh what I have left?
       TECH: Eh *huh*! Okay. Ho:ld your breath...

Thus, complaints are sometimes offered without laughter and yet are responded to playfully. In this example, the technician's breathy affirmation "Eh *huh*!" plays along with the patient's question about "skwooshing." In this sense, one might hear a "complaint" and respond to it as a playful utterance, just as one might wrap a coat around a bundle and, in so doing, help to define its outward presentation. Of course, the other party can refuse to take up the playful bid, but with the risk of being received as a "sour puss."

In summary, "complaints" described here are often coated within what appears to be a collaboratively managed production of meaning. The following analysis shows how the content, placement, and responses to "complaints" identify them as candidate laughables different from "troubles talk."

Content of "Complaints"

Schegloff (1986) observed that conversations are often far less ambiguous to participants than to onlookers. That point is well illustrated here. What seems a rather straightforward complaint is often followed by joint laughter, suggesting that the ambiguous difference between "playful" and "serious" is managed quite smoothly by interactants. The overlaps in the following exchange show the collaborative laughter immediately following what might otherwise be treated as a protest or challenge.

(NNNN)
    PATIENT: Are you sure you have the camera
             on for my exam? ⌈hhh   Oops! ⌈((playful tone))
       TECH: ⌊eh huh huh ⌊Oops! ((playful))

Although people may not always expect the laughs that a "complaint" draws, some statements seem worded to be funny. Humor is indicated by (among other things) the use of exaggeration and colloquial terms. In Ex. MMMM what the caregiver calls "compression" the patient dubs "skwooshing," and adds an exaggerated threat to breast size with "what I have left." Another patient (Ex. PPPP) punctuates her "complaint" with the prolonged word "smashed."

(MMMM)

> TECH: °Okay.° Mm. This hand'll go this way over there.
> ➤   Good. Hh. Here comes some <u>compression</u>. It's
>   gonna kinda press right here. If you need to bend
>   your knees, you can. It's kinda (   ).
>   (.9) ((machine noise)) Doin' *okay?*
> PATIENT: Umhmm.
>   ((machine noise))
> ➤   Goina skwoosh what I have left?
> TECH: Uh *huh!* Okay. Ho:ld your breath.

(PPPP)

> TECH: Hold your breath. Don't breathe or move. (3.4)
>   Brea:the.
>   (2.4)
> PATIENT: You feel like you <u>can't</u> breathe once you get
> ➤   all- (.2) sma::shed ⌜inta that!   huhhhh
> TECH: ⌞ huh huh huh hhh ⌟

A speaker may cue others' laughter by planting laughter particles within an utterance or immediately after it (Jefferson, 1979). The current examination of "complaints" supports the finding that speakers often cue laughter in another way as well. A straight-faced speaker may invite laughter through what Glenn (1989) called "exaggeration or idiosyncratic word choice" (p. 137). Similarly, Jefferson asserted that "contrast pairs" (p. 81) may flag an utterance as a candidate laughable. The exaggerated contrast between the medical term *compression* and patients' use of "skwoosh" and "smashed" may signal that the utterances are meant as other than serious. The hearer displays an understanding of the utterance as playful, even though it does not include planted laughter. And the "complainer," by joining the laughter, vocally endorses that interpretation. In summary, the difference between Jefferson's troubles talk and the episodes described here may be explained, in part, by the content of the utterances—*how* they are delivered considering where they are delivered.

Placement

It is also revealing to examine where "complaints" are located relative to their causes. Following are two "complaints" managed as *serious* rather than playful.

(QQQQ)

    PATIENT: Boy this isn't particularly COMfortable is it?

    TECH: No its not real- um a a fun way to have to lie for
             a long time but (1.3) I'm akshully pretty speedy so

(RRRR)

    PATIENT: Mmmh. Just a hair ⌐ah back off just a hh (.4)
    TECH: └ °mhmm?°

    PATIENT: Okay (.2) That's ⌐good.
    TECH: └°Mmhm. Okay.°
             Hold your breath
             ((machine noises))

In both cases, the complaint is registered during or before the conditions it describes. The hearer responds with an explanation or makes the requested adjustment. By contrast, many laughter-coated complaints are voiced after a delay or after the completion of an uncomfortable procedure. They are uttered too late to alter what has occurred. In this way laughter coated complaints are less immediate than serious complaints.

(PPPP)   TECH: Hold your breath. Don't breathe or move. (3.4)
                      Brea:the.
                      (2.4)

        PATIENT: You feel like you can't breath once you get all- (.2)
                 sma::shed   ⌐inta that!   huhh⌐hh
        TECH: └huh huh huh hhh┘

(NNNN)   ((rustling and machine noises))

        PATIENT: Are you sure you have the camera on
                 for my exam? ⌐hhh   Oⱷps! ⌐((playful tone))
        TECH: └ eh huh huh│ └Oops! ((playful))
             ((machine noises))

        TECH: °Okay° (   ). Okay.
             Now relax this arm. There you go.

By delaying a "complaint" it may be interpreted as more of a comment than a protest. Both exclamations of "Oops!" in Ex. NNNN are delivered in playacting tones, as depicting what someone might say who had left the machine off, not as serious reactions to real mistakes. The question—occurring well into the exam—is not treated as a serious one, and the subject returns to procedural matters. As examples here indicate, laughter-coated complaints are typically initiated after several seconds of silence or machine noise. They are not represented as spontaneous outbursts. Indeed, their overwhelming placement after conversational lapses suggests that playful complaints may serve significantly as silence-breakers. One maxim of conversation is that *somebody* should say *something* (Sacks et al.,1978), and what topic is more immediate than the unignorable unpleasantness of the exam?

It is also interesting to note what follows laughter-coated complaints. Technicians, presumably oriented toward completing the exam, follow almost every playful exchange with "okay," "now," or "alright" and a subsequent return to serious instruction-giving.

(OOOO)

      PATIENT: ... An' you're goin' to mash the other un?

         TECH: eh-huh-huh. O:h yea::h!

      ➡   °Okay.° This hand'll go this way over there.

(SSSS)

         TECH: Now (.9) keep all these muscles loose over here=

      PATIENT: =An' don' hang on tight

         TECH: Uh huh ⌈huh huh huh. Iss hard to ⌉

      PATIENT: ⌊huhhhh hhuhhh huhuhhhuhhhuh ⌋

         TECH: =when I'm just mashin' ya back against it an yer about ta fall over, issen it?

      PATIENT: My lih'l fat body dudn't want.
               (1.8)

  ➡TECH: O::kay. Let's lean forward and push back against it.

In both excerpts, the technician's use of "okay" follows a playful exchange, and directly precedes a return to serious medical talk. Schegloff (1986) remarked on the use of "anyway" to serve a similar purpose. In Schegloff's terminology, words such as *okay* and *anyway* may be used as "misplacement markers," displaying that a speaker's next utterance is somewhat "out of place" or is relevant to a previous utterance, not the most recent one. As conversational segues, misplacement markers may mitigate the abruptness of a topic shift, or the abandonment of a conversational aside. In the medical dialogue examined, it is a relatively simple affair to switch between playful episodes and serious medical talk. The use of a misplacement marker such as "okay" or "alright" usually serves the purpose.[2] This is remarkably economical compared to the intricate process of extricating oneself from a troubles talk segment. Jefferson (1986a) said that "A primary orientation to a troubles-telling is that from it, there is nowhere else to go; that getting off a troubles-telling is tantamount to getting out of the conversation itself" (p. 191). Thus, it seems that troubles talk is treated to greater conversational distinction and magnitude than laughter-coated complaints. Laughter-coated complaints, although not a linear part of conversation, are nevertheless smoothly embedded in it. Furthermore, the cause of a laughter-coated complaint has often been removed prior to its utterance. Presumably, the speaker is not oriented toward relief but something else. Combined with idiosyncratic word choices, that "something else" may be managed as a bid for play or laughter.

In summary, laughter-coated complaints are somewhat removed from the medical talk surrounding them. A lapse before, and a transition word after the "complaint" display it as a side sequence. Troubles talk, by contrast, is not managed as an aside, but as a complete conversation. Furthermore, that the cause of a laughter-coated complaint is so quickly eliminated distinguishes it as a rather fleeting, momentary trouble. This is quite different from troubles related by many participants in Jefferson's (1986b) study, who speak of physical injury, heartache, property damage, and the like.

Responses

Based on the conversations considered here, the meaning of a "complaint" is mutually managed, with great influence granted to the hearer/respondent. By laughing at a "complaint," a recipient may bid for playful treatment, a bid nearly always seconded with joint laughter by the "complainer." Technicians often respond in playful ways even when "complaints" seem particularly ambiguous. In the following example, the technician treats the patient's utterance as humorous and invites playful agreement with the tag question "issen it?"

---

[2] Interestingly, examples of seriously managed complaints (Ex. PPPP and QQQQ) are not followed by transition words such as "okay." This suggests that laughter-coated complaints are taken as departures from medical talk in a way that serious complaints are not.

(SSSS)   TECH: Now (.9) keep all these muscles loose over here=

➡ PATIENT: =An' don' hang on tight

                  TECH: Uh huh ⌈huh   huh   huh. Iss   hard   to ⌉
             PATIENT: ⌊huhhhh hhuhhh huhuhhhuhhhuh⌋

                  TECH: =when I'm just mashin' ya back against it an yer
                             about ta fall over, issen it?

             PATIENT: My lih'l fat body dudn't want.
                             (1.8)

                  TECH: O::kay. Let's lean forward and push back against it.

"An' don' hang on tight" might be treated as a serious complaint. It
contains no unusual word choice and it occurs within the instruction
sequence. Nevertheless, the technician responds with laughter, perhaps
"allowed to" by the statement's ambiguity or cues unavailable here. As
shown, the patient quickly joins the laughter and returns a quip about
her "lih'l fat body."

In the following instance, a playful question ("havin' fun yet?") is
introduced in the wake of a seriously managed complaint ("back off").

(RRRR)   PATIENT: Mmmh. Just a hair ⌈ah back off just a hh (.4)
                  TECH: ⌊ °mhmm?°

             PATIENT: Okay (.2) That's ⌈good.
                  TECH: ⌊°Mmhm. Okay.°
                             Hold your breath
                             ((machine noises))

                  TECH: Okay (.2) Now (.) lets do your right side next. Are
             ➡   you hhavin' fun yet?

             PATIENT: Oh yeah. Uh ⌈huh huh ⌉huh
                  TECH: ⌊huh huh ⌋

In other cases, technicians "suggest" humorous complaints before patients comment. In the following example, the technician forecasts the
patient's discomfort and playfully frames the offense as a way to take
"your mind off yer compression."

(PP)   TECH: Now this corner right here is just gointa poke
                             you right here. And this corner right here is gointa poke
                             up under your arm. (.8) Now it's pretty
                             uncomfortable (1.3) but it takes your mind off yer
                             compression.

PATIENT: Uh huh huh huh ⌈huh ⌉
TECH: ⌊huh ⌋

In summary, participants in the conversations described demonstrate a penchant for managing "complaints" in a playful rather than a serious way. In the language of CA, preferential actions are those judged by members to be most affiliative and least confrontational. (Recall the "sour puss" reputation of the woman who would not laugh.) Preferred utterances are usually stated without preface or hesitation, unlike dis-preferred actions that are often hesitant, indirect, and weak (Pomerantz, 1986). The prevalence and smooth management of laughter-coated complaints suggests their preferential status in the situations examined.

A difference between laughter-coated complaints and Jefferson's troubles talk may lie in the participants' roles relative to the trouble. In the breast center study, the technician is a well-meaning offender, and the patient but a temporarily discomfited beneficiary. Considering social sanctions against complaining too loudly over what is explicitly a voluntary procedure done for one's own good, laughter may be pre-ferred to serious management of "complaints." This may be particularly true when the person receiving the complaint (here, the caregiver) is also the perpetrator of the offense. By contrast, in Jefferson's (1986b) episodes of troubles telling, serious responses seem preferred, perhaps to signify the hearer as a "compassionate person" or "good friend," and presumably not to blame for the troubles. This may also explain why Dr. Lane (see chapter 12, this volume) more frequently responds to "com-plaints" with serious attention. She is not usually to blame for the patient's distress. Overall, it seems that playful exchanges offer an accepted means of "complaining" and responding to utterances about an uncomfortable but beneficial situation, particularly when one con-versational partner is responsible for the grievance.

OVERVIEW AND SIGNIFICANCE

There appears to be a playful element not generally recognized in "complaining" behavior. Distinguishing between "serious" and "playful" complaints seems to involve some degree of conversational cuing and a great deal of mutual management. By wording a "complaint" in an exaggerated or unusual way, one may "suggest" that it be interpreted as other than serious. Furthermore, a belated "complaint," particularly for a momentary discomfort, may not carry the same call to action as a spontaneous protest. It may be taken more as a conversational device than a bona fide request for mercy or sympathy. Thus, complaints may be managed as playful to avoid the negative associations of griping.

Furthermore, an ambiguous "complaint" may serve as a type of conversational litmus paper, testing what it is popularly called the chemistry between people—their willingness and ability to interact in certain ways. In offering an ambiguous "complaint," a speaker calls on the other party to display his or her understanding of it. A conversational partner who responds to ambiguous complaints with laughter displays a willingness, perhaps a preference, for play. Serious complaints may reflect negatively on both parties, casting one as a "difficult patient" and the other as an "insensitive caregiver." This double hex no doubt applies to many situations in which the recipient of a complaint may be seen as its cause.

A participant may also "suggest" a complaint in advance, negotiating for playful treatment of what might otherwise stir serious complaining. Thus, it is obvious that a complaint is both embedded and collaborative; it is interpreted in light of what comes before and after it, and circumstances of the before and after are interactively managed by both participants. The creation of a play sequence seems to rely strongly on the collaboration of participants, a conclusion well supported by Ragan (1990) in her study of verbal play during gynecological exams.

Considering these factors, one may better understand how conversants distinguish between laughter-coated complaints and the troubles talk as identified by Jefferson (1986b). Talk about troubles, even when it includes embedded laughter, may differ in wording. It may describe misfortune of greater magnitude and more lasting effect. One may have a perceived right or need to talk about serious troubles—a liberty not granted for momentary discomforts. Furthermore, one may engage in playful complaining with relative strangers (such as radiology technicians) but restrict troubles talk to chosen listeners.

This study is not meant to imply that laughter-coated complaints are taken only as play. It is difficult to say what physical changes are made to accommodate the "complaints" either immediately or in subsequent actions. A limitation of this study is the invisibility of inaudible cues. Having been present when the audiotapes were recorded, I was aware of many instances of raised eyebrows, smiles, and significant looks that are not accessible in the transcripts. Nevertheless, this focus on audible conversation may yield insights that would have been overlooked had the scope been larger.

The current study, combined with Jefferson's substantial work on conversational laughter, adds credence to an observation made by Schenkein (1971):

> For even an apparently simple, artless, nonproblematic utterable such as heheh there exists to be consulted a vast configuration of conversational machinery for its appropriate use, and, upon the occasion of its use some very subtle and elegant interactional activities can be accomplished. (p. 371)

This study advances the idea that "complaining" is a versatile art form, intricately managed. In the examples given here, laughable complaints allow conversants to simultaneously display grievances and interpersonal alliance. Consequently, laughter-coated complaints may present a compelling way to interactively manage the dialectic between hurting and helping in medical encounters.

VI

Conclusions

Chapter 22

▼

Summary

In conclusion, it seems that people are involved in quite a lot of what we might call *joking around* or *monkey business*, and far from being the primitive enterprise these terms suggest, humor use is actually a sophisticated means of organizing and influencing social transactions. This is true even in the institutional atmosphere of health care transactions. Or perhaps it is true especially in health care settings. I have made the point several times that people typically do not associate humor with medical settings. The two seem incompatible—one fun and informal, the other usually frightening and institutional. Here I would like to elaborate on a point that usually escapes notice: Perhaps humor shows up in medical settings precisely because the two are incompatible. It is difficult to imagine an experience that is both frighteningly institutional and funny. Like the popular optical illusion in which one can see a vase or two faces, but not both at the same time, humor may have a Gestalt effect that leads us—if only momentarily—into perceiving the situation in a radically different way. I think this is a proposal worth considering as we assess the implications of the analyses just posed. In this chapter, I present a summary of my conclusions. A few cautions about humor use are presented in chapter 23. A discussion of the limitations and strengths of this multimethod analysis takes place in chapter 24. Finally, implications for practical application and future research are discussed in chapter 25.

Following is a brief summary of the conclusions reached by the collection of analyses in this book. The implications of these conclusions are discussed more fully in chapters 25 and 26.

Phenomenological analysis (Part II) reveals that "funny" is essentially a constituent of awareness and perception—not a predictable response to a particular kind of stimulus. In light of this, I suggest that theories of humor based on stimulus–response suppositions are inherently capricious. The claims they make are beleaguered by the common presence of things that are funny to some people but not to others, funny once but not twice, or are not funny at all until days or years later. I suggest that a unifying theory of humor is possible if we consider that humor does not lie within a stimulus at all, but rather within consciousness. More specifically, I propose the Surprise Liberation Theory of Humor: To consider something funny, we must begin with an "expectation," perceive a surprising deviation from that "expectation," and experience the deviation as pleasurable and liberating.

Viewed ethnographically (Part III), joking around seems to serve the same functions in a variety of settings. It represents a way to mitigate embarrassment, soften or sidestep complaints, display identification, solicit feedback, and good-naturedly insist on compliance with unpleasant routines. But the tones and topics of humor use are sometimes very different. As described, "torture" humor in the physical therapy departments studied is bold and public—a contrast to the mild humor of the breast center and doctor's office. Several factors may account for this difference, including the length and nature of treatment, status differences between patients and caregivers, goals, and privacy. Overall, physical therapists' bold use of rapport-building humor may reflect their familiarity with patients and their need to socialize and motivate patients.

Viewed as speech communities (Part IV), the seven health care settings studied fall into two camps. One camp is characterized by adherence to an individualistic Code of Dignity. Within that code, participants seek to create a non-threatening environment, molded as much as possible to each patient's unique preferences. Caregivers take great pains not to offend patients, and they adopt relational strategies that congratulate patients for seeking medical attention. Participants in the breast center and doctor's office uphold this code.

Participants in other settings display adherence to a more collectivistic Code of Compassion. Within the hospital and the outpatient physical therapy department, a greater premium is placed on enlisting cooperation with prescribed routines. Caregivers quickly display a sense of intimacy or familiarity with the patients. When they do not do this, patients use humor to campaign for more personal treatment. Overall, transactions are bolder and more persuasive and participants are willing to risk momentary offenses in the interest of longterm goals.

A closer look at three medical transactions (chapter 20) shows how participants collaboratively organize/interpret each experience using humor. In one sequence, humor is used to rekey a distressful episode as a playful one, with the effect of soothing the patient and gaining his cooperation. In another sequence, a semi-nude patient talks about her breasts in a humorously animated way that seems to reduce her vulnerability to embarrassment. Finally, a patient and caregiver negotiate the terms of an ambiguous frame using playful utterances to draw a fuzzy line between interpersonal conflict and play. In each episode, humor appears to minimize the consequences of participating in threatening or disagreeable activities.

Finally, CA (chapter 21) reveals the conversational mechanisms used to manage laughter-coated complaints. Examples show how participants use idiosyncratic words, delayed placement, and suggestive feedback to flag some "complaints" as candidate laughables. Participants are also shown suggesting playful complaints in advance, negotiating for playful treatment of what might otherwise stir serious complaining.

In summary, humor is shown to be a versatile and widely used communication technique in the settings studied. Within the data of this study there are both striking similarities and distinctions. Humor is used for similar purposes overall, but the forms it takes differ widely across some settings. All in all, humor seems intricately involved in the organization of many medical experiences in ways that reflect/affect cultural expectations.

Chapter 23

▼

A Few Cautions

An important ramification of this book is that humor is a potent and potentially risky venture. What is appropriate in one setting may be offensive in another. Following are some cautions about the potentially negative effects of humor and some suggestions for using it appropriately.

Although humor can help build rapport, it can also be hurtful. Burton (1986), founder of the national Nurses for Laughter organization, cautioned that sarcastic, mocking, and degrading humor worsens rather than improves therapeutic communication. In a similar way, Emerson (1969) warned that jokes about sensitive topics may hurt people's feelings and make them feel victimized. Particularly when the initiator has more power than the recipient, the recipient may perceive little recourse in such situations. The social calamity of allowing a jest to flop may seem so daunting that would-be challengers feel forced into displays of acquiescence with viewpoints that offend them.

In her work with children, Wooten (1995) reported that teasing is common and not usually harmful. But humor can wound, she warned, particularly when individuals are the butts of jokes because of their physical or racial differences. Then humor serves to distance and belittle people rather than put them at ease.

From an organizational aspect, humor is not always indicated either. Based on a survey of nurses, White and Howse (1993) suggested that humor is a valued technique in some health care situations but not all. The nurses surveyed judged humor to be moderately helpful in boosting morale and improving employee cohesiveness. They did not feel humor would strengthen communication between staff and physicians nor serve to express management's appreciation of staff members' efforts. The authors concluded: "Employees are sensitive to how their work is valued. Use of humor in this situation could be construed as trivializing the severity of work issues" (p. 86).

Also at issue is the receipt of ill-considered humor. Caregivers must not only monitor the propriety of their own humor, but prepare for those times when they will be *recipients* of inappropriate humor (Erdman, 1993). Unseemly humor may take the form of belligerent put-downs or sexually harassing statements. Negative humor might also include sarcasm, teasing, and slanderous belittling (Perrin, 1995).

Although caregivers must be careful not to cause offense, they may do well to resist offense as well. Erdman (1993) encouraged caregivers to cultivate a healthy appreciation for patients' diverse humor styles. She described the surprising aplomb of a patient dealing with the regretful necessity of a hysterectomy. The woman playfully suggested a list of contraceptive items to be auctioned off. She also sent out invitations for a "Coming Out Party" and assured well-wishers there would be "plenty of womb for everybody." Another patient joked with his nurses that—in light of his quickly approaching death—he was watching movies on fast forward and bathing his dog in the drive-through carwash. Erdman reported that "the nurse was at first caught off guard by the patient's comments, but the humor opened the door to further communication about death between the nurse and this patient" (p. 59).

Based on the analyses in this book, the equivocal nature of humor is both its greatest strength and weakness. The same ambiguity that makes humor useful at forgiving a complaint or glossing embarrassment leaves little recourse to the person pierced by a humorous barb. Although this scenario has never been apparent in my observations of patient–caregiver transactions, surely it happens. We have all seen people sidestep responsibility for hurtful jests by proclaiming "I was only joking!" The power differential between patients and caregivers makes sensitive use of humor particularly important. Following are a few suggestions for using humor appropriately.

SUGGESTIONS

As shown in this book, the appropriateness of humor can only be judged in context. What one culture embraces, another disdains. However, humor scholars offer some basic guidelines to help increase sensitivity and use humor to best advantage.

Many suggest that humor users be nonaggressive in their conversational quips. Richman (1995) wrote that: "The distinction between *laughing with* and *laughing at* is a valid one. A good rule of thumb for the therapist is when in doubt, don't" (p. 273). Similarly, Hillman (1994) suggested that caregivers laugh *with* rather than *at* patients.

Burton (1986) offered three guidelines for appropriate humor: (a) do not use it in the middle of a crisis situation, (b) be sensitive to other people's preferences and willingness to engage in humor, and (c) be wary that people may overhear laughter and think you're laughing at *them*.

In an article for at-home caregivers, Pasquali (1991) advised that bedside humor is appropriate among people experiencing mild to moderate (but not extremely high) anxiety, those with similar senses of humor, and in those instances when the subject of the humor is the initiator or the situation, not the other person. Pasquali encouraged caregivers to take humor breaks to moderate their stress levels.

Humor may be found in a variety of places. Simon (1989) recommended humor as a "high touch" way to counterbalance the alienating effects of "high tech" medicine, simultaneously reducing the stress on both patients and caregivers. She suggested collecting and sharing humorous but nonthreatening cartoons, videos, books, cards, and games. Erdman (1993) also suggested personalized laughter first-aid kits including funny books, tapes and videos, Play-Doh, bubbles, colors, games, water guns, and the like. But she went one step further, providing a sample "prescription for humor" on an authentic-looking prescription form with the following directions:

> Remember to laugh at least once a day. Laughter will open you up and let life's experiences flow through you. If you do not laugh regularly, you may suffer from HUMORRHOIDS. This is a condition that starts with a hardening of the attitudes and may actually lower your laugh expectancy. Suggested cures include taking a mild laughsitive every day or laughing at one's own everyday unintended humor. These should restore you to regular hilarity. (p. 66)

In summary, it seems that humor has serious effects, both good and bad. The ambiguity that masks embarrassment and conflict can also cloak insults and put-downs. Humor users do well to proceed with caution and respect, avoiding utterances that demean others.

Chapter 24

▼

Limitations and Strengths

LIMITATIONS

In different sections, I have already written of the limitations of each perspective. As I have said, many of the gaps left by one method are filled in by another. A few overarching limitations remain, however.

First, I cannot escape the reflexiveness of language. In describing medical transactions, I contribute to yet another communication event, which itself has a context and implications. Paraphrasing Bateson, Bochner (1981) expressed the dilemma this way: "The end product [of scientific reporting] can never be anything more or less than maps of maps of maps" (p. 66). I cannot fully know how the reader will take these words, sitting where he or she is, seeing them written and bound in just such a way. But it is certain that the context of the writing and the reading of this piece contribute something more or different than existed in the original phenomena. As I see it, this is unavoidable, but a limitation nonetheless.

Second, however much I wish to be nonreductionistic, I readily concede that holism in a pure sense is unattainable. The analyses I present cover only a small fraction of what lies within the data. For instance, it is probably impossible to catalog every metacommunicative cue in even 5 minutes of conversation, much less fully understand and explain its significance (which does not negate the fruitfulness of striving to that end). That social actors achieve practical understandings with each other without being constantly overwhelmed or perplexed makes them fascinating subjects for study, and reveals (I think) how inadequate science is to fully explain them.

Finally, I am limited by the ways in which I have collected data. Notes and audiotapes are once removed from the phenomena, and cannot encompass every aspect of what occurred. I am also limited by the absence of a visual recording. Although I address some aspects of nonverbal cuing, my analysis relies largely on fieldnotes written in real time. It would be more precise and thorough to have videotapes of the transactions that I might repeatedly review, as I have the audiotapes. Surely much nonverbal activity has gone unrecognized. I accepted this limitation because it was not practical or permissible to videotape the transactions I observed. Hopefully, future researchers can find a way to overcome this limitation and fill in some of the gaps I leave.

In summary, this is but an imperfect account of the transactions as they actually occurred. I am limited by language, data-gathering procedures, and the restrictions of time and space. However, these limits are offset by many strengths, described here.

STRENGTHS

Many years of field study and analysis have gone into this book in an effort to make it as thorough as possible. Following are the overall strengths as I see them.

First, the data set is broad in scope. It includes consideration of many types of patients and caregivers in a range of settings and situations. This breadth is unusual; to date, health communication scholars have focused almost entirely on physicians and to a small degree on nurses. Particularly in light of the differences revealed here, it seems important to expand the focus of health communication research.

Second, because the study examines naturally occurring phenomena, it encompasses many facets of communication, and is perhaps more transferable to real-life problems and situations than many studies. Furthermore, by including contextual examples, portions of the data are also made immediately available for review. This may help in a scientific way to ensure that the analyses are valid. I also hope that it helps in a practical way to make the study more readable and "real" for practitioners interested in gaining practical knowledge from it.

Third, I believe the study profits from meticulous data-gathering techniques. As described in chapter 9, I made disciplined efforts to be unobtrusive and to solicit participants' viewpoints without influencing them.

Fourth, I have tried to minimize the effects of my personal biases, and to be honest about them as much as possible (see Philosophy Statement, Appendix D). I have also tried to be up-front about the assumptions and limitations of the perspectives I have employed, presenting that information before each analysis. In this way I hope to promote in the reader an informed skepticism that will show my conclusions in their truest light.

Finally, and perhaps most importantly, this study benefits from the use of multimethod analysis. By examining the data from different perspectives, I am able to say something about both structural and contextual issues. I have tried to use each method to best advantage, yielding a collection of analyses that consider humor as an element of consciousness, a cultural phenomenon, a communication technique, and an organizing property of social interaction. To my knowledge, the thoroughness of this collection is unprecedented in humor research.

Chapter 25

▼

Suggestions for Application

PRACTICAL APPLICATION

I would like to end this examination where it began, with an examination of the questions posed by practitioners and researchers. In these last pages I restate some of those questions, and based on what I have learned, suggest answers and directions for continued inquiry.

Is it Appropriate to Use Humor in Medical Settings?   Like most good questions, there can be no easy answer to this one. After observing hundreds of patients and dozens of caregivers, I have rarely seen a transaction devoid of humor. Judging by participants' displayed acceptance of humor, I propose that, yes, humor is appropriate in most medical settings. But I caution that humor has many faces and many voices and appropriateness is a complex construct.

One of the most important implications of this book is that humor is culturally and situationally reflexive. It does not function the same way in every setting. For instance, it is acceptable in the settings observed here for complaints to be laughingly managed in the physical therapy department but not usually in the doctor's office. To know whether humor is appropriate or not, one must consider the assumptions and values of the people involved. As shown, these values are often reflected in cultural codes that make it feasible for many people to shape and display the same assumptions and values. But in instances of intercultural communication, appropriateness may be a more problematic issue.

And even among members of the same community, situations arise that require novel interpretations of the code.

My advice to practitioners is to tread lightly until other participants display that they are willing to collaborate in this type of communication. I also reiterate the position I stated in chapter 1 that the decision to use humor is rightfully a personal and situational one. I believe those who too zealously prescribe specific humor routines may lead their followers down culturally unacceptable paths. I do think it conceivable—indeed, I greatly hope—that accounts such as this one will give people useful ideas about using humor, but these ideas can only be used effectively if one exercises a healthy sensitivity to context (including the expectations of one's conversational partner). Considering this, appropriateness becomes a process of evaluating the expectations of other participants, the nature of one's relationship to them, and the goals and setting of the transaction.

Is Humor Use Consistent With Medical Professionalism? Again, appropriateness is at issue. Certainly it would seem unprofessional to use some types of humor in some settings. But one implication of this study is that the traditional image of a stoic, objective caregiver is a restrictive and unrealistic standard. If we view competence from the ethnographic perspective discussed in Part IV, the best communicators are those who maximize goal achievement without violating cultural expectancies. Considering the many objectives to be served by humor and the culturally diverse contexts caregivers occupy, I believe we would do well to help them develop versatile communication repertoires. Although I do not believe that a caregiver must use humor to be effective, the data supports that humor is a versatile communication technique with implications directly related to many health care objectives (e.g., gaining cooperation, maintaining rapport, overcoming embarrassment, etc.). In light of this, if humor is inconsistent with professionalism, we may wish to reconsider our ideas about professionalism.

What Functions Does Humor Serve in Health Care Contexts? Relative to existing literature, this study supports claims that humor in medical settings may reduce face threats (Ragan, 1990); display mutual identification between patients and caregivers (Beck & Ragan, 1992); reduce embarrassment, bolster rapport, and encourage attentiveness (Smith-Dupré, 1992). I elaborate on the implications of these findings and others in the following sections.

First of all, humor often seems to encourage a meaningful engagement between patient and caregiver. That is, humor may call forth signs of emotional warmth and personal attention from an otherwise distracted partner. The data shows that a bid for humor is often returned with eye contact, smiles, laughter, and return bids for humor. This effect usually lasts throughout the transaction, and may be an effective way to diminish a sense of unreciprocal intimacy or emotional distance. It may also be a way for patients to interrupt the flow of closed-ended questions that restrict their input in medical transactions.

Humor may also be a way of soliciting feedback. For instance, patients may present their feelings in funny/serious ways to see how a caregiver will respond. In the breast center data, some fears expressed this way were treated as serious concerns, others were "laughed off" as representing not real threats. It is suggested that ambiguously stated fears may be collaboratively treated as laughables if they contain potentially comical exaggerations, or if laughter seems an appropriate way to emphasize that the cause of the fear is inconsequential. Either way, humor presents a nonthreatening way to solicit information.

Humor may also represent an acceptable way to comment on a threatening or embarrassing situation. Within the role of animated "commentator," a participant can make fun of otherwise embarrassing matters, and even good-naturedly complain. This is evident in the way that mammography patients joke about breast size and physical therapy patients joke about torture. The animation of humor seems to flag the participants' behavior as somewhat theatrical—a lamination that may shield the "naked I" and make participants feel less personally vulnerable. Within this guise, relatively nonthreatening avenues for giving and receiving feedback are opened.

Judging by existing literature and situated interview data, humor may enhance patient and caregiver satisfaction. Studies suggest that patients prefer doctors who are affiliative (Buller & Buller, 1987; Street & Wiemann, 1987) and involved and expressive (Street & Wiemann, 1987)—qualities that may be associated with humor use. Interviews within this study suggest that patients typically prefer caregivers who joke around with them, and caregivers, in turn, say they gravitate to good-humored patients.[1]

Finally, in a more abstract way, humor and play seem to allow participants to negotiate a pleasing equilibrium between institutionalism and individuality[2] and between hurting and helping. Humor allows

---

[1]Although we cannot make generalizations based on the interviews done in this study, the data suggests that the link between humor use and satisfaction might be worth pursuing using different methods.

[2]An idea commented on more fully by Glenn and Knapp (1987, p. 50).

participants to collaboratively "break the rules" together. As such, it may defy institutional edicts while accentuating the solidarity of individuals. It may also key a hurtful episode as a playful or benevolent one, suggesting a solidarity inconsistent with adversarial roles. Huizinga (1970) suggested that play creates a particular sense of social order: "It [play] creates order, *is* order. Into an imperfect world and into the confusion of life it brings a temporary, a limited perfection" (p. 29). Humor, like play, occupies a middle ground between anarchy and rigidity. When neither extreme is acceptable, it is a persuasive force drawing the transaction toward a more comfortable medium.

In summary, humor seems to be a particularly persuasive technique, useful in diminishing many of the obstacles to effective medical communication. In terms of Barnlund's (1976) 10 universal obstacles to communication, humor may present an effective way to minimize social status differences, emotional distance, and one-way communication. It also seems to provide a means of recruiting personal attention, giving and soliciting feedback, and reducing emotional barriers.

What Are the Risks of Using Humor in Medical Settings?

I have suggested that the ambiguity of humor serves as a strategic medium of negotiation, allowing participants a range of interpretations and next moves. But where ambiguity is already elevated (as in intercultural transactions or instances of extreme emotion), humor may complicate matters to a calamitous degree. For instance, it may be safe among same-community members to imply as a patient that you do not really think it is funny that your back hurts so. But if another person, missing the serious implications of your voice and gestures, assumes from your chuckle that you do find it funny, confusion and dissatisfaction are likely to result. Likewise, if a caregiver smiles or chuckles while delivering treatment advice, the patient may wonder whether the caregiver *really* means what he or she says or is only joking around. Misunderstandings of this type are possible in any setting, but are especially consequential when someone's health is at stake.

I also made the point (see chapters 10 and 11) that caregivers who are ostensibly to blame for a patient's temporary grievances may be granted license to treat those grievances in a playful way (at least on one level). This is a sophisticated social maneuver that relies on both parties' cooperation, but there is room for misunderstanding. For instance, what results when a harried caregiver begins to feel that patients are complaining about her rather than to her? In other words, what if the caregiver thinks patients are blaming her for their troubles? And what if they are? What mixed signals might humor send in a situation such as that?

Honestly, I do not know. Whether by chance or by design, I have yet to see a transaction in which a participant seemed visibly frustrated or annoyed by the presence of humor. I think the possibility is a real one, however, and worth pursuing. We might ask whether and how humor use thwarts the goals of a medical transaction, and how the organization of the transaction is affected by this. We might also question how if no instances of this can be found, participants so consistently avoid negative repercussions. Following are more ideas for future research.

IMPLICATIONS FOR FUTURE RESEARCH

Avenues to Explore

One advantage of an inductive inquiry such as this one is that it presents a complex array of factors worth further exploration. Following are several implications of the preceding analyses.

First, this book illuminates the importance of physical surroundings and treatment routines. Researchers and practitioners alike may do well to consider the differences between communal arrangements (less structured, more interactive, more hectic) and private rooms (restricted communication, more privacy).

They might also consider how communication is affected by the nature of an exam and the topics being discussed. The same caregiver acts differently during some exams than others. In short, the line the participants take (e.g., serious or joking) is prescribed to some extent by the activities in which they are engaged. Some activities such as troubles talk seem to suggest that participants be serious and sympathetic, while others that require nudity permit or require them to joke around. This difference is missed if we are too quick to assume that caregivers and patients all and always act alike. It also means that simplistic approaches to communication training may be of limited utility. Indeed, communication "cure-alls" may restrict caregivers' repertoires more than they improve them.

Third, we might also consider how the roles played by interactants are defined by their communication and the activities in which they engage. For instance, as the number of health maintenance organizations rise, we might do well to consider the differences between assymptomatic clients and traditional patients. Clients may have different motivations and expectations that affect health care transactions. (Compare the luxuries and decorum of the breast center with traditional medical settings!) With an emphasis on preventing (rather than curing) health crises, health care clients may feel more actively involved, and perceive that they have a right/need to ask questions, and to choose and switch caregivers. This suggests a different imperative for caregivers, who may become more competitive and more solicitous. Moreover, it would not be surprising if these expectations spill over into issues concerning patienthood as well.

This study suggests that clues about participants' perceptions of their roles and others are available in their talk. For instance, breast center caregivers speak of "clients" rather than "patients." And through their use of humor, physical therapy participants refer to themselves metaphorically as "torturers" and "slaves." In some ways, the topics of humor often seem to offer an insightful peek at the images and symbols entertained by participants. Taken seriously, these images and symbols may help us better understand the relationships between patients and caregivers.

Finally, in an overall sense, this book supports that humor is an informative arena for communication research. It seems to serve some very real and important functions. Because it is ambiguous and usually affiliative, it allows people to negotiate and receive feedback without incurring negative sanctions. This seems particularly important in light of the importance and uncertainty of medical setting transactions.

Chapter 26

▼

Parting Observations

FRUITFUL HEALTH
COMMUNICATION RESEARCH

I hope this study stands as encouraging evidence that there is still much to learn about health-related communication. Patient–caregiver relationships are not identical across situations. Communication is apparently affected by many factors, including the physical setting in which the patient and caregiver find themselves, the topics they discuss, the nature of the exam and the emotions associated with it, the length of their transactions and their relationship, the goals of the medical organization, the degree of patient–caregiver interdependence, and the amount of hurting and helping required. Additionally, this collection of analyses suggests that communication with physicians makes up a relatively small (and nonrepresentative) portion of health care transactions. Furthermore, physicians themselves may not be as similar as the literature suggests. In light of this, it seems particularly myopic that current literature is dedicated nearly entirely to physician–patient communication. I believe we will arrive at fruitful understanding only when we acknowledge and take into account the complexities of health-related communication.

My observations convince me that we—as social actors—are primarily rational in the way we conduct ourselves. That is, we do things for reasons, reasons that reflect our best efforts to assess a situation and predict the consequences. To assess one aspect of a patient or caregiver's circumstances—or to assume that their circumstances are always the same—is unrealistic. To think that we can change one aspect of the situation and accomplish sweeping change is likewise naive. However, I do not suggest that we throw up our hands and walk away. Instead, researchers truly interested in change must take a wide angle look at medical situations. Then—rather than immediately asking "What is wrong here?" and "How can it be fixed?"—begin by asking with nonjudgmental curiosity: "What is happening here?" and "Why is it happening?"

In my opinion, communication scholars are often too quick to judge medical transactions by criteria external to them, then propose solutions that are inconsistent with the challenges perceived by participants. I am reminded of a television comedy[1] in which a character wise to the ways of magic cautions a neophyte to the effect of: "Watch how you use your powers. Flood the Sahara; drain the ocean." Communication scholars have been quick to assume that doctors are overbearing because they do not know how to act in more affiliative ways. It may not drain the ocean to flood the medical field with communication skills training, but if we implement communication strategies without considering the complex goals of medical transactions we may be discouraged to find we have created droughts we never imagined.

From my perspective, ignorance may be one obstacle to effective medical communication. But it is almost certainly the case that communicating as participants do serves (or seems to serve) some quite rational purposes. Before we understand the implications of "what is happening" and "why it is happening," we are in a poor position to begin to fix medical communication (if fixing is what it needs). Perhaps we as communication scholars have shied away from a wide angle look at medical communication because it seems too overwhelming, and because we may be forced to confront the discouraging possibility that we cannot fix it. We can, at best, provide tools for those who might fix it, work for those changes that are locally manageable by patients and caregivers, and contribute in a responsible way to larger efforts for systemic change.

Toward that end, I propose several approaches that I believe offer great promise for yielding the type of informed, useful information we might wish to accrue about health-related communication.

First, approach medical communication from a relational perspective, viewing it as a collaborative process. It is simple and tempting to blame/applaud either the caregiver or the patient, but a close look at

---

[1] Dare I quote *I Dream of Jeannie?*

any conversation shows that neither party acts alone. Barnlund (1981) put it rather poetically when he wrote: "This reactive cosmology in which people are cast inevitably as victims or victimizers is, in my view, one of the vastly underestimated sources of twentieth century malaise" (p. 90). We may do better to consider how both parties contribute to health communication than too quickly to point fingers at the caregivers.

Second, foster an interactive loop between research and practice. When researchers and practitioners are involved in dialogue, both stand to gain. Practitioners are in a place to suggest real-life questions and concerns, and to comment on the wisdom and efficacy of research conclusions. Involved in this way, researchers are in a better position to understand and actually contribute to health communication. This is not to say that all research must be bound to practical application, but we are certainly fooling ourselves if we claim to understand medical communication without understanding medical contexts.

Finally, be wary of value judgments. Considering what remains to be understood, I believe it is risky to impose external value judgments on medical phenomena. For example, it is tempting from an individualistic (Nacirema) viewpoint to wish that hospital caregivers would treat patients more as individuals. But if we wish to campaign for that change, we must take into account the complex bureaucracy of hospitals, and the difficulties involved in adapting routines to fit so many individual preferences. Within the current system it may indeed be more compassionate and realistic to socialize the patient to the hospital than to try to tailor individualized routines, many of which are not controlled by the caregiver. Thus, although I *am* interested in improving medical communication, I advise careful, thorough consideration of the issues involved.

Concerning humor, the examples quoted here are a small fraction of those collected. Nearly every transaction I have observed included humorous exchanges. Overall, there is encouraging evidence that humor is a defensible component of medical communication, and used appropriately, an effective means of pursuing multiple goals in real-life settings. Moreover, evidence suggests that many caregivers and patients are remarkably adept at changing the tone and timing of their humor to suit particular occasions and relationships. Their front line skills at handling difficult situations may offer valuable insights for medical participants and for others who are less often part of tense or embarrassing encounters.

The literature supports a growing awareness that communication not only affects, but is inextricably intertwined with issues of health and medicine. Patients and caregivers face many barriers to effective communication, but there is some promise that these barriers can be minimized or overcome, with important results. Humor is a promising communication technique and there are certainly many more yet to be fully explored. The challenge is to be both explorer and guide in this newly identified and important arena. In taking on the challenge, scholars accept something of the life-and-death responsibility of medicine. I suggest that useful research begins with practical questions posed by the unique, real-life requirements of medical transactions. The stakes have never been higher, nor the potential greater for communication research.

Appendix A

▼

The Relationship Between
Conversational Context
and Structure

One might say that this book moves from an examination of conversational meaning to an examination of conversational structure. The move requires a change in focus and a change in methodology. Moerman (1988) put it quite succinctly when he wrote: "A conversation analyst takes events to be orderly unless proven otherwise. An ethnographer takes them to be meaningful" (p. 23).

In light of this, the question arises: Is context informative when examining structure? This point has been debated, with CA purists (cf. Sacks 1986a; Schegloff, 1991) insisting that contextual details distract from, and do not assist, microanalytic analysis. They do not argue that conversation exists autonomously from context; rather, they find it more interesting that fundamental conversational mechanisms exist that enable conversants to adapt to different contexts (Zimmerman & Boden, 1991). Some others (cf. Moerman, 1988) argue that conversations are embedded in, and influenced by, contextual considerations, and they cannot be understood in isolation. In health communication, this dual attention to discourse and context characterizes the work of Sue Fisher, M. A. Paget, Alexandra Todd, and Candace West. They resist a separation of structure and meaning, working from the position that the two are mutually reflexive. Their lens is not so microscopic as some conversation analysis, and their description not so thick as some ethnography.

For example, their focus on institutional authority (Fisher, 1984), medical misunderstandings (Paget, 1993), and asymmetric power relationships (Fisher, 1993; Todd, 1993; West, 1993) is more socially critical and less microanalytic than the purists' interest in turn-transition points (Sacks et al., 1978).

Having been influenced by work in both camps, I cannot decry either. In my experience, to meld ethnography and conversation analysis effectively, one must strive for a compromise between the two—a method more often called discourse analysis than CA. This is not a wholly regrettable compromise. It brings up methodological questions such as Schegloff's (1991) challenge: How does one determine which aspects of the context are salient, and precisely what is their effect? But it also sidesteps some of the limitations of either method, mainly the criticism that CA is a purely theoretical endeavor, and ethnography is a purely descriptive one. Moreover, to avoid compromising the methods—to be very thickly descriptive and very microanalytic in the same paper—is, I believe, to lose focus of either. It is not easy to present either ethnographic or CA in a few words, and the paper soon reads like a series of lengthy digressions.

But there is another alternative, provided one has adequate data and space in which to pursue it. A rich ethnography and a microanalytic study of conversation may stand side by side as I present them here. In this way, I believe that each lends credence to the other (just as in actual conversation, structure and meaning are interdependent.) CA can provide rigorously empirical support to ethnography, and ethnography can soften the bare bones aspect of conversation analysis, which can sometimes be so detailed and microanalytic as to seem inconsequential. This can be done without compromising the benefits of either method. In this book, for instance, it helps to know, when a woman exclaims "You're gonna skwoosh what I have left!" that she is undergoing breast compression for a mammography. It is not necessary to know that to appreciate the structure of the utterance, but perhaps it does help the reader appreciate how the utterance-as-structured affects, not only the sequence of the conversation, but the tone and overall effect of the transaction. In doing conversation analysis, I leave these inferences to the reader, or refer him or her to the ethnographic sections that more directly assess meaning. Thus, this book is somewhat circular, with conclusions in any one section providing implications for all other sections in no prescribed, linear fashion.

In summary, I propose that the reader who reads the entire book is likely to get the most out of every section. However, I do think a person interested solely in one topic or method can flip to that chapter and understand it. Who is to say that personal experiences do not provide a more than adequate context for understanding the events described here? I hope that is the case. My aim is to present analyses the reader may challenge or (more hopefully) accept, based on the data I have presented and the transferability of these insights to other contexts and situations.

Appendix B

▼

Transcription Guide

The following transcription conventions are based on the system initiated by Jefferson. The information presented here is adapted in part from Atkinson and Heritage (1986), using examples from my own data.

Simultaneous Utterances

Simultaneous utterances are linked with brackets.

```
PATIENT:  Are you sure you have the camera
          on for my exam? ⌈hhh         ⌈Oops! ⌈((playful tone))
   TECH:                  ⌊eh huh huh        ⌊Oops!
```

Silences

Silences are timed in tenths of seconds and noted in parentheses.

```
TECH:  Hold your breath. Don't breathe or move. (3.4)
       Brea:the.
```

Untimed intervals are described in double parentheses ((pause)) and micropauses are indicated by (.).

Characteristics of Speech Delivery

Punctuation marks are used to mark inflections, not necessarily the ends of phrases or sentences.

205

. A period denotes a drop in tone.
? A question mark denotees a rising inflection.
! An exclamation point denotes vocal animation.
- Dashes indicates abrupt stops in speech or strings of stammered words (I-I-I want to).

Extended sounds

A colon indicates an extension of the sound or syllable it follows (go:sh). The more colons, the longer the stretch (sma::shed).

Emphasis

Words emphazed in speech are underlined in the transcripts.

> TECH: Eh huh! Okay. Ho:ld your breath....

Volume

Utterances spoken more loudly than others are shown in capital letters.

> PATIENT: Boy this isn't particularly COMfortable is it?

Utterances spoken more quietly than others are surrounded by degree signs.

> TECH: °Okay.° Mm. This hand'll go this way over there

Audible Breaths

Audible breaths are indicated by (hhh).

> PATIENT: Mmmh. Just a hair ah back off just a hh (.4)

Descriptions and Unintelligible Sounds

Descriptions and unintelligible sounds are presented in double parentheses and unintelligible sounds in empty single parenthesis.

> PATIENT: ((laughing)) No. I don't do that ever night.
> Maybe a glass o' wine. . . .
>
> TECH: . . . kinda (   ).

Appendix C

▼

Discovery Model

I. Humorous speech act
   A. What is the topic of the humorous message?
   B. What words and nonverbals accompany humor?
   C. What are the various keys, tones, or manners in which humor is delivered?
   D. What participants are involved?
   E. What categories do humor users fall into?
   F. In what situations is humor typically used/not used?
   G. How does the setting help define humor use?
   H. What styles of humor can be identified?
   I. What are the ends, goals, and purposes of humor?
   J. What specific behaviors accompany humor use?
   K. How do the following aspects of the patient–caregiver relationship affect humor use?
      1. Length of transaction (so far and expected)
      2. Age difference
      3. Status difference
      4. Common interests
      5. Race
      6. Gender
II. Attitudes toward humor
   A. Does humor differ according to one's role/age?
   B. What types of people are most apt to initiate or respond to humor?
   C. What makes the message funny?
   D. What personal characteristics contribute to humor?

E. What are the social consequences of failed humor?

F. When is it okay to use risky humor?

G. When is it rewarding to use humor?

H. When is it rewarding to respond to humor?

I. What personality traits and characteristics are associated with humor use?

J. What is management's attitude toward those who use humor? Toward those who don't?

K. What is the patient's attitude?

L. What is the caregiver's attitude?

III. Competence

A. Can a person learn to be funny?
If so, how?
If not, why not?

B. When does humor skill develop?

C. What factors contribute to humor competence?

D. Who should use humor? Who shouldn't?

E. What happens if no one laughs?

F. Is formal training offered on humor use?
On other types of patient–caregiver communication?

IV. Compliance and socialization

A. Does the organization have an explicitly stated policy on humor?
On other types of patient–caregiver communication?

B. How do staff members get patients to follow rules?

C. How does the staff handle quarrelsome patients?

D. How do patients express complaints?

E. How does the staff handle embarrassing situations?

F. How do patients handle embarrassing situations?

G. How does the staff handle nonresponsive patients?

H. How do patients act if they feel ignored?

Appendix D

▼

Philosophy Statement

I approach the study of patient–caregiver interaction believing there are many ways of being a successful communicator. Success depends on the context, personalities, and goals involved in any transaction. Therefore I am easily exasperated by scholars who prescribe medical communication reforms without first learning about medical contexts. It is one thing to theorize that a caregiver should speak the patient's language. But it is quite another thing to tell the caregiver how to do that, and how to do it without sacrificing other objectives. To do that, we must take into account the context and multiple goals of medical encounters.

In my opinion, communication scholars too often ignore their own advice. They have much potentially valuable advice to give medical caregivers, but in delivering it they neglect to speak the caregiver's language. There has been little attempt to tailor health communication theory to suit the practical objectives of medicine. My goal is to span the boundaries between medicine and communicology, with respect for the world views of both.

My objectives are somewhat reformatory, but I shy away from specific prescriptions for change. I believe there is no one communication technique that works in all situations. Rather, the best communicators are those with flexible and varied repertoires. My work is fueled by the conviction that human action is not deterministic, but largely the result of strategically made decisions. My reform, then, is not to overthrow the system but to make choices available to people so they may have more communication tools with which to accomplish their objectives.

Furthermore, I do not subscribe to the view of patient and caregiver as underdog and dominator. Observing hundreds of medical transactions, I have seen very few really deplorable communicators. I have seen fewer still who seemed malicious in their incompetence. However, I frequently encounter both caregivers and patients with limited communication repertoires. Some handle embarrassing situations gracefully, but become aloof and uncommunicative in the face of a devastating diagnosis. Unfortunately, caregivers—particularly physicians—often have minimal opportunities to observe themselves or their peers. Patients, often struck dumb by intimidation, often offer little feedback to their caregivers, and tend to acquiesce meekly to the caregiver's agenda. I believe, if it were practical to do so, most patients and caregivers would adopt a more constructive variety of communication techniques.

My focus here is on humor as a communication technique. I don't profess that humor serves every purpose. But I do believe that humor is an effective, flexible communication tool. By studying it in natural medical settings, I hope to be able to speak about humor in a language caregivers (and perhaps others) can understand. Using words rather than numbers, I attempt to de-mystify humor somewhat.

I seek, not some monolithic truth about humor, but a well-rounded perspective of humor use. I hope to show what purposes conversational humor serves in medical settings, and how humor can be recognized and created. The more I observe humor, the less mysterious it seems to me, and the more I believe that it is a communication skill worth serious attention.

References

Adams, E. R., & McGuire, F. A. (1986). Is laughter the best medicine? A study of the effects of humor on perceived pain and affect. *Activities, Adaptations & Aging, 8,* 157–175.

Alberts, J. (1990). The use of humor in managing couples' conflict interactions. In D. D. Cahn (Ed.), *Intimates in conflict: A communication perspective* (pp. 105–120). Hillsdale, NJ: Lawrence Erlbaum Associates.

Armour, R. (1972). A short course in geriatric medicine. *Geriatrics, 29,* 120–129.

Arnston, P. H., & Philipsborn, H. F. (1982). Pediatrician–parent communication in a continuity-of-care setting. *Clinical Pediatrics, 21,* 302–305.

Atkinson, J. M., & Heritage, J. (Eds.). (1986). *Structures of social action: Studies in conversation analysis.* Cambridge, MA: Cambridge University Press.

Baker, L. (1987). Families and illness. In M. A. Crouch & L. Roberts (Eds.), *The family in medical practice: A family systems primer* (pp. 97–111). New York: Springer-Verlag.

Banner, M. G. (1988, Fall-winter). Comic relief. *Saratoga Style,* p. 93.

Barnlund, D. C. (1976). The mystification of meaning: Doctor–patient encounters. *Journal of Medical Education, 51,* 716–725.

Barnlund, D. C. (1981). Toward an ecology of communication. In C. Wilder-Mott & J. H. Weakland (Eds.), *Rigor & imagination: Essays from the legacy of Gregory Bateson* (pp. 87–126). New York: Praeger.

Bateson, G. (1956). The messages "this is play." In B. Shaffner (Ed.), *Transactions of the second conference on group processes* (pp. 145–242). New York: Josiah Macy, Jr. Foundation.

Bateson. G. (1972). *Steps to an ecology of mind.* New York: Ballantine.

Baxter, L. A. (1992). Forms and functions of intimate play in personal relationships. *Human Communication Research, 18,* 336–363.

Beck, C. S., & Ragan, S. L. (1992). Negotiating interpersonal and medical talk: Frame shifts in the gynaecologic exam. *Journal of Language and Social Psychology, 11,* 47–61.

Beckman, H. B., & Frankel, R. M. (1984). The effect of physician behavior on the collection of data. *Annals of Internal Medicine, 101,* 692–696.

Ben-Sira, Z. (1976). The function of the professional's affective behavior in client satisfaction: A revised approach to social integration theory. *Journal of Health and Social Behavior, 17,* 3–11.

Ben-Sira, Z. (1980). Affective and instrumental components in the physician–patient relationship: An additional dimension of interaction theory. *Journal of Health and Social Behavior, 21,* 170–180.

Berk, L. S., Tan, S. A., Fry, W. F., Napier, B. J., Lee, J. W., Hubbard, R. W., Lewis, J. W., & Eby, W. C. (1989). Neuroendocrine and stress hormone changes during mirthful laughter. *American Journal of the Medical Sciences, 298,* 390–396.

Berlyne, D. E. (1960). *Conflict, arousal, and curiosity.* New York: McGraw-Hill.

Berlyne, D. E. (1969). Laughter, humor, and play. In G. Lindzey & E. Aronson (Eds.), *The handbook of social psychology* (2nd ed., Vol. 3, pp. 795–852). Menlo Park, CA: Addison-Wesley.

Betcher, R. W. (1981). Intimate play and marital adaptation. *Psychiatry, 44*, 13–33.

Bochner, A. (1981). Forming warm ideas. In C. Wilder-Mott & J. H. Weakland (Eds.), *Rigor & imagination: Essays from the legacy of Gregory Bateson* (pp. 65–83). New York: Praeger.

Bogden, R., & Taylor, S. J. (1975). *Introduction to qualitative research methods.* New York: Wiley.

Bost, L., & Foltz, A. (1990, October). Make way for the laugh mobile. *Parks and Recreation*, pp. 64–66.

Bradney, P. (1957). The joking relationship in industry. *Human Relations, 10*, 179–187.

Brewer, J., & Hunter, A. (1989). *Multimethod research: A synthesis of styles.* Newbury Park, CA: Sage.

Brukman, J. (1975). "Tongue play": Constitutive and interpretive properties of sexual joking encounters among the Koya of South India. In M. Sanches & B. G. Blount (Eds.), *Language, thought, & culture: Advances in the study of cognition* (pp. 235–268). New York: Academic Press.

Buckeley, W. F., Jr. (1990). Norman Cousins, RIP. *National Review, 42*, 14–15.

Buller, M. K., & Buller, D. B. (1987). Physicians' communication style and patient satisfaction. *Journal of Health and Social Behavior, 28*, 375–388.

Burgoon, J. K., Pfau, M., Parrot, R., Birk, R., Coker, R., & Burgoon, M. (1987). Relational communication, satisfaction, compliance-gaining strategies, and compliance in communication between physicians and patients. *Communication Monographs, 54*, 307–359.

Burton, D. L. (1986). Laughter and humor in critical care. *Dimensions of Critical Care Nursing, 5*, 162–170.

Bush, D. F. (1985). Gender and nonverbal expressiveness in patient recall of information. *Journal of Applied Communication Research, 13*, 103–117.

Buss, A. R. (1979). Dialectics, history, and development: The historical roots of the individual-society dialectic. In P. B. Baltes & O. G. Brim, Jr. (Eds.), *Life-span development and behavior* (Vol. 2., pp. 313–333). New York: Academic Press.

Byrne, D. (1958). Drive level, response to humor, and the cartoon sequence effect. *Psychological Reports, 4*, 439–442.

Callen, M. (1990). *Surviving AIDS.* New York: Harper Collins.

Carroll, J. L., & Shmidt, J. L., Jr. (1992). Correlation between humorous coping style and health. *Psychological Reports, 70*, 402.

Cheatwood, D. (1983). Sociability and the sociology of humor. *Sociology and Social Research, 67*, 324–338.

Coleman, W. E., Jr. (1983). The struggle for control in health care settings: Political implications of language use. *Et cetera, 40*, 401–408.

Coles, R. (1989, June). Day by day: Humor as antidote. *New Choices*, pp. 85–86.

Comstock, L. M., Hooper, E. M., Goodwin, J. M., & Goodwin, J. S. (1982). Physician behaviors that correlate with patient satisfaction. *Journal of Medical Education, 57*, 105–112.

Coombs, R. H., & Goldman, L. J. (1973). Maintenance and discontinuity of coping mechanisms in an intensive care unit. *Societal Problems, 20*, 342–355.

Coser, R. L. (1959). Some social functions of laughter: A study of humor in a hospital setting. *Human Relations, 12*, 171–182.

Coser, R. L. (1960). Laughter among colleagues: A study of the social functions of humor among the staff of a mental hospital. *Psychiatry, 23*, 81–95.

Cousins, N. (1976). Anatomy of an illness (as perceived by the patient). *The New England Journal of Medicine, 295*, 1458–1463.

Cousins, N. (1979). *Anatomy of an illness as perceived by the patient.* New York: W. W. Norton.

Cupchik, G., & Leventhal, H. (1974). Consistency between expressive behavior and the evaluation of humorous stimuli: The role of sex and self-observation. *Journal of Personality and Social Psychology, 30*, 429–442.

Danzer, A., Dale, J. A., & Klions, H. L. (1990). Effect of exposure to humorous stimuli on induced depression. *Psychological Reports, 66*, 1027–1036.

Danziger, S. K. (1980). The medical model in doctor–patient interaction: The case of pregnancy care. In J. A. Roth (Ed.), *Research in the sociology of health care* (Vol. 1, pp. 263–304). Greenwich, CT: JAI.

Davis, J. M., & Farina, A. (1970). Humor appreciation as social communication. *Journal of Personality and Social Psychology, 15*, 175–178.

DesCamp, K. D., & Thomas, C. C. (1993). Buffering nursing stress through play at work. *Western Journal of Nursing Research, 15*, 619–627.

Dillon, K. M., Minchoff, B., & Baker, K. H. (1985). Positive emotional states and enhancement of the immune system. *International Journal of Psychiatry in Medicine, 15*, 13–18.

Drass, K. A. (1988). Discourse and occupational perspective: A comparison of nurse practitioners and physician assistants. *Discourse Processes, 11*, 163–181.

Dubin, R. (1978). *Theory building.* New York: The Free Press.

Duncan, H. D. (1962). *Communication and social order.* New York: Oxford University.

Ellis, M. J. (1973). *Why people play.* Englewood Cliffs, NJ: Prentice Hall.

Emerson, J. P. (1969). Negotiating the serious import of humor. *Sociometry, 32*, 169–181.

Erdman, L. (1993). Laughter therapy for patients with cancer. *Journal of Psychosocial Oncology, 11*, 55–67.

Fang, W. L., Hillard, P. J. A., Lindsay, R. W., & Underwood, P. B. (1984). Evaluation of students' clinical and communication skills in performing a gynecological examination. *Journal of Medical Education, 59*, 758–760.

Fennell, R. (1993). Using humor to teach responsible sexual health decision making and condom comfort. *Journal of American College Health, 42*, 37–39.

Finney, J. W., Brophy, C. J., Friman, P. C., Golden, A. S., Richman, G. S., & Friman, A. F. (1990). Promoting parent–provider interaction during young children's health-supervision visits. *Journal of Applied Behavior Analysis, 23*, 207–213.

Firth, R. (1977). Routines in a tropical disease hospital. In A. Davis & G. Horobin (Eds.), *Medical encounters: The experience of illness and treatment* (pp. 143–158). New York: St. Martin's Press.

Fisher, S. (1984). Institutional authority and the structure of discourse. *Discourse Processes, 7*, 201–224.

Fisher, S. (1993). Reflections on gender, power and discourse. In A. D. Todd & S. Fisher (Eds.), *The social communication of doctor–patient communication* (2nd ed., pp. 287–299). Norwood, NJ: Ablex.

Fox, R. C. (1959). *Experiment perilous.* Glencoe, IL: The Free Press.

Frankel, R. M. (1984). From sentence to sequence: Understanding the medical encounter through microinteractional analysis. *Discourse Processes, 7*, 135–170.

Frankel, R. M., & Beckman, H. B. (1989). Conversation and compliance with treatment recommendations: An application of micro-interactional analysis in medicine. In L. Grossberg, B. J. O'Keefe, & E. Wartella (Eds.), *Rethinking communication: Vol. 2. Paradigm exemplars* (pp. 60–74). Newbury Park, CA: Sage.

Friedman, H. S., & DiMatteo, M. R. (1979). Health care as an interpersonal process. *Journal of Social Issues, 35,* 1–11.

Fuller, D. S., & Quesada, G. M. (1973). Communication in medical therapies. *Journal of Communication, 23,* 361–370.

Garfinkel, H. (1967). *Studies in ethnomethodology.* Cambridge, MA: Polity Press/Basil Blackwell.

Geertz, C. (1973). *The interpretation of cultures.* New York: Basic Books.

Glaser, B. G., & Strauss, A. L. (1967). *The discovery of grounded theory: Strategies for qualitative research.* New York: Aldine de Gruyter.

Glenn, P. J. (1989). Initiating shared laughter in multi-party conversations. *Western Journal of Speech Communication, 53,* 127–149.

Glenn, P. J., & Knapp, M. L. (1987). The interactive framing of play in adult conversations. *Communication Quarterly, 35,* 48–66.

Glesne, C., & Peshkin, A. (1992). *Becoming qualitative researchers: An introduction.* White Plans, NY: Longman.

Goffman, E. (1956). Embarrassment and social organization. *American Journal of Sociology, 62,* 264–271.

Goffman, E. (1967). *Interaction ritual.* New York: Pantheon Books.

Goffman, E. (1974). *Frame analysis: An essay on the organization of experience.* New York: Harper Colophon.

Goldstein, J. H. (1987). Therapeutic effects of laughter. In W. F. Fry, Jr. & W. A. Salameh (Eds.), *Handbook of humor and psychotherapy: Advances in the clinical use of humor* (pp. 1–20). Sarasota, FL: Professional Resource Exchange.

Goodman, J. (1983). How to get more smileage out of your life: Making sense of humor, then serving it. In P. McGhee & J. H. Goldstein (Eds.), *Handbook of humor research: Vol 2. Applied studies* (pp. 1–21). New York: Springer-Verlag.

Goodwin, M. H. (1990). *He-said-she-said: Talk as social organization among Black children.* Bloomington: Indiana University Press.

Gurwitsch, A. (1964). *The field of consciousness.* Pittsburgh, PA: Duquesne University Press.

Gutman, J., & Priest, R. (1969). When is aggression funny? *Journal of Personality and Social Psychology, 12,* 60–65.

Halley, F. M. (1991). Self-regulation of the immune system through behavioral strategies. *Biofeedback and Self-Regulation, 16,* 55–74.

Harvey, C. W. (1989). *Husserl's phenomenology and the foundations of natural science.* Athens: Ohio University.

Hayworth, D. (1928). The social origin and function of laughter. *Psychological Review, 35,* 367–384.

Heritage, J. (1984). *Garfinkel and ethnomethodology.* Cambridge, MA: Polity Press.

Hillman, S. (1994). The healing power of humour at work. *Nursing Standard, 8,* 31–34.

Hom, G. L. (1966). Threat of shock and anxiety in the perception of humor. *Perceptual and Motor Skills, 23,* 535–538.

Huizinga, J. (1970). *Homo ludens.* New York: Harper & Row.

Hymes, D. H. (1962). The ethnography of speaking. In T. Gladwin & W. C. Sturtevant (Eds.), *Anthropology and human behavior* (pp. 13–53). Washington, DC: Anthropological Society of Washington.

Hymes, D. H. (1967). Models of the interaction of language and social setting. *Journal of Social Issues, 23,* 8–28.

Hymes, D. H. (1972). Models of the interaction of language and social life. In J. J. Gumperz & D. Hymes (Eds.), *Directions in sociolinguistics: The ethnography of communication* (pp. 35–71). New York: Holt, Rinehart & Winston.

Jefferson, G. (1979). A technique for inviting laughter and its subsequent acceptance or declination. In G. Psathas (Ed.), *Everyday language: Studies in ethnomethodology* (pp. 79–96). New York: Irvington.

Jefferson, G. (1986a). On stepwise transition from talk about a trouble to inappropriately next-positioned matters. In J. M. Atkinson & J. Heritage (Eds.), *Structures of social action: Studies in conversation analysis* (pp. 191–222). Cambridge, MA: Cambridge University.

Jefferson, G. (1986b). On the organization of laughter in talk about troubles. In J. M. Atkinson & J. Heritage (Eds.), *Structures of social action: Studies in conversation analysis* (pp. 364–369). Cambridge, MA: Cambridge University.

Kahn, W. A. (1989). Toward a sense of organizational humor: Implications for organizational diagnosis and change. *The Journal of Applied Behavioral Science, 25*, 45–63.

Kambouropoulou, P. (1926). Individual differences in the sense of humor. *American Journal of Psychology, 37*, 268–278.

Katriel, T., & Philipsen, G. F. (1981). "What we need is communication": "Communication" as a cultural category in some American speech. *Communication Monographs, 48*, 301–317.

Korsch, D. M., & Negrete, V. F. (1972). Doctor–patient communication. *Scientific American, 227*, 66–74.

Kuiper, N. A., & Martin, R. A. (1993). Humor and self-concept. *Humor International Journal of Humor Research, 6*, 251–270.

Lambert, R. B., & Lambert, N. K. (1995). The effects of humor on secretory immunoglobulin A levels in school-aged children. *Pediatric Nursing, 21*(1), 16–19.

Lammers, B. H. (1991). Moderating influence of self-monitoring and gender on responses to humorous advertising. *The Journal of Social Psychology, 131*, 57–69.

Lane, S. D. (1983). Compliance, satisfaction, and physician-patient communication. In B. Westley (Ed.), *Communication yearbook* (Vol. 7, pp. 772–799). Newbury Park, CA: Sage.

Lefcourt, H. M., Davidson-Katz, K., & Kueneman, K. (1990). Humor and immune-system functioning. *Humor, 3*, 305–321.

Lefcourt, H. M., & Martin, R. A. (1986). *Humor and life stress: antidote to adversity.* New York: Springer-Verlag.

Lesserman, J., & Luke, C. S. (1982). An evaluation of an innovative approach to teaching the pelvic examination to medical students. *Women & Health, 7*, 31–42.

Leventhal, H., & Cupchik, G. C. (1975). The informational and facilitative effects of an audience upon expression and evaluation of humorous stimuli. *Journal of Experimental Social Psychology, 11*, 363–380.

Lincoln, Y. S., & Guba, E. G. (1985). *Naturalistic inquiry.* Newbury Park, CA: Sage.

Linstead, S. (1985). Jokers wild: The importance of humour in the maintenance of organizational culture. *The Sociological Review, 33*, 741–765.

Long, B. E. (1985). A study of the verbal behavior of family doctors. *International Journal of the Sociology of Language, 51*, 5–25.

Long, D., & Graesser, A. (1988). Wit and humor in discourse processing. *Discourse Processes, 11*, 35–60.

Martin, R. A., & Dobbin, J. P. (1988). Sense of humor, hassles, and immunoglobulin A: Evidence of a stress-moderating effect of humor. *International Journal of Psychiatry in Medicine, 18*(2), 93–105.

Martin, R. A., & Lefcourt, H. M. (1983). Sense of humor as a moderator of the relation between stressors and moods. *Journal of Personality and Social Psychology, 45*, 1313-1324.

McGhee, P. E. (1979). *Humor: It's origin and development.* San Francisco: Freeman.

McGhee, P. E. (1983). The role of arousal and hemisphere lateralization in humor. In P. E. McGhee & J. H. Goldstein (Eds.), *Handbook of humor research. Vol. 1. Basic issues* (pp. 13-37). New York: Springer-Verlag.

McKinlay, J. B. (1975). Who is really ignorant—physician or patient? *Journal of Health and Social Behavior, 16*, 3-11.

McWhinney, I. (1989). The need for a transformed clinical method. In M. Stewart & D. Roter (Eds.), *Communicating with medical patients: Vol. 9. Interpersonal communication* (pp. 25-40). Newbury Park, CA: Sage.

Metcalf, C. W. (1987). Humor, life, and death. *Oncology Nursing Forum, 14*, 19-21.

Metts, S., & Cupach, W. R. (1989). Situational influence on the use of remedial strategies in embarrassing predicaments. *Communication Monographs, 56*, 151-162.

Miller, F. C. (1967). Humor in a Chippewa tribal council. *Ethnology, 6*, 263-271.

Moerman, M. (1988). *Talking culture: Ethnography and conversation analysis.* Philadelphia: University of Pennsylvania.

Moody, R. A. (1978). *Laugh after laugh: The healing power of humor.* Jacksonville, FL: Headwater Press.

Nezu, A. M., Nezu, C. M., & Blissett, S. E. (1988). Sense of humor as a moderator of the relationship between stressful events and psychological distress: A prospective analysis. *Journal of Personality and Social Psychology, 54*, 520-525.

Nofsinger, R. E. (1991). *Everyday conversation.* Newbury Park, CA: Sage.

Nussbaum, J. F. (1989). Life-span communication: An introduction. In J. F. Nussbaum (Ed.), *Life-span communication: Normative processes* (pp. 1-4). Hillsdale, NJ: Lawrence Erlbaum Associates.

O'Connell, W. E. (1987). Natural high therapy and practice: The humorists's game of games. In W. F. Fry, Jr. & W. A. Salameh (Eds.), *Handbook of humor and psychotherapy: Advances in the clinical use of humor* (pp. 55-80). Sarasota, FL: Professional Resources Exchange.

Ottenberg, S. (1990). Thirty years of fieldnotes: Changing relationships to the text. In R. Sanjek (Ed.), *Fieldnotes: The makings of anthropology* (pp. 139-160). Ithaca, NY: Cornell University Press.

Paget, M. A. (1993). On the work of talk: Studies in misunderstandings. In A. D. Todd & S. Fisher (Eds.), *The social communication of doctor–patient communication* (2nd ed., pp. 107-126). Norwood, NJ: Ablex.

Pasquali, E. A. (1991). Humor: Preventive therapy for family caregivers. *Home Healthcare Nurse, 9*, 13-17.

Perrin, K. M. (1995). Laugh at stress! Creative methods for teaching stress management. *Journal of Health Education, 26*, 309-310.

Peterson, J. H., Jr. (1975, January). Black–white joking relationships among newly integrated faculty. *Integrated Education*, 33-37.

Peterson, K. E. (1992). The use of humor in AIDS prevention, in the treatment of HIV-positive persons, and in the remediation of caregiver burnout. In M. R. Seligson & K. E. Peterson (Eds.), *AIDS prevention and treatment: Hope, humor, and healing* (pp. 37-57). New York: Hemisphere.

Philipsen, G. F. (1975). Speaking "like a man" in Teamsterville: Culture patterns of role enactment in an urban neighborhood. *Quarterly Journal of Speech, 61*, 13-22.

Philipsen, G. F. (1992). *Speaking culturally: Explorations in social communication.* Albany: State University of New York Press.

Polkinghorne, D. (1983). *Methodology for the human sciences: Systems of inquiry.* Albany: State University of New York Press.

Pomerantz, A. (1986). Agreeing and disagreeing with assessments: Some features of preferred/dispreferred turn shapes. In J. M. Atkinson & J. Heritage (Eds.), *Structures of social action: Studies in conversation analysis* (pp. 152–164). Cambridge, MA: Cambridge University.

Porterfield, A. L. (1987). Does sense of humor moderate the impact of life stress on psychological and physical well-being? *Journal of Research in Personality, 21,* 306–317.

Porterfield, A. L., Mayer, S., Dougherty, K., Kredich, K., Kronberg, M., Marsee, K., & Okazaki, Y. (1988). Private self-consciousness, canned laughter, and responses to humorous stimuli. *Journal of Research in Personality, 22,* 409–423.

Raddcliff-Brown, A. (1959). On joking relationships. In *Structure and function in primitive society.* Glencoe, IL: The Free Press. (Original work published 1940)

Ragan, S. L. (1990). Verbal play and multiple goals in the gynaecological exam interaction. *Journal of Language and Social Psychology, 9,* 67–84.

Ragan, S. L., & Glenn, L. D. (1990). In D. O'Hair & G. L. Kreps (Eds.), *Applied communication theory and research* (pp. 313–330). Hillsdale, NJ: Lawrence Erlbaum Associates.

Rawlins, W. K. (1989). A dialectical analysis of the tensions, functions, and strategic challenges of communication in young adult friendships. *Communication Yearbook, 12,* 157–189.

Richman, J. (1995). The lifesaving function of humor with the depressed and suicidal elderly. *Gerontologist, 35,* 271–273.

Robinson, V. M. (1975). *Humor and the health professions: Cultivating humor as a tool in teaching, communication and intervention in the helping process by health professionals.* Unpublished doctoral dissertation, University of Northern Colorado, Greeley.

Robinson, V. M. (1983). Humor and health. In. P. E. McGhee & J. H. Goldstein (Eds.), *Handbook of humor research. Vol. II. Applied studies.* New York: Springer-Verlag.

Rosenblatt, P. C. (1981). Ethnographic case studies. In M. B. Brewer & B. E. Collins (Eds.), *Scientific inquiry and the social sciences* (pp. 194–225). San Francisco, CA: Jossey-Bass.

Roter, D. (1989). Which facets of communication have strong effects on outcome—A meta-analysis. In M. Stewart & D. Roter (Eds.), *Communicating with medical patients: Vol. 9. Interpersonal communication* (pp. 183–196). Newbury Park, CA: Sage.

Sacks, H. (1986a). Notes on methodology. In J. M. Atkinson & J. Heritage (Eds.), *Structures of social action: Studies in conversation analysis* (pp. 21–28). Cambridge, MA: Cambridge University Press.

Sacks, H. (1986b). On doing "being ordinary." In J. M. Atkinson & J. Heritage (Eds.), *Structures of social action: Studies in conversation analysis* (pp. 413–429). Cambridge, MA: Cambridge University Press.

Sacks, H., Schegloff, E. A., & Jefferson, G. (1978). A simplest systematics for the organization of turn-taking in conversation. In J. Schenkein (Ed.), *Studies in the organization of conversational interaction* (pp. 7–55). New York: Academic Press.

Sanjek, R. (1990). *Fieldnotes: The making of anthropology*. Ithaca, NY: Cornell University Press.

Saville-Troike, M. (1982). *The ethnography of communication: An introduction* (2nd ed.). New York: Basil Blackwell.

Schatzman, L., & Strauss, A. L. (1973). *Field research: Strategies for a natural sociology*. Englewood Cliffs, NJ: Prentice-Hall.

Schegloff, E. A. (1986). On some questions and ambiguities in conversation. In J. M. Atkinson & J. Heritage (Eds.), *Structures of social action: Studies in conversation analysis* (pp. 28–52). Cambridge, MA: Cambridge University.

Schegloff, E. A. (1991). Reflection on talk and social structure. In D. Boden & D. H. Zimmerman (Eds.), *Talk and social structure: Studies in ethnomethodology and conversation analysis* (pp. 44–70). Berkeley: University of California Press.

Schegloff, E. A., & Sacks, H. (1973). Opening up closings. *Semiotica, 7*, 289–327.

Schenkein, J. N. (1971). Towards an analysis of natural conversation and the sense of heheh. *Semiotica, 6*, 344–377.

Schutz, A. (1967). Common-sense and scientific interpretation of human action. In M. Natanson (Ed.), *Alfred Schutz, collected papers 1: The problems of social reality* (pp. 3–47). The Hague: Matinus Nijhoff. (Original work published 1962)

Schwartz, H., & Jacobs, J. (1979). *Qualitative sociology: A method to the madness*. New York: The Free Press.

Scott, S. (1992, Winter). Bill Cosby. How humor heals. *Vim & Vigor*, pp. 14–19, 58–59.

Seckman, M. A., & Couch, C. J. (1989). Jocularity, sarcasm, and relationships. *Journal of Contemporary Ethnography, 18*, 327–344.

Sherzer, J., & Darnell, R. (1972). Outline guide for the ethnographic study of speech use. In J. J. Gumperz & D. Hymes (Eds.), *Directions in sociolinguistics: The ethnography of communication* (pp. 548–551). New York: Holt, Rinehart & Winston.

Shurcliff, A. (1968). Judged humor, arousal, and the relief theory. *Journal of Personality and Social Psychology, 8*, 360–363.

Shuy, R. W. (1993). Three types of interferences to an effective exchange of information in the medical interview. In A. D. Todd & S. Fisher (Eds.), *The social communication of doctor-patient communication* (2nd ed., pp. 17–30). Norwood, NJ: Ablex.

Siegel, B. S. (1983). *Love, medicine, and miracles*. New York: Harper & Row.

Simon, J. M. (1989). Humor techniques for oncology nurses. *Oncology Nursing Forum, 16*, 667–670.

Simon, J. M. (1990). Humor and its relationship to perceived health, life satisfaction, and morale in older adults. *Issues in Mental Health Nursing, 11*, 17–31.

Smith-Dupré, A. A. (1992). *Humor in the hospital: An ethnographic study of the communicational aspects of humor shared by patients and caregivers*. Unpublished master's thesis, University of Southwestern Louisiana, Lafayette.

Spiegelberg, H. (1982). *The phenomenology movement: A historical introduction* (3rd ed.). Martinus Nijhoff: The Hague.

Spradley, J. P. (1979). *The ethnographic interview*. New York: Holt, Rinehart & Winston.

Street, R. L., Jr., & Wiemann, J. M. (1987). Patient satisfaction with physicians' interpersonal involvement, expressiveness, and dominance. In M. L. McLaughlin (Ed.), *Communication yearbook* (Vol. 10, pp. 591–612). Newbury Park, CA: Sage.

Suchetka, D. (1992, February 26). Prescription: Take two jokes and call me in the morning. *The Advocate*, pp. 1C–2C.

Sumners, A. D. (1990). Professional nurses' attitudes toward humor. *Journal of Advanced Nursing, 15*, 196–200.

Todd, A. D. (1993). Exploring women's experiences: Power and resistance in medical discourse. In A. D. Todd & S. Fisher (Eds.), *The social communication of doctor–patient communication* (2nd ed., pp. 267–285). Norwood, NJ: Ablex.

U.S. Department of Health and Human Services. (1983). *National healthcare expenditures study* (DHHS Publication No: PHS 83–3361). Washington, DC: U.S. Government Printing Office.

Van Maanen, J. (1988). *Tales of the field: On writing ethnography*. Chicago: University of Chicago Press.

Vinton, K. L. (1989). Humor in the workplace: It's more than telling jokes. *Small Group Behavior, 20*, 151–166.

Waitzkin, W. (1984). Doctor–patient communication: Clinical implications of social scientific research. *Journal of the American Medical Association, 252*, 2441–2446.

Watzlawick, P., & Beavin, J. (1977). Some formal aspects of communication. In P. Watzlawick & J. H. Weakland (Eds.), *The interactional view* (pp. 56–71). New York: Norton.

Weir, D. (1977). The moral career of the day patient. In A. David & G. Horobin (Eds.), *Medical encounters: The experience of illness and treatment* (pp. 135–142). New York: St. Martin's Press.

West, C. (1993). "Ask me no questions . . ."– An analysis of queries and replies in physician–patient dialogues. In S. Fisher & A. Todd (Eds.), *The social organization of doctor–patient communication* (2nd ed., pp. 127–157). Norwood, NJ: Ablex.

Weston, W. W., & Brown, J. B. (1989). The importance of patients' beliefs. In M. Stewart & D. Roter (Eds.), *Communicating with medical patients: Vol. 9. Interpersonal communication* (pp. 77–85). Newbury Park, CA: Sage.

White, C., & Howse, E. (1993). Managing humor: When is it funny—and when is it not? *Nursing Management, 24*, 80, 84, 86.

Wicker, F., Barron, W., & Willis, A. (1980). Disparagement humor: Dispositions and resolution. *Journal of Personality and Social Psychology, 39*, 701–709.

Wieder, D. L. (1974). *Language and social reality: The case of telling the convict code. Approaches to Semiotics*. The Hague: Mouton.

Williams, L. (1990, November 5). Treating the funny bone. *Time*, pp. 17–22.

Wolff, H. A., Smith, C. E., & Murray, H. A. (1934). The psychology of humor: A study of responses to race-disparagement jokes. *Journal of Abnormal and Social Psychology, 28*, 341–365.

Wooten, P. (1995). Jest for the health of it! Finding comedy in chaos. *Journal of Nursing Jocularity, 5*, 46–47.

Young, P. T. (1937). Laughing and weeping, cheerfulness and depression: A study of moods among college students. *The Journal of Social Psychology, 8*, 311–334.

Zijderveld, A. C. (1983). Trend report: The sociology of humour and laughter. *Current Sociology, 31*, 1–100.

Zillmann, D. (1983). Disparagement humor. In P. McGhee & J. H. Goldstein (Eds.), *Handbook of humor research* (Vol. 1, pp. 85–108). New York: Springer-Verlag.

Zillmann, D., Rockwell, S., Schweitzer, K., & Sundar, S. S. (1993). Does humor facilitate coping with physical discomfort? *Motivation and Emotion, 17*(1), 1–21.

Zimmerman, D. H., & Boden, D. (1991). Structure-in-action: An introduction. In D. Boden & D. H. Zimmerman (Eds.), *Talk and social structure: Studies in ethnomethodology and conversation analysis* (pp. 3–21). Berkeley, CA: University of California Press.

Ziv, A. (1984). *Personality and sense of humor.* New York: Springer.

Zola, I. K. (1983). *Socio-medical inquiries: Recollections, reflections, and reconsiderations.* Philadelphia: Temple University Press.

Author Index

Subject Index